Mediation and other forms of Alternative Dispute Resolution

Covering both the principles and practice of Alternative Dispute Resolution (ADR), this important new textbook equips students not only with a contextual understanding of the role of ADR in adjudicating civil disputes but also with the different forms of mediation and ADR available and the key issues in their application.

Providing theoretical and practical insights, the book begins with a critical examination of the tenets on which ADR is based, where it sits in relation to civil law, and how it is applied in different national contexts. It discusses the various areas in which mediation or arbitration can be applied, from family mediation to restorative justice, and includes chapters on the ethics of mediation and its psychology, as well as an introduction to online dispute resolution (ODR). The concluding chapter offers some thoughts on the benefits and challenges of mediation.

Featuring a glossary of key terms, detailed case law, end-of-chapter problem questions, and advice around listening skills during a mediation process, *Mediation and other forms of Alternative Dispute Resolution* is an essential textbook for any student approaching ADR for the first time and offers practitioners an opportunity to reflect on the context of ADR.

Michael Bartlet is a mediator and senior lecturer in ADR and public law at SOAS, University of London.

Mediation and other forms of Alternative Dispute Resolution

Michael Bartlet

Routledge
Taylor & Francis Group
LONDON AND NEW YORK

Designed cover image: Viesinsh / Getty Images ®

First published 2025
by Routledge
4 Park Square, Milton Park, Abingdon, Oxon OX14 4RN

and by Routledge
605 Third Avenue, New York, NY 10158

Routledge is an imprint of the Taylor & Francis Group, an informa business

British Library Cataloguing-in-Publication Data
A catalogue record for this book is available from the British Library

Library of Congress Cataloging-in-Publication Data
Names: Bartlet, Michael, author.
Title: Mediation and other forms of alternative dispute resolution / Michael Bartlet.
Description: Abingdon, Oxon [UK] ; New York, NY : Routledge, 2024. | Includes bibliographical references and index.
Identifiers: LCCN 2024033998 | ISBN 9780367632557 (hardback) | ISBN 9780367610814 (paperback) | ISBN 9781003112617 (ebook)
Subjects: LCSH: Mediation. | Dispute resolution (Law)
Classification: LCC K2390 .B37 2024 | DDC 347/.09—dc23/eng/20240724
LC record available at https://lccn.loc.gov/2024033998

ISBN: 978-0-367-63255-7 (hbk)
ISBN: 978-0-367-61081-4 (pbk)
ISBN: 978-1-003-11261-7 (ebk)

DOI: 10.4324/9781003112617

Typeset in Times New Roman
by Apex CoVantage, LLC

For my wife, Alex, and daughters, Evie and Bea.

Contents

Table of Cases

Table of Statutes and Statutory Instruments

United Kingdom

Austria

Australia

China

Hong Kong

Ghana

India

Ireland

Italy

New Zealand

USA

Table of Treaties, Directives, Regulations, and Conventions

Glossary

ADR (Alternative Dispute Resolution) Processes for resolving disputes that are alternative or complementary to court adjudication. Many of these processes include a neutral third party supporting a negotiation settlement. The term is generally used to include arbitration and sometimes internal dispute resolution.

Arbitration Process by which parties to a dispute contract to be bound by the decision of an arbitrator or arbitral board who will make a binding determination of the issue brought before them.

Bargaining Process of making and responding to specific 'offers' that are capable of acceptance by the other party or parties taking place within the broader context of negotiation.

Caucus Meetings Term generally used in the USA for confidential individual meetings held between one party and the mediator

Civil Mediation Voluntary, flexible, and confidential third-party facilitated negotiation in hich the parties remain in control of the decision to settle and the terms of resolution. It can take place either in prospect of litigation or as an attempt to settle litigation.

Collaborative Law Process of negotiating the resolution of a dispute by which the lawyers, their clients, and experts work in a multi-disciplinary way to negotiate financial and other arrangements outside the court process. The lawyers of parties to a dispute make a commitment not to represent their clients in court proceedings should the process break down.

Community Mediation Process of facilitated dialogue used for resolving disputes between neighbours or in a community setting. Agreements are generally made as commitments in good faith.

Confidentiality Protection of personal or private information from disclosure without the express consent of the party concerned.

Conflict Generalised state of disequilibrium between individuals and groups, more amorphous and less clearly defined than a dispute.

Dialogue Thinking together. Interaction and exchange between individuals and groups of different cultures. Dialogue is premised on increasing mutual understanding of complex issues rather than creating consensus.

Dispute Contest between individuals or groups involving identification of parties and a specific wrong for which one (or more) individuals attempt to hold another person, other people, or an institution accountable.

Early Neutral Evaluation Voluntary, without-prejudice process by which parties and their legal teams put their case to a neutral party to obtain an evaluation of what might happen if the case goes to trial.

Evaluative Mediation Style of mediation in which the mediator takes a role in evaluating the respective claims of the parties.

Facilitative Mediation Style of mediation in which the mediator enables, encourages, or supports dialogue between the parties in the support of settlement of a dispute but does not take a role in evaluating the respective claims of the parties.

Family Mediation 'Process in which those involved in family relationship breakdown, change, transitions or disputes, whether or not they are a couple or other family members, appoint an impartial third person, a Mediator, to assist them to communicate better with one another and reach their own agreed and informed decisions typically relating to some, or all, of the issues relating to separation, divorce, children, finance or property by negotiation' (Family Mediation Council definition).

Financial Dispute Resolution Form of facilitated evaluative negotiation offered by district judges in the context of family break-ups or disputes.

Mandatory Mediation Mediation in which one or both parties are required to participate. The mandate may be either at the discretion of a judge or categorical, in which all disputes of a particular kind are subject to mediation.

Mediation Third-party facilitated negotiation.

Narrative Mediation Style of mediation which prioritises mutual understanding of the narratives or stories of the parties involved.

Negotiation Dialogue between parties taking place with the goal of reaching agreement on a specific issue or issues.

Ombudsman Official with authority to investigate complaints about public (and sometimes private) decisions and to propose remedies.

Online Mediation Any dispute resolution process taking place online.

Privilege Legal doctrine according to which confidential information cannot be shared with a court or other parties.

Problem-Solving Mediation Style of mediation in which the mediator plays a proactive role in helping the parties shape a resolution to their dispute.

Reconciliation Ending hostility or restoring amicable relations between parties to a dispute.

Reparation Act of repairing or making amends for damage caused.

Resolution Agreement in relation to the matters in dispute

Restorative Justice Form of ADR often taking place in the context of a criminal offence, giving those who have caused harm the opportunity to acknowledge the impact of their behaviour, to listen to those they have harmed, and potentially to make reparations. It is in essence relational and involves dialogue between the victim and offender.

Settlement Agreement between parties to a dispute as a way of disposing of or concluding litigation.

Transformative Mediation Style of mediation which prioritises the relationship between the parties over the settlement of the dispute between them.

Acknowledgments

Writing this book would not have been possible without the support of friends, family, and colleagues. I would like to acknowledge my appreciation to the following for their help and advice: Simon Keyes for many discussions about mediation and the development of the book; Gillian Caroe who has taught on the SOAS ADR course and helped with comments on negotiation, civil mediation, and mediation ethics; Hiro Aragaki and Charles Seaford for their comments on negotiation; Neil Morgan, Tracey Fox, and Heidi Bartlet for commenting on a chapter on mediation psychology; Victoria Harris, Mike Nellis, Tim Newell, Kimmet Edgar, Jamie Buchan, and Alison Scott-Baumann have offered helpful comments on various aspects of community mediation and restorative justice; Marion Liebmann has both commented in detail on community mediation and restorative justice and helped me track down historical material in this area; Andrew Goodman for his comments, corrections, and practical suggestions on civil mediation and mediation ethics; Omer Shapira for his reading and helpful critical commentary on mediation ethics; Samia Bano and Marianne Roberts for their thoughtful comments in helping me expand my horizon on family mediation; Stephen Barker for discussion of a mediation observation with him and his thoughtful comments on a chapter on mediation ethics; Chula Rupasinha for providing a case study illustrating civil mediation; Robert McCracken for commenting on a chapter on mandatory mediation; Frank Eijkman and Peter Leyland for their comments on hybrid forms of ADR; Michael Patchett-Joyce and my SOAS colleagues Emilia Onyema, Martin Lau, and Mashood Baderin for their insightful comments on arbitration; Michael Palmer, Ding Qi, Nuhu Yidana, and former students, Shreeja Kumar, Adnan Shaikh, Kudrat Dev, Pedro Medina, and Brandon Lin for discussion of mediation in a comparative context; and John Bray for providing an historical example of mediation in Nepal and Bhutan. I would like to thank Resolve West for their permission to include a case study on restorative justice; CEDR for permission to reproduce their 'model mediation agreement' and Family Mediation Council (FMC) for permission to reproduce their code of practice in an appendix. I would like to express my thanks to SOAS for the opportunity to take study leave in autumn 2023 to work on the book and my appreciation to my wife, Alex, and children, Evie and Bea, for their patience in making this project possible.

All remaining errors are my own responsibility.

1 Introduction

Definition of Terms

In addition to formal processes of adjudication, any society requires processes that resolve disputes not by appeal to an authoritative umpire but by encouraging parties to re-engage with each other as a way of enabling them to resolve their own differences.

Mediation, as the dominant form of alternative dispute resolution (ADR), is the primary focus of this book. Before looking at the history of mediation, it may be helpful to define these central terms. Mediation derives from *mediare*, Latin for 'to be in the middle.' 'Mediation' is, in essence, 'third party facilitated negotiation.' It is about supporting people in having difficult conversations, especially, but not exclusively, in finding resolution to disputes. For the Center for Effective Dispute Resolution (CEDR 'Mediator Handbook' 7th Edition (2019)):

> Mediation is a **flexible** process conducted **confidentially** in which a **neutral** person actively assists parties in working towards a negotiated agreement of a dispute or difference, with the **parties in ultimate control** of the decision to settle and the terms of the resolution.

Article 3 of Directive 2008/52/EC of the European Parliament and of the Council on Certain Aspects of Mediation in Civil and Commercial Matters defines mediation as:

> a structured process, however named or referred to, whereby two or more parties to a dispute attempt by themselves, on a voluntary basis, to reach an agreement on the settlement of their dispute with the assistance of a mediator.

Alternative dispute resolution (ADR) is a broader term covering all forms of dispute resolution other than court adjudication. The *Glossary of the White Book* (the authoritative legal text regarding rules of civil procedure in the High Court and County Court of England and Wales) defines ADR as the 'collective description of methods of resolving disputes otherwise than through the normal trial process.' While most of these processes involve a third party as a facilitator or advisor and the parties remain in control of the outcome, there are also adjudicative options,

DOI: 10.4324/9781003112617-1

including arbitration and binding expert determination, in which this is not the case. Some commentators would also include Internal Complaint's procedures in the definition of ADR.

It may also be helpful to define some other terms as used in this book. 'Conflict' is used to cover a general disequilibrium, whether between individuals or groups of people. 'Dispute' is used to refer to a far more focused contest between individuals or groups involving identification of parties and a specific wrong for which one (or more) individuals attempt to hold another person, people, or institution accountable. 'Resolution' is used broadly to describe agreement in relation to matters in dispute. 'Resolution' does not necessarily imply a restoration of friendly relations, whereas 'reconciliation' describes the ending of hostility and some degree of harmony in relations. 'Settlement' is largely coterminous with 'resolution' but is used to refer, in particular, to an agreement which disposes of litigation.

For the legal philosopher Fuller (1971), the defining characteristic of mediation is its capacity

> to re-orientate the parties toward each other, not by imposing rules on them, but by helping them achieve a new and shared perception of their relationship, a perception that will redirect their attitude and dispositions toward one another.

This will be most effective when brought about not through formal rules but by persuading the parties to adopt a relationship of mutuality and understanding that will give them the capacity to meet future contingencies.

The significance of 're-orientation' is central to the anthropologist Curle's (1990) conception of mediation as 'a *psychological* effort' to change perceptions both of the conflict and adversary to the extent that 'protagonists gain some hope of a reasonable resolution and as such are more prepared to negotiate seriously' (Curle 1990). Not all mediation is premised on a future continuation of relationships, and there are often cases in which the goal may be an amicable or stoic separation of ways and decoupling of mutual goals. In family mediation, even when couples no longer relate to each other as spouses, they often remain as co-parents, and in this context, there is space for a transformation of relationships based on a mutuality of needs, responsibilities, and interests.

This book examines the practice of mediation and the way it exists in a complex, 'symbiotic,' 'complementary,' or 'dialogic' relationship with the courts in a variety of different contexts. While mediation is often seen as existing in 'the shadow of the law' (Mnookin and Kornhauser 1979) or, indeed, more narrowly, 'in the shadow of the court,' many processes of mediation predate the development of the modern system of legal adjudication.

Judges and lawyers have always played a role in helping parties settle. Abraham Lincoln exhorted litigants to 'Persuade your neighbours to compromise whenever you can. Point out to them that the nominal winner is often the loser in fees, expenses and cost of time.' Mahatma Gandhi is quoted as saying,

> I realised that the true function of a lawyer was to unite the parties. A large part of my time during the 20 years of my practice as a lawyer was occupied

> in bringing about private compromises of hundreds of cases. I lost nothing thereby – not even money, certainly not my soul.

Civil lawyers sometimes present litigation as but one part of a wider process of 'litigotiation' (Galanter 1984), in which litigation is seen as a strategy for strengthening a corporate bargaining position rather than an end in itself.

Modern ADR

Courts have never been the sole, or even the dominant, location for the resolution of disputes. Court capacity and the volume and nature of disputes in a complex economy are such that this could never be the case. Even of those cases in which disputes are filed with courts, less than 5% go to trial. Research in the USA suggests that parties are almost twice as likely to comply fully with mediated outcomes as with judgments imposed by the court after adjudication (McEwen and Maiman 1984).

While court adjudication may set the paradigm, influence the tone, and determine the boundaries of how disputes are constructed and resolved via precedent, the majority of disputes are resolved or 'settled' through a process of negotiation.

The mediation movement initially gathered momentum in the developed West with idealism of the 1960s and a desire to create better access to justice. In the early 1970s, San Francisco community boards advocated a communitarian vision of justice and self-governance (Palmer and Roberts 2020). The movement was given academic authority and momentum by the intervention of Frank Sander in the National Conference on the Cause of Popular Dissatisfaction with the Administration of Justice (The Pound Conference in 1976) with his visionary concept of the 'multi-door courtroom' where adjudication would become one among many processes for the resolution of conflict.

Mediation was given impetus within civil procedure in the USA with the imprimatur of the Supreme Court's Chief Justice Warren Burger after his visit to the Peoples' Republic of China (PRC) at the invitation of the Ministry of the Interior in 1981, which included an opportunity to observe a people's mediation committee at work. Warren Burger famously called on those involved in civil litigation in the USA to search for a 'better way' (Burger 1982).

At an institutional level, in the UK, the Heilbron/Hodge Report (1993) made the case for settlement as a primary goal of the civil justice system. This then became a premise of the Woolf Report and subsequent changes to civil procedure in the 1990s. For Lord Neuberger, 'the philosophy of litigation should be primarily to encourage settlement of disputes whether through the court process or by alternative means of dispute resolution' (Allen 2018).

Mediation and Adjudication

Values

Litigation and mediation seek to fulfill rather different purposes and reflect different concepts of justice. While mediation empowers participants by placing what is most important to them centre stage in negotiating an agreed settlement, only adjudication can form the basis of an 'authoritative public decision' that creates a precedent for determining analogous disputes.

Adjudication appeals to values of impartiality and objectivity and the authority of precedent, focusing on the facts rather than the people in a forum of 'public' decision-making. Mediation, by contrast, prioritises participant-led decision-making and is voluntary, confidential, and informal, and its decisions are often based on interests rather than rights. Often, but not invariably, mediation seeks to maintain relationships and is future focused, looking to agreed outcomes. Adjudication is more focused on an analysis of what has happened in the past, although damages may include an element of future consequences.

Mediation Values

- **Voluntary – implies neither coercive nor violent**
- **Confidential**
- **Informal**
- **Impartial**
- **Interest based (rather than rights)**
- **Decisions non-binding until agreed by all parties**
- **Maximises value**
- **Maintains relationship where possible**
- **Future focus**

Judicial values

- **Impartiality**
- **Objectivity**
- **Authority of precedent**
- **Focus on facts rather than people**
- **Public decision-making**
- **Consistency with other cases**
- **Rights based (rather than interests)**

Mediation is often spoken of as operating 'in the shadow of the law' (Mnookin and Kornhauser 1979), in the sense that the outcomes of a negotiated settlement will depend on the legal merits of a case and a prediction of how a court might decide an issue if it were to come to be decided in a court.

Styles of Mediation

Styles of mediation will vary according to context and an implicit tension between the significance given to the relationships of the parties and the substance of the dispute. At one end of the continuum, facilitated 'dialogue' may involve a conversation that seeks greater mutual understanding, without any goal of convergent expectations leading to agreement. At the other, as in some online mediation platforms, parties may agree to settle a dispute without ever meeting. Some commentators describe mediation as taking place on a spectrum between 'facilitation' and 'evaluation.' Riskin (1996) offers a more sophisticated analysis that provides for a matrix comprising two axes, one of *goals* between 'broad' and 'narrow' and the other of *strategies* between 'facilitation' and 'evaluation.' A mediator's style may not only vary according to the legal context but also shift between stages of a mediation. A mediator adopting a 'narrow evaluative' style might seek to broaden the problem by exploring broader underlying interests. A mediator adopting a 'broad facilitative' style, if unable to facilitate a comprehensive settlement, might narrow the focus to identify smaller areas on which agreement might be possible.

Boulle and Nessic (2001) describe four models of mediation: 'settlement,' 'facilitative,' 'therapeutic,' and 'evaluative.' Other styles commonly referred to include 'problem solving,' 'narrative mediation,' and 'insider partial mediation' (especially in relation to diplomacy). Many mediators develop an eclectic style and acknowledge explicitly the disputants' contribution to the process as well as the substance of the negotiation. Carroll and Mackie (2021) identify 27 variations of mediation. The following section aims to briefly set out some of the characteristics of the principal styles of mediation.

Facilitative Mediation

Facilitative mediation is the dominant form of modern UK/US mediation. This is sometimes referred to as pure mediation, and for commentators such as Love (1997), any element of evaluation compromises the integrity of the process. The mediation takes place in a mixture of joint sessions with both parties and individual (or caucus [USA]) meetings, including individual disputants and the mediators. Smaller meetings in a corporate context might include a meeting of both parties' lawyers or specialists (construction engineers, accountants, etc.) from both sides. While those in dispute are responsible for the substance of negotiations, mediators take responsibility for the process although they may seek the parties' advice on how to proceed and who should be included in meetings.

Evaluative Mediation

Evaluative mediation is modelled on US-style settlement conferences. The mediator supports the parties in evaluating their claims in light of what a court might determine by enabling the parties to 'reality test' their claims. In some forms of evaluative mediation, especially in the USA and the Pacific Rim, mediators may make either informal or formal recommendations in encouraging the parties to settle their claims.

Transformative Mediation

In transformative mediation, priority is put on the relationships between the parties. Bush et al. (2004) describe a form used in community mediations, in which disputes are viewed not as problems at all but as 'opportunities for moral growth and transformation.' Mediation offers an opportunity for transforming 'conflict interactions,' leading to a 'virtuous circle' of communication that affirms 'empowerment' and 'recognition.' According to this model, a mediation is successful when it leads to more humanising, constructive, connecting, positive communication, despite the issues between the parties remaining unresolved.

Narrative Mediation

Narrative mediation derives from the work of Winslade and Monk (2000) on narrative therapy. The narrative metaphor draws attention to the ways in which we use stories to make sense of our lives and relationships. Descriptions of problems are repeated in formulaic terms. Such saturated problem narratives have often been rehearsed and elaborated by participants until they structure and organise their interpretation of the world. Narrative mediators focus on the parties' stories (both their narratives of the conflict and the underlying interpretive frameworks which frame their understanding of the world) and then help the parties deconstruct the 'conflict-saturated' narrative and create a more constructive alternative story, which the parties use as a platform to build a more positive interaction.

Problem-Solving Mediation

In problem-solving mediation, the mediator asks the parties to explore the original cause of the dispute and discuss ideas for solution. The dispute is seen as a problem to be solved by mutual agreement and creative thinking. The mediator is able to bring logic and clarity from an independent perspective and help as an agent of reality in checking the various actions that are necessary for the settlement to be fulfilled. While the mediator may suggest possible solutions, it is vital to the integrity of the process that this is done with a light touch and that both the definition of the problem and its solution are derived from the parties' preferences. Mediators may not know the reasons for parties choosing a particular solution and prematurely telling the parties a seemingly 'obvious' solution may undermine party autonomy and deny the disputants the learning experience of coming up with their own agreement.

One Genus, Many Species

Mediation has developed as an alternative and a response to a powerful and dominant discourse of adjudication. Mediation will be most effective where there is a combination of strong social cohesion and a high degree of mutuality combined with reticence towards the role of the judiciary in adjudicating and enforcing a settlement to a dispute. While mediation has the potential to empower participants by placing what is most important to them centre stage and can affirm relationships in negotiating an agreed settlement, it cannot form the basis of an authoritative public decision that creates a precedent for determining analogous disputes.

Mediation is the dominant form of ADR considered in this book, not least for its capacity to enhance human relationships. It may be helpful to consider mediation as one point on a continuum from unassisted negotiation to arbitration, in which disputants agree to nominate a third party to adjudicate their dispute. In expert evaluation, parties may agree to the appointment of an expert for evaluation of a particular aspect of a dispute. While lawyers are not generally present in community mediation, in civil disputes, they play a significant role.

Forms of dispute resolution combining mediation and arbitration (Med-Arb) lie on the boundary between non-adjudicative and adjudicative forms of ADR. Disputants agree to submit their dispute to an arbitrator in the event of mediation failing to produce an agreed outcome. In expert determination, parties may agree to the appointment of an expert for a binding determination of a particular aspect of a dispute. In pure arbitration, parties agree to the appointment of an arbitrator who will make a decision for them.

Fitting the Forum to the Fuss

Flexibility is a hallmark of ADR as a variety of practices. Sander and Goldberg (1994) suggest that while mediation is the default process, two lines of enquiry should guide disputants' choice of forum: 'What are the disputants' goals in forum choice?' and 'What are the obstacles to settlement, and in what forum might they be overcome?' What the parties want out of a dispute will determine the applicability of various ADR techniques. Where vindication is the priority, court adjudication may be the preferred outcome. Where a definitive view of merits is significant, early neutral evaluation or a mini-trial may be effective. Mediation is especially useful where a continuing relationship is a priority.

Mediation Ground Rules

Mediation is, in essence, third-party facilitated negotiation and can be applied in a huge variety of contexts. While its style and context may vary, forms of mediation share a set of principles and practices. What are often referred to as the 'ground rules' of mediation are not invariable, and one of the first tasks of a mediator is to establish or articulate this shared understanding. In community mediation in particular, agreeing on these rules as a first step may help create momentum for establishing more skillful communication.

Common to most forms of mediation are the following ground rules:

Mediation is voluntary. Parties are free to discontinue the mediation if and whenever they choose.

Mediation is confidential. Everything that is said in the mediation will be confidential to those in the mediation, and nothing said in individual meetings with a mediators will be disclosed to the other party without the party's explicit permission.

Offers in mediation are made on a **without-prejudice** basis; any offers made are **non-binding** and cannot be disclosed to a court if it not possible to come to an agreement.

The mediator acts as an **impartial** facilitator.

Courtesy. Parties agree to listen to one another courteously and with respect, especially when not agreeing with what is being said.

Mediation requires good faith. Parties agree to come to the mediation with an intention of coming to an agreement and a willingness to compromise. Mediation is generally more informal than court adjudication.

Conclusion

The development of mediation has been influenced by a diversity of factors that include tensions within the court system to manage caseloads and pressure from below for an alternative to adjudication that is more empowering and satisfying to disputants. Greater psychological and anthropological awareness of the dynamics of conflict and disillusion with the judicial system have fed into a willingness both to reinvigorate traditional forms of dispute resolution and to develop innovative forms in jurisdictions in developed countries and the Global South. Mediation has sometimes been described as 'a practice in search of a theory.' While not offering such a theory, this book will invite readers to reflect on how forms and styles of mediation vary according to context and suggest that the role of the mediator is one that requires a very different analysis of relationships than that conventionally adopted in a law school.

While mediation may take heterogeneous forms, common to them and distinct from the process of adjudication are the consensual nature of the practice and the consequent function of reinforcing social solidarity.

Questions

1. **What do you see as the values that inform mediation and adjudication?**
2. **What are the purposes of ground rules in mediation, and what do you consider to be the most significant?**
3. **What are some of the principal factors that have led to the development of mediation?**
4. **Discuss in pairs some of the contexts in which mediation might be most effective and those in which it might not be appropriate.**

2 Theories of Conflict and the Principles of ADR

Conflict is an inherent aspect of life. Conflict is present within individuals; between their competing motivations, desires, emotions, and drives; between individuals with perceived or substantive incompatible goals; between groups or classes in society; over finite resources or distribution of social, economic, or political power; and between nation-states or blocs of nations. How we define conflict will also influence how we respond to it. For Wall (1985), it is defined in terms of goals and perceptions: 'a process in which two or more parties attempt to frustrate the attainment of the other's goals. The factors underlying conflict are threefold: interdependence, differences in goals and differences in perceptions.' For Schelling (1960), conflicts are 'bargaining situations in which the ability of one participant to achieve his ends is dependent on the choices or decisions that the other participant makes.'

Conflicts are dynamic, complex, and fluid and define social relations at every level from the community to the nation-state. Conflict may be as much an opportunity as a threat. Conflict is an inevitable aspect of social development as vested interests protect themselves and seek to protect their interests and power. Movements for the abolition of slavery; for race, gender, and sexual equality; and for democratic participation or the representation of workers' rights all inevitably involve conflict. While the effective resolution of conflict can lead to a transformation and enhancement of social justice, ineffective conflict management can lead to stasis and repetitive cycles of injustice.

For the purpose of this chapter, conflict is understood as a generalised state of disequilibrium and a 'dispute' as a more specific and developed contest, whether over limited resources or values between clearly delineated parties. While disputes often focus on legal causes, conflicts relate more broadly to 'human relations and transaction' (Menkel-Meadow 2017). Conflict is frequently amorphous, fluid, and ill defined, lacking the precision and formal boundaries of disputes. It is only through a series of transformations that conflicts become formalised as disputes and through a set of cultural changes that they are given a legal imprimatur and reproduced before the court as a cause for settlement. Disputes require the identification of parties and a specific wrong, involving a breach of normative values for which one person (or more) attempt to hold another person, people, or institution accountable.

DOI: 10.4324/9781003112617-2

Societies accord different priorities to social harmony and show very different attitudes towards the desirability of conflict, as either a threat or an opportunity for social change, which may lead to what Palmer and Roberts (2020) have referred to as 'grievance apathy' (the unwillingness of persons who perceive themselves to have suffered an injurious experience caused by another party to pursue their grievance against that party) or, more neutrally, a reticence to resort to litigation. While, for instance, American individualism may value legal assertiveness as a laudable hallmark of democratic entitlement, the Chinese values of Confucianism emphasise duty as a positive social value and disparage the claiming of rights. The victim of a failed operation in the NHS may be unwilling to formalise a complaint out of a commitment to the public service values of the NHS rather than out of apathy as conventionally understood according to the US model.

Disputes are the culturally contingent way in which conflict takes shape in a specific social context. For Felstiner et al. (1980–1981), the initial transformation of conflict involves the identification of an 'injurious experience.' They (1980–1981) describe a process of 'naming,' 'blaming,' and 'claiming,' in which 'injurious experiences' are first recognised and then attributed to a particular cause for which a claim is made and subsequently framed in legal language. In the first transformation, an unperceived injurious experience (UNPIE) becomes identified as a perceived injurious experience or PIE – naming. Subsequent transformation occurs when an injurious experience (PIE) is identified as a grievance that is the responsibility of another – blaming. A grievance only becomes a dispute when it is resisted or refused, leading to a contest between the parties. There may be further changes, including grievance processes, of various degrees of formality, before a claim is framed as a dispute and organised, through rules of civil procedure, as a case that is given legal impress – claiming. In interpersonal (and other) conflicts, transformations take place as a party making a claim, attempts to enlist supporters – with various degrees of neutrality – to support or endorse their position. A similar process may be conducted by those against whom a claim is made. The enlistment and co-option of allies – and, at times, their refusal to be enlisted, thereby becoming 'third parties' – may clarify issues at the cost of entrenching positions and making it harder for either party to back down without losing face.

Whether an injurious experience is transformed into a dispute will depend on many factors. Level of education, confidence, and availability of resources – see, for instance, the impact of trade unions in employment disputes or law centres in cases of housing and welfare rights – are significant factors, as are previous experiences of similar problems, leading to pattern recognition. The availability of legal aid and accessibility of legal fora may increase levels of dispute recognition at the point at which underlying issues are being addressed. While the existence of a community mediation scheme may help resolve intransigent conflicts, it may have the unintended consequence of increasing levels of grievances by providing for more accessible fora. Community disputes may be a symptom of underlying structural problems regarding, for instance, poorly insulated housing stock or poor social landlords.

For Felstiner et al. (1980–1981) a healthy social order minimises barriers inhibiting the emergence of grievances and disputes and preventing their translation into claims for redress. This itself, however, is a socially embedded value. The individual's experience of 'entitlement' to 'enjoy certain experiences and be free from others' is a function of ideology, of which law is only one component. The consumer's dissatisfaction with a product or service may have been influenced by organisations such as Which (the consumer's association) in the UK or campaigns of activists like Ralph Nader in the USA, who assert that consumers have a right to expect high-quality treatment. Significant legal change, for instance *Brown v Board of Education* (1954) in the USA, the Race Relations Act 1976, or Equality Act 2010 in the UK may sometimes offer a way of transforming ideology to create a sense of legitimate entitlement.

Levels of education, expectations of entitlement, and political culture may all have an impact on how latent conflict is shaped and formalised into a dispute. In the UK mining industry in the 19th century, poor health was accepted as an occupational hazard. This was not just a matter of 'grievance apathy' but a combination of medical ignorance and lack of political education and union organisation. Advances in medical science and political and union organisation may lead to strategic claims being brought before courts for pneumoconiosis and subsequent improvements in occupational health.

Further transformation takes place with the advent of courts and counsel. Courts transform what may be perceived as an indivisible conflict into a tangible contest over specific identified (often financial) issues. Various degrees of formality may impede access to the courts, except where complex procedural law is followed. In England, an equitable jurisdiction tempered the inflexibility of the law by providing for non-financial remedies on the balance of equities but prior to the Judicature Acts (1875), parallel systems of courts, as satirised in the case of *Jaundyce v Jaundyce* in Dicken's *Bleak House* (1852–1853), could stymie the most determined litigator while in absolutist pre-revolutionary France, judges would only consider that which was in the file in their docket; from the point of view of a judge, '*Quod non est in actis non est in mundo*' ('What is not in the file doesn't exist').

By the time a dispute is filed in court, there will have been a huge psychological and professional investment of time and resources, and the costs incurred may often be significantly greater than the sum in dispute. Lawyers select material for a case according to professional criteria of relevance and filter that material according to their 'theory' of a case: What happened? What rule breaches were involved? Who was responsible? In a final stage, judges further organise cases by both selecting the law that is to be interpreted and defining the body of evidence to which it is to be applied.

Anthropologists interpreting conflict in pre-colonial societies identify a variety of modes of dealing with conflict, including ritualised negotiation and third-party decision making (Palmer and Roberts 2020). In highly integrated, mutually dependent cultures, conflict is likely to be more socially costly, and there may be highly developed processes for the settlement of disputes. In 'low-context' cultures, conflict may take a very direct and belligerent form, whereas in 'high-context' cultures, conflict may be inferred from more nuanced changes in behaviour. Courts are not the exclusive mechanisms of conflict resolution, and third-party decision-making can take place independently of the organisation of the modern secular state.

Theories of Conflict

Friedrich Hegel (1770–1831)

Hegel developed a theory of social change involving a triangular process of thesis, antithesis, and synthesis which, in turn, becomes the context for further social change. This theory offers a paradigm of the process of mediation in which one party proposes a perspective (thesis), and the other responds with a contrary position (antithesis). The mediator attempts to facilitate a resolution (synthesis) that integrates the perspectives of both parties.

Karl Marx (1818–1883)

Marx applied Hegel's theory of the dialectic to social classes in a philosophy of 'dialectical materialism.' Marx's analysis focuses on how relationships between people and classes are shaped by their relative positions in relation to the means of production. Conflict is the agent of social change. In Marxism, the capitalist economy manifests itself in conflict between the ruling class (bourgeoisie), who own and control the means of production, and the working class (proletariat), who depend on selling labour in return for wages. Conflicts over wealth and resources can bring about a transcendence of self-interest among the poorest in society. According to a Marxist analysis, law is not socially neutral but serves to justify and consolidate the interests of the most powerful.

George Simmel (1858–1918)

Simmel identified the way in which conflict and 'common enmity' serve as agents of social solidarity. He envisages the role of mediator as universal and as a symbol of society. The role of mediator as non-aligned facilitator is conceptually distinct from that of the partisan supporter and the arbitrator with determinative authority. The presence of a mediator subtly changes the behaviour of disputants in the model of calm and detachment it provides and the capacity that they bring to invite the parties to shape a more reasoned and considered account of their perspectives. From a conversation between friends to the family of three, there is no triad in which a dissent between two elements does not occur and in which the third member does not play a mediating role. In this non-aligned, non-determinative role,

> A gesture, a way of listening, the mood that radiates from a particular person, are enough to change the difference between two individuals so that they can seek understanding, are enough to make them feel their essential

commonness which is concealed under their acutely differing opinions and to bring this divergence into the shape into which it can be ironed out the most easily.

(Simmel 1950)

Kenneth Boulding (1910–1993)

As editor of *The Journal of Conflict Resolution*, Boulding integrated different areas of academic expertise, including anthropology, psychology, and sociology, in considering human behaviour as shaped by various constructed world views (images). New information is processed according to a 'world view' and may change or inform this framework. His 'evolutionary world view' is distinct from the 'dialectic' approach of Marx and the 'structural' approach of Galtung (discussed later). For Boulding, poverty, destitution, and deprivation belong to systems that are only 'peripherally related to the structures that produce violence' (Boulding 1977). Writing in the context of the Cold War, he considered war an inherent consequence of the sovereign state system that could be prevented by the reform of international organisation and the development of research and information capability.

Johan Galtung (1930–2024)

Galtung (1969) was a Norwegian sociologist who envisaged conflict, at a micro or macro level, as a process in which attitudes and behaviour are in a state of constant flux. Conflict is 'a dynamic process in which structure, attitudes and behaviours are constantly changing and influencing one another.' Parties organise in the context of this structure to pursue their interests, and the conflict develops a momentum of its own. In 'structural violence,' the structures of society and their institutional arrangements deny civil, legal, and political rights and create conditions of poverty, destitution, or inequality. These conditions carry within them the seeds of further violent behaviour (Galtung 1990). Resolving conflict involves dynamic interventions that lead to a de-escalation of conflict behaviour with the potential for a transformation of relationships. Galtung distinguishes between 'direct violence' or 'structural violence,' in which social structures or institutions prevent the satisfaction of basic human needs, and 'cultural violence' in the hegemony that maintains unjust relationships, whether by language, religion, or other ideologies (Ramsbotham et al. 2016).

At a macro level, peace enforcement is the coercive settlement by a dominant party. Peace-making activities can be identified with the search for creative and sustainable outcomes of the conflict which aim to change the attitudes of the protagonists. Peace-building activities can be identified with building structural and cultural peace, seeking to overcome the contradictions at the heart of the conflict. Galtung contested Boulding's focus on the 'upper side of human history' (that of the developed world) and considered 'a removal of structural violence' a necessary condition to obtain a stable peace. He advocated a process of dialogue or 'soft negotiation,' suggesting that only by genuine dialogue between the parties (*dia logos*, or 'by the word') is it possible to reach a transformation that transcends the interests of both (Galtung 1987, 2004).

Louis Coser (1913–2003)

For Coser (1956), conflict is rooted in the struggle over limited resources and the aim of 'eliminating' the rival group. Conflict becomes 'a struggle between opponents over values and claims to scarce, status, power and resources.' He follows Simmel in understanding conflict as fulfilling a cohesive and bonding function in defining social groups and Dewey in seeing conflict as a '*sine qua non*' of reflection and ingenuity. Conflict prevents ossification of structures by exerting pressure for creativity and innovation. Conflict between vested interests and new strata and groups competing for their share of wealth, power, and influence is a source of social vitality. Whether conflict leads to changes within a system (reform) or the formation of a new system (revolution) will depend on the rigidity of a system and its resistance to change. Coser considers conflict dysfunctional only for societies in which there is insufficient toleration or institutionalisation of conflict. Highly intense conflicts that threaten to 'tear apart' society arise only in rigid social structures.

Morton Deutsch (1920–2017)

For Deutsch (1973), conflict 'takes place wherever incompatible activities occur. One party is interfering, disrupting, obstructing, or in some other way making another party's actions less effective.' Conflict may be constructive in the context of an effective cooperative problem-solving process, in which it is seen as a mutual problem to be resolved. It may be destructive in a competitive process, in which the parties become locked in a 'struggle to determine who wins and who loses,' and the outcome of the struggle is a loss for both parties. Deutsch advocates an 'interactive problem-solving process,' at the heart of which is 'reframing the conflict as a mutual problem to be resolved (or solved) through joint cooperative efforts' (Deutsch et al. 2014: 30, 31).

Paradigms of Conflict

Coleman (Chapter 30 in Deutsch et al. 2014) offers five paradigms for considering intractable conflict. Each paradigm is supported by its own evidence and implies its own methods of questioning. The **realist paradigm** adopts a political metaphor and understands conflict resulting from rational strategic choices made under the conditions of a politics of hatred, manipulation, dominance, and violence. It dismisses other interpretations as naïve or idealistic. Change is primarily effected through coercive command and control and distributive bargaining strategies. The realist paradigm underpins many international efforts at political mediation. The **human relations paradigm** uses a social metaphor to understand intractable conflict as the result of destructive relationships and envisages fear, mistrust, and misunderstanding as primary obstacles to constructive engagement. Change can be brought about through developing a better quality of relationships fostered by psychological understanding, influence, and education, considering integrative negotiation as a route to resolving conflict. The **pathology paradigm** applies a medical metaphor to understanding conflict as a disease. This presents conflict as a complex and inter-related system that can be analysed, treated, and understood. Change may be effected by outside experts or specialists who may have the knowledge, training, and distance from the 'patient' to diagnose and treat the problem. The **postmodern paradigm** deploys a communications metaphor to portray intractability as rooted in the way we make sense of the world. Change depends on challenging assumptions, critical reflection, dialogue, and confrontation, developing disputants' awareness of complexity. The postmodern paradigm underpins some of Lederach's thinking on mediation (Lederach 1997) and Winslade's and Monk's (2000) theory of narrative mediation. The **systems paradigm** uses a biological metaphor which sees conflict as living entities made up of complex and interdependent entities which are parts of other increasingly complex entities. A marital conflict, for instance, is located in a family, a community, an ideology, and a culture. Change occurs in response to shifts in the underlying patterns or structures of organisation.

Responses to Conflict

Individuals and groups respond to conflict in a multiplicity of ways. At the most basic level, there may be resistance to accepting an uncomfortable conflict, especially where this involves a challenge to those in authority. This may lead to strategies of avoidance, denial, or 'deflection,' in which it is more comfortable to blame those who are not responsible for an injurious experience. At an extreme level, individuals may identify with the aggressor, as recognised in studies of the experience of POWs in Korea and Japan. Withdrawal of cooperation or non-compliance may be adopted – for instance, in union strategies – to bring attention to grievances such as a union action short of a strike.

More proactive responses to a dispute may lead to strikes in an employment context. This, in turn, may develop into confrontation and subsequent negotiation, whether bilateral or assisted. Where negotiation fails, disputants may refer to various levels of political authority, including umpiring, court adjudication, and reference to public decision-making. This can involve the institutionalisation of third-party decisions, which Austin's 'command theory' (Austin 1832) identifies as the essence of law, where morality contained in legal norms is enforced with the backing of the state.

Conflict Styles

Various commentators have sought to explain the relationship between personality and conflict. Blake and Mouton (1964), in an employment context, classified five methods of responding to interpersonal conflicts based on the tension between an individual's concerns for 'self' and 'others' or focus on 'agenda' and 'relationship' (Kraybill 2013). Concern for self could be characterised as 'assertiveness' and concern for others as 'empathy' or 'cooperativeness.' Others have identified a similar tension between 'competition' and 'cooperation' (Deutsch 1973). Thomas and Kilmann (1977) created a measurement device for use in human resources. The Thomas-Kilmann Conflict Mode Instrument (TKI) is based on employees choosing between paired statements to assess an individual's choice of conflict methods. According to this model, there are five distinct conflict styles or methods:

1. Avoiding (withdrawing), showing low concern for self and others;
2. Accommodating (smoothing), showing low concern for self but high concern for others;
3. Competing (forcing, dictating, dominating), showing high concern for self but low concern for others,
4. Collaborating (problem solving), showing high concern for self and high concern for others; and
5. Compromising (integrating), showing medium concern for self and others.

While each style may have its own advantages, individuals' dispositions may vary according to social and professional context. Protagonists are more likely to yield to higher-status individuals while dominating those in lower-status positions and compromising or collaborating with those of an equal status. Our style may also be influenced by that of the person we are negotiating with. It is hard to compromise with an avoidant negotiator and even harder to collaborate. Kraybill

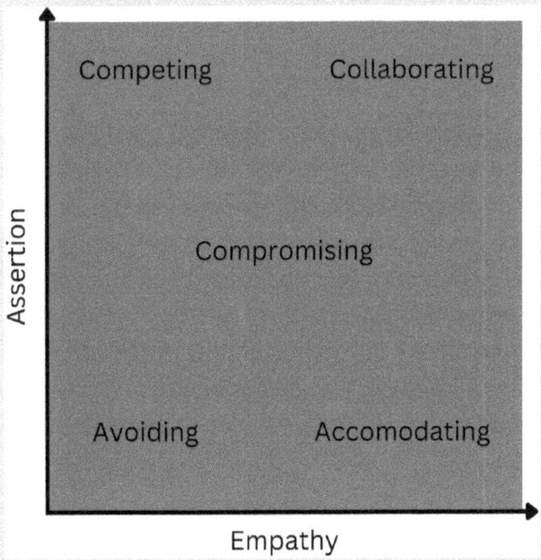

Figure 2.1 Horizontal axis: Empathy/regard for others/cooperativeness/relationship; vertical axis: Regard for self/assertiveness/agenda

(2013) makes the significant distinction that our response to conflict may change when we are faced with intransigence and uses two sets of questions to evaluate our responses in 'calm' and 'stormy' situations.

While there is no universally better style, collaborating is likely to increase long-term goodwill and maximise benefit. Accommodation on an issue that is more important to the person you are negotiating with than to you may help build relationships in issues that are not of particular significance; compromise may be less costly in terms of time and resources than finding the best collaborative solution. Becoming more aware of our conflict styles and those of the people we are negotiating with may increase our effectiveness as a negotiator. As a mediator, an awareness of what is happening in negotiation may enable us to make more skillful interventions in guiding parties towards a negotiated settlement.

Bilateral and Multilateral Disputes

According to Fuller (1978), disputes may involve multiple parties, multiple issues, and complex matrices of relationship. The most appropriate form of resolution will depend on the form of the dispute. Polycentric disputes and those requiring the allocation of resources are inherently problematic for both adjudication and mediation, which requires the presence or representation of all parties involved. While those disputes with a contractual basis involving reciprocity may be uniquely amenable to the negotiation involved in mediation, those involving common purpose and voting on decisions are more suitable to a political process involving election while adjudication is most appropriate to cases involving authoritative determination of claims of right and accusations of guilt requiring presentation of proofs and reasoned argument. For Fuller (1978), 'Wherever successful human association depends upon spontaneous and informal collaboration, shifting its forms with the task at hand, there adjudication is out of place except as it may declare certain ground rules applicable to a wide variety of activities.'

Recent legal scholarship suggests that although legal disputes may be presented as bilateral, this may be an artificial construction. Even a simple claimant/defendant case in contract may involve insurers, employees, vendors, suppliers, agents, family members, and business partners. Work by scholars such as Susskind et al. (2005) and Menkel-Meadow (2012) consider that multilateral disputes call for a more sophisticated analysis of dispute resolution but do not make mediatory processes impossible. Fuller's distinction between processes requiring 'adjudication' and 'election' may be more blurred than he suggests. The techniques of multi-party dispute resolution are indeed the skills and building blocks of deliberative democracy.

Conflict Dynamics

In both bilateral and multilateral disputes, conflicts develop dynamics independent of the intentions of the parties. Once a case is prepared for court, the investment of professional time and resources (and even responsibilities to the legal aid board) may inhibit settlement.

Multilateral dispute conflicts may develop a momentum of their own independent of the parties. Taylor (1969) argues that the origins of the First World War were rooted in the great powers' belief that if they possessed the capacity to mobilise their armed forces faster than their rivals, this would serve as a deterrent to prevent war and allow them to achieve their policy aims. When the crisis of Sarajevo came in 1914, none of the major parties consciously sought war. The general staff of the great powers had developed an elaborate timetable for swift mobilisation, and pressure to mobilise faster than their rivals created an inexorable movement towards war.

The dynamics discussed by Taylor may be equally true of preparing a case for trial in which cycles of escalating threat and counterthreat lead to a context in which the costs of litigation outweigh the value of what is being litigated, schedules of discovery and interlocutory hearings create self-fulfilling expectations, principals lose control of the process, and backing down becomes almost impossible.

Curle (1971) considered that creative resolution of intractable conflict follows several distinct phases. He identified a four-stage process of conflict resolution in which conflict is first hidden and in which some parties are unaware of imbalances and injustices, which are subsequently brought to the surface through development of awareness or collective 'conscientisation' (Freire 1970), leading to a potential confrontation. Negotiation has the potential to rebalance the dynamics of power where a change of the perception of the protagonists leads to a restructuring of relationships and the potential for sustainable peace.

Discourse

Habermas (1979, 1990, 1996) describes communication as the source of political authority, in which law becomes a form of social mediation between facts and norms. Discourse is politically legitimate where agreement is arrived at freely and uncoerced. His ground rules for an 'ideal speech situation' as the source of that authority are congruent with those for public mediation (Habermas 1979). Menkel-Meadow highlighted that the 'conditions for ideal speech look remarkably like the ground rules for most mediations.' According to his theory of 'communicative action' (Habermas 1990), these require:

1. Every subject with the competence be able to speak and participate.
2. Everyone be able to challenge an assertion.
3. Everyone be able to introduce an assertion.
4. Everyone be able to express their attitudes, desires, and needs.
5. No speaker may be prevented or coerced from exercising these rights.

In these conditions, authentic communication affirms recognition and respect and facilitates listening and evaluation of options without coercion, domination, or structural violence. While remaining an ideal for dialogue, this represents the touchstone of 'unconstrained communication,' which a mediator aims to facilitate in negotiation (Menkel-Meadow 2012).

Conclusion

Understanding the forms of conflict and styles both facilitates effective negotiation and offers a helpful context in which to consider the kind of 'difficult conversations' that mediators may encourage. Such an understanding will help shape the strategies of both disputants and mediators. In the subsequent chapters on forms of mediation, we will consider how mediation styles are influenced by the context of the conflict, preferences of the parties, and mediator orientations.

Questions

1. **How would you define 'conflict,' and what words do you associate with it?**
2. **What words do you associate with a 'dispute,' and what are its essential characteristics?**
3. **How does a 'conflict' differ from a 'dispute,' and how does it become one?**
4. **What factors facilitate and inhibit settlement of conflicts without resort to litigation?**
5. **How would you describe your 'conflict style' at home, in a social situation, and in a professional context?**
6. **How do you find that your 'conflict style' changes when you are under pressure?**

Further Reading

Deutsch, M., Coleman, P. & Marcus, E., D., eds (2014) *The Handbook of Conflict Resolution: Theory and Practice* (3rd ed). Jossey Bass Publishers.

Lederach, J. P. (2005) *The Moral Imagination: The Art and Soul of Building Peace*. Oxford University Press.

Menkel-Meadow, C. J. et al (2005) *Dispute Resolution: Beyond the Adversarial Model*. Aspen.

Ramsbotham, O., Woodhouse, T. & Miall, H., eds (2016) *Contemporary Conflict Resolution* (4th ed). Polity Press.

3 Negotiation

Negotiation

Negotiation, for the purposes of this chapter, is defined as a 'dialogue between two or more parties with the intention of reaching agreement.' Parties to a negotiation may have closely aligned or diametrically opposed interests and objectives, but common to all negotiation is the desire to reach an agreed outcome. All effective mediator interventions are designed to facilitate or influence the underlying process of negotiation between parties. Mediators subscribing to a Western facilitative model of mediation would characterise their intervention as solely 'facilitative.' In practice, many mediators seek to go beyond this and influence the process to ensure congruence with ideological, legal, or community norms.

Negotiation Theory

Negotiation involves two overlapping processes: a 'cyclical' process of exchange of information and a 'developmental' process involving distinct phases or sequences as parties recalibrate their expectations, and possibly their objectives, in the light of what they learn (Gulliver 1979). The combination of the two creates a 'negotiation dance' (Lax and Sebenius 1986), in which periods of antagonism alternate with co-ordination as both parties try to push each other to their bottom line while consolidating their advantage and maintaining the possibility of conclusive agreement.

Without this 'negotiation dance,' accepting a party's first offer, at a level at which they would subsequently be prepared to agree, might leave the offeror considering whether they had been too generous and the acceptor thinking they might have done better.

Requirements for Negotiation

Negotiation requires a shared medium and effective communication to identify and evaluate options leading to convergence or compatibility of outcomes. A distinction is sometimes made between 'negotiation,' involving the entire

DOI: 10.4324/9781003112617-3

interaction between the parties, and 'bargaining,' the making of and response to specific 'offers' that may be accepted by the other party or parties. Generally, parties to a negotiation will have a sense of its boundaries and devise strategies according to their analysis of risk and their alternatives to a negotiated agreement, whether it be acquiescence to the status quo, continuing litigation, or some other alternative form of action. ADR commentators encourage parties to weigh their minimal satisfaction against their 'best alternative to a negotiated agreement (BATNA)' (Palmer and Roberts 2020). A party's BATNA is the choice they will make as their 'resistance point': the quantification of the point at which they no longer wish to negotiate. But negotiators' behaviour may also be influenced by their assessment of their worst alternative to a negotiated agreement (WATNA), the non-chosen, forced, or feared outcome that might arise if compromise is not reached.

These are not fixed co-ordinates, and their boundaries may shift. Parties will make a decision on their alternative to continuing to negotiate on the basis of their hopes and fears of the likely outcome if negotiations break down. The so-called WATNA will be of particular significance to risk-averse negotiators. A skilled negotiator may try to manipulate an adversary into thinking that their alternatives are constrained, and they will be more likely to achieve their worst fears rather than their best hopes if the negotiations break down. The point at which agreement is reached will depend on the relative strength of the respective parties and the potential spectrum of possible agreements (a positive negotiation range) in which both parties consider themselves better off than not reaching an agreement. The zone of potential agreement (ZOPA) covers the area within which it is potentially mutually advantageous for parties to agree – in which they might achieve the minimum for which they would be prepared to settle. While much thinking about negotiation comes from psychology and business models, negotiation is increasingly seen as a component of the training of barristers and solicitors.

Both parties in a negotiation will have an idea of a possible ZOPA, but assumptions will be made on imperfect information, and there may at times be a negative negotiating range, in which case, unless one party modifies their resistance point, there is no prospect of a potential agreement.

Positive Negotiation Range

A puts his house on the market for £500,000, and B makes an initial offer of £450,000. A is, in fact, willing to sell for £470,000 and B to offer up to £480,000. The initial positive negotiating range ZOPA is £10,000.

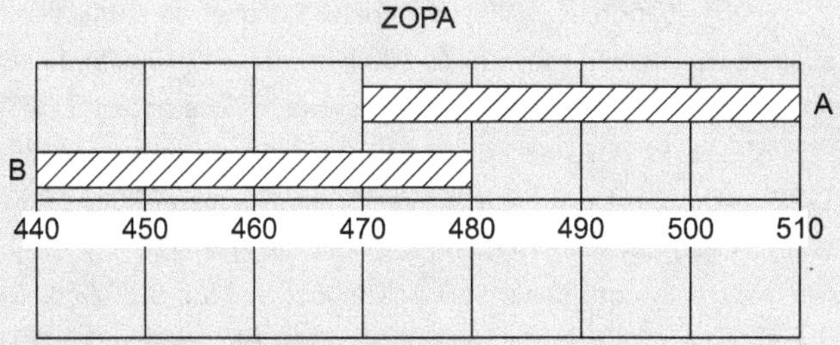

Buyer willing to pay £480,000
Seller willing to accept £470,00
ZOPA £470 to £480,000

Figure 3.1 Positive negotiation range

Negative negotiation range

A is, in fact, only willing to sell for £480,000 and B to offer up to £470,000. There is a negative negotiation range of £10,000.

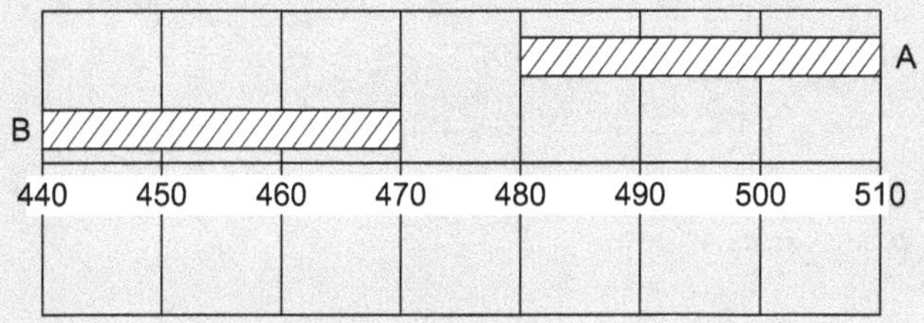

Buyer willing to pay £470,000
Seller willing to accept £480,00

Negative negotiating range £470 to £480,000

Figure 3.2 Negative negotiation range

But where exchange of additional information – for instance, a buyer's survey and valuation – provides a mortgage valuation of the property of £480,000 and the seller becomes aware of defects (which will cost £20,000 to remedy) of which they were previously unaware, goodwill and an effective exchange of information can shift this to a positive negotiation range. A is now willing to remedy the defects, (maybe at a lower cost of £10,000) and to drop his price by £5,000, and B, on the basis of the higher valuation, is willing to increase his offer to £480,000. This then creates a positive negotiation range of £5,000 between £475,000 and £480,000.

Neither party to the negotiation will be aware of the actual ZOPA. B may be willing to offer and A to accept a range of prices between £475,000 and £480,000 GBP, so there is a positive zone of potential agreement of £5,000. But an over-optimistic A may consider that B will, in fact, be willing to pay £490,000, and an over-assertive B may consider that A will, in fact, sell for £450,000. A will then consider that there is a ZOPA of £15,000 (between £475,000 and £490,000) and B that there is a ZOPA of £30,000 (between £480,000 and £450,000). In these circumstances, an unskillful exchange of offers may lead to A rejecting an initial offer of £475,000, even though he might subsequently be willing to accept this figure.

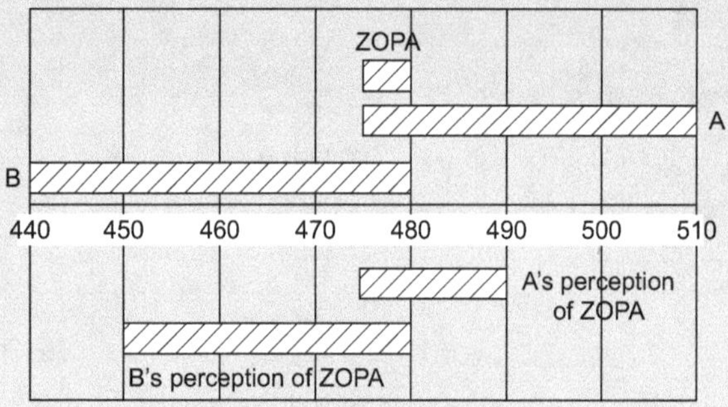

Figure 3.3 A's and B's perception of negotiating range and potential point of convergence

With good communication and further exchange of information, (provided B is the only potential buyer, and A is the only seller of a house that meets B's needs), subsequent offers should lead to a convergence in the ZOPA of £475,000 to £480,000, but miscommunication, alternate buyers and sellers, or pride may mean that a mutually advantageous bargain is lost.

Stages of Negotiation

Gulliver (1971, 1988) drew on cross-cultural research to describe the interplay of 'cyclical' and 'developmental' processes, envisaging negotiation as involving eight partly overlapping phases:

1. Search for an arena for negotiation
2. Formulation of an agenda and definition of issues
3. Preliminary statements of demands and offers and the exploration of the dimensions and limits of the issues

4. Narrowing of the differences, agreements on some issues, and the identification of the more obdurate ones
5. Preliminaries to final bargaining
6. Final bargaining
7. Ritual confirmation
8. Implementation

In its training manual, CEDR (2019) simplifies this to 'preparation,' 'opening,' 'exploration,' 'bargaining,' and 'concluding.'

Positional or Distributive Negotiation

Positional negotiation is the default process in individualistic free-market societies. In positional negotiation, both parties justify extreme positions and make mutual incremental concessions in a process leading to the convergence of positions towards a point of compromise at a hypothetical middle point. Positional bargaining is the premise of a developed individualised commercial system and is a zero-sum game, in which it is assumed that one party's gain is another party's loss in distribution of finite and quantifiable resources. Positional bargaining has the benefit of simplicity and, in consumer cases in which there is little continuity of relationship between the parties, may represent the reality of their experience and be an effective model for negotiation.

A range of tactics are often deployed to maximise the share of the cake in positional bargaining. Negotiators frequently withhold sensitive information to justify extreme postures and use bluffs and threats. Concessions are made slowly, grudgingly, and only in response to movements from the other side.

Anchoring

Individuals' judgments and decisions may be affected by an arbitrary or apparently irrelevant starting point. Tversky and Kahnenen (1974) demonstrate its effect in an exercise estimating the proportion of Africa nations that were members of the UN. In negotiation, initial offers serve as 'anchors' that play a significant role in shaping negotiators' perceptions of the bargaining range. The concept of anchoring suggests that the first person who makes an offer or concession may exhibit a powerful influence in shaping how the process subsequently develops. The concept is a challenge to the received wisdom in negotiation that it is generally best not to make the first move as this may be seen as a sign of weakness. It may be unwise to make the first move if the party you are negotiating with knows more about you and your case than you do about their case. But anchoring is a powerful heuristic that exerts an influence over the range of subsequent negotiations. In distributive bargaining, adopting an extreme anchor creates space for subsequent concessions towards a subsequent hypothetical midway point of convergence. Once an extreme anchor has been set by the offeror, there is then an incentive to make a similarly extreme counteroffer – or second anchor – in order to shift the centre point in the counterofferor's direction.

Resisting Anchoring

Adopting an equally extreme position risks destabilising the process. Techniques for countering anchoring include 'walking away,' a classic market trader's strategy of withdrawal from the process, or rigorous questioning to drill down into the reasons for an initial starting point. Lax and Sebenius (2006) suggest an effective strategy may be to courteously but firmly reject the initial offer while changing the 'metric' or the terms of reference of the negotiation. In valuing a company, for instance, they give the example of countering an offer based on a prices/earnings valuation with a different valuation method: e.g. discounted cash flow analysis (DCF), which looks at the overall valuation of the company rather than its profits. In negotiating an employment contract, a nanny, given what she considers a low-pay offer, might counter by seeking to negotiate on the basis of weekly take-home pay rather than pretax salary. Research suggests that anchoring operates as an unconscious process, but it may be possible to restore integrity to the process by challenging the opposing position with the use of effective questions to establish reasons for the position and establishing your own proposal on the basis of detailed evidence and rigorous analysis (Lax and Sebenius 2006).

Integrative, Principled, or Problem-Solving Negotiation

Integrative bargaining works because parties to a negotiation will value different facets of the negotiation subject matter in different ways. Integrative bargaining seeks to maximise value by understanding what is important to each party. In a labour dispute, for example, there may be a distributional tension over the proportion of profit to be distributed to share-holders and the level of employee wages, but if a union is concerned primarily with job security and total compensation while management is concerned with minimising labour costs and increasing productivity, a negotiated settlement on the basis of profit sharing and innovation may be possible (Birke and Fox 1999).

Negotiation almost inevitably involves what Lax and Sebenius (2006) have termed the 'negotiator's dilemma': the tension between creating and claiming value. Much of the literature on negotiation, especially in relation to mediation, has been influenced by the work of Fisher and Ury, who popularised the pioneering work of Mary Parker Follett regarding 'mutual gains' in the 1920s, and the work of Walton and McKersie (1965) in the field of industrial relations. Fisher and Ury (1983) set out the following four principles in their manual of negotiation, *Getting to Yes*:

1. Separating the People From the Problem

Doing so maintains dignity and self-respect. It enables those in a dispute to build a more collaborative approach in which they can, metaphorically, sit on the same side of the table in seeking to find a solution to the subject matter of the negotiation or dispute. Parties are encouraged 'to be hard on the problem and soft on the people' (Fisher and Ury 1983). Doing so requires a greater development of interpersonal skills than positional bargaining and fosters problem-solving skills.

2. Negotiating on the Basis of Principle and Focusing on Interests Rather Than Positions

This kind of negotiation is premised on a distinction between 'positions' and 'interests.' While positions are the 'claims' made by a party, 'interests' are the reasons for the underlying concerns or needs that those positions are intended to meet. This enables parties to investigate beneath stated aspirations to underlying needs and preference. By doing so, where parties ascribe different values to various components of a dispute, it may be possible to find a resolution that leaves everyone better off.

3. Generating Multiple Options for Mutual Gain

This maximises collaboration and expands the size of cake that is to be shared. Generating options can take place via 'brainstorming' but will also require a detailed knowledge of both parties' interests that can only be built up via questioning and information exchange.

4. Establishing Objective Criteria

This develops trust and enables a reasoned discussion where judgments are less likely to be clouded by emotions. Objective criteria enable an assessment of the utility of any compromise and appeal to an innate sense of fairness, which encourages collaboration. By providing reasons for demands made or concessions given, objective criteria provide a basis for modifying those expectations if the reasoning is found to be flawed or incomplete.

Collaborative bargaining encourages the parties to listen carefully and discover what is most significant to each other. In this process of 'active listening,' skilled negotiators will be attuned not only to the facts but also to the emotional overlay with which they are presented.

Parties are encouraged to be clear about their own BATNA, the point at which they would walk away from the table. Knowing your BATNA enables a critical evaluation of options and clarity about what is needed in any agreement. It can also help resist extreme anchoring and 'salami slicing' by an aggressive bargainer who seeks to make last-minute demands.

Strengths of 'Principled Negotiation'

The model of principled negotiation has a number of strengths as a framework for mediation, in which the mediator has a responsibility to both parties to a dispute.

It provides a helpful tool for analysing a dispute and differentiating between ephemeral details and the nub of a conflict. It may be particularly helpful to a 'facilitative' style of mediation in which the mediator seeks to facilitate collaboration while those in a dispute take responsibility for its resolution.

Separating the people from the problem appeals to a mediator's psychological skill set. It creates a tone conducive to settlement and helps build social cohesion.

Focusing on interests rather than positions can maximise mutual advantage. The metaphor of dividing a lemon illustrates the point. Two people want the same fruit but for different reasons: one wants the lemon skin for flavouring a pudding and the other the juice for making a honey and lemon drink. If they bargain solely on the basis of positions, they may end up dividing the lemon. If, on the other hand, they listen to each other's interests, they may be able to share the lemon in a more mutually beneficial way. In practice, there is seldom such an elegant solution of which negotiators are blithely unaware, but there are often multiple elements in a negotiation or a dispute which are valued in different ways. By basing a negotiation on 'interests' rather than 'positions,' the greatest mutual advantage can be achieved. Outcomes in which the overall utility is maximised are sometimes referred to as 'Pareto efficient' after the Italian economist Vilfredo Pareto (1848–1923), who developed the concept of economic efficiency and income distribution. In a Pareto optimal outcome, no negotiating party could derive a greater benefit without it creating a loss for another party. In principled negotiation, parties are encouraged to develop the most effective trade-offs to maximise the size of the cake.

As Menkel-Meadow (1993) summarises: 'By identifying needs and interests, the parties may learn the important psychological fact that if people have complementary, rather than identical value systems, they will be able to achieve joint gains, without having to give anything up.' It is attuned to 'creating value' and therefore maximises opportunity for successful negotiation. The use of objective criteria helps resolve unnecessary conflict and creates a superordinate structure than is shared by both parties, preserves and facilitates relationships, and educates parties in pre-empting unnecessary conflict.

Critiques of 'Principled Negotiation'

Fisher and Ury's work has been criticised for being 'naïve' and 'idealistic' while others have taken issue with its conceptual distinction between 'interests' and 'positions.' Contentious, litigated business disputes are often almost exclusively about the size of the cake.

Galtung (2004) questions its assumption about the conceptual distinction between positions and interests. The authors 'seem to believe that the parties can revise their positions if the theories linking their positions to their interests do not hold water,' arguing that for a European 'to challenge his theory that positions derive from his interests will easily lead to a theory conflict so intractable that the original positions will be forgotten.'

Principled negotiation has been treated as the theoretical underpinning for much mediation theory. It will not necessarily be the most applicable model. In some disputes, there may be little room for creating value – especially where there is a scarce resource and little prospect of a future relationship. It may be of less relevance to an 'evaluative' style of mediation, in which the 'shadow of the court' is at its sharpest.

White (1984) has criticised the focus on 'mutually profitable adjustment' to the exclusion of the distributional side of bargaining. In responding to this, Fisher agreed that with 'single issue negotiations among strangers and where each side is protected by competitive opportunities, haggling over position may be better than joint problem solving.'

'Principled negotiation' assumes a degree of goodwill that may have been irreparably eroded by a breakdown of relationships. Collaboration requires the commitment of both parties. It may lead to a collaborative negotiator being manipulated by an unscrupulous partner who is unwilling to mutualise concessions. An unscrupulous party may take advantage of a freely given information exchange in subsequent litigation. Where one party is significantly more powerful than another, their interests may be best served by adopting a positional style.

In prioritising value creation over value division, it is better suited to business relationships undamaged by the imminence of litigation. Lowenthal (1982) considers that most negotiations include competitive and collaborative elements of negotiation. A negotiator seeking to turn a competitive process into a collaborative one faces 'the dilemma that that most of the gestures of good will, openness, and reassurance suggested in the literature may be interpreted by a competitive opponent as a sign of weakness or a willingness to make concessions.' Gifford (1985) recognises the difficulty of moving between cooperative and competitive behaviour and considers that the combination of strategies will 'typically occur only at different phases of negotiation or on easily separable and distinct issues.' Reliance on a third-party facilitation may minimise risk by exploring possibilities in provisional terms and recognising that collaboration requires universal consent.

In some disputes (e.g. 'family' and community), the people or the relationship between them are the problem and cannot be separated from it. In other disputes, objective criteria may be elusive, implausible, or impossible.

Barriers to Success

Fear and suspicion often impede effective negotiation and bargaining. The danger of distrust is illustrated in the paradigm of the 'prisoner's dilemma': two suspects are accused of being accomplices in a crime, but there is insufficient evidence to secure a conviction. A judge tells each that if he offers evidence against his accomplice, he will be let off with a year's sentence, and his accomplice will be imprisoned for five. If both make statements against each other, they will both be imprisoned for five years, but if neither makes a statement, they will both be imprisoned for a lesser offence and serve two years. The dilemma is one of trust and communication. If both colleagues remain loyal, they will maximise mutual advantage but betrayal may lead to greater individual reward. Trusting his colleague risks the maximum sentence if he is betrayed. Mistrust often leads to results that are less mutually beneficial than they might have been with greater trust and better communication.

Insights from game theory suggest that cooperation maximises individual returns. On the basis of empirical research based on a version of the 'dilemma,' in which parties do not meet each other, Axelrod (1980) identifies the most effective negotiating strategy as consistent, cooperative but revocable behaviour, in which a party begins by collaborating, is willing to retaliate if the other party is competitive or adversarial, and is also consistent and willing to forgive such defections.

Tensions in negotiation include those between creating and distributing value, between empathy and assertion, and between 'principals' and 'agents,' in which repeat players may prioritise the interests of favoured clients and pursue the interests of others less vigorously in the hope of gaining strategic advantage and maximising the overall utility of a bargaining relationship. The drive for distributive advantage may at times be a barrier to a deal being made or a dispute settled as hard-bargaining tactics can lead to ineffective outcomes (Mnookin 2003).

Power in Negotiation

There are many different aspects of power in a negotiation, and its distribution may vary between parties as a negotiation develops. Types of power include hierarchical position, relative economic and financial position. knowledge of the subject matter or the dispute, capacity to withdraw cooperation, relative legal strength of positions, analysis of reputational risk, capacity to pursue alternative means, charisma, understanding of the psychology of opposing parties, degree of influence over the negotiation process, and pattern recognition or experience of similar or analogous contexts.

While both (or all) parties in a negotiation may appeal to normative arguments of fairness, fairness may mean different things to different people who will select their own criteria. In an employment context, for instance, it may include 'equity,' 'equality,' 'precedent,' and long service. Disputants will tend to be self-interested in their choice of criteria.

The distribution of power in negotiation may shift during the process. In a litigated case of personal injury, for instance, the ability to withstand legal costs may be subject to stepped thresholds, and above those thresholds, the insurer will be a significant factor in negotiation in a way that they weren't before. There may be significant internal ambivalences in cases involving sensitive personal details, an employee may be very reluctant to be cross-examined in an employment tribunal but have no anxiety about reputational risk, or, conversely, a respondent may be subject to significant reputational risk but very concerned to establish a precedent in a particular class of cases.

Even those with apparently no bargaining power may be able to assert their priorities. A colleague who was climbing in Colombia had her very expensive photographic equipment stolen by armed FARC guerrillas. The guerillas were under 18 and jittery, and she felt her partner might seem to be a threat. She was nevertheless able to calm them down by listening, take the heat out of the situation, and persuade the guerillas to give her the film cannisters in the camera and bag. The film of their trip was of great interest to her but of no value to the guerillas.

Culture in Negotiation

Culture, in the sense of the 'set of attitudes, values, beliefs and behaviours' shared by a group of people (Matsumoto 1996), will inevitably play a role in the 'negotiation dance,' whether the term is applied to a nation, group, or business culture.

Legal anthropologists (Barton 1919; Evans Pritchard 1940; Felstiner et al. 1980–1981; Gulliver 1979; Palmer and Roberts 2020) writing about conflict in non-industrial societies identify a diversity of modes of dealing with conflict, including ritualised negotiation and third-party decision-making. In highly integrated, mutually dependent cultures, conflict is likely to be more costly, and there may be more highly developed forms of leverage for the settlement of disputes than in more individualistic industrial societies.

Culture and cultural expectations influence and determine the positions, needs, interests, and assumptions of the parties to a negotiation. Expectations about the negotiation process and what it entails will, in part, be culturally determined. Cultural norms will shape the legal, social, economic, and political institutions of the location of the negotiation table and the forum in which any agreement is to be implemented (Goldberg et al. 2012).

The anthropologists Douglas (1973) and Hall (1976) offered binary descriptions of culture. Douglas (1973) proposed a distinction between 'group' or inclusion (the claim of groups over members) and 'grid' or classification (the degree to which social interaction is subject to rules). Hall (1976) developed the concept of high- and low-context cultures. Messages in a high-context culture carry more 'implicit' meanings with more information than the spoken words while in low-context cultures, the messages have a more explicit reference with less implied beyond the words used. In low-context cultures, conflict may take a very direct and belligerent form, whereas in high-context cultures, conflict may be inferred from more nuanced changes in behaviour. In this context Australia, the USA, and Scandinavia would be considered classically low-context cultures in which verbal communication is more explicit and Asian, Latin American, and Arabic cultures typically high context, where verbal meaning is more subtle, implicit, and nuanced. Hofstede (2001), in his research into the behaviour of IBM trainees globally, derived a model of six dimensions of culture:

1. Power distance, related to the different solutions to the basic problem of human inequality;
2. Uncertainty avoidance, related to the level of stress in a society in the face of an unknown future;
3. Individualism versus collectivism, related to the integration of individuals into primary groups;
4. Masculinity versus femininity, related to the division of emotional roles between women and men;
5. Long-term versus short-term orientation, related to the choice of focus for people's efforts: the future or the present and past; and
6. Indulgence versus restraint, related to gratification versus control of basic human desires related to enjoying life.

Hofstede's research suggests that 'power distance' index scores (inequality) are higher for Latin, Asian, and African countries and lower for Germanic and English-speaking Western countries. 'Uncertainty avoidance' (fear of change) tends to be higher in

European countries and lower in English-speaking, Nordic, and Chinese-culture countries. 'Individualism' tends to prevail in developed and Western countries while 'collectivism' prevails in less-developed Eastern European and Eastern countries. 'Masculinity,' or the acceptance of traditional gender roles, is high in Japan, in German-speaking countries, and in some Latin countries like Italy and Mexico; moderately high in English-speaking Western countries; low in Nordic countries and in the Netherlands; and moderately low in some Latin and Asian countries like France, Spain, Portugal, Chile, Korea, and Thailand. East Asian countries are more likely to be 'long term' oriented. The USA and Australia are more likely to be 'short term' oriented. The USA is likely to be far higher on 'indulgence' while 'restraint' prevails in Asia and the Muslim world. The research was conducted in the immediate aftermath of the fall of communism in Eastern Europe and illustrates, at least in relation to collectivism, the inter-relationship of cultural and political norms.

Culture will always be socially and psychologically distributed in a group (Avruch 1998). While Western cultures, which will be low on the power/distance dimension (more equal and individualistic), will think about power in terms of BATNA, social status is more likely to be significant in more hierarchical Asian cultures. In Japanese culture, for instance, where the web of responsibility and obligations is more developed, disputants are more likely to defer to those of higher social status who, in return for privilege and prestige, accept an obligation to look after more vulnerable members. According to Adler (1996), the dynamics of relationship between buyer and seller in Japan may replicate that of a father/son relationship. The seller (son) does not negotiate as an equal but carefully explains his situation and asks for the buyer's (father) help because he will have no room for bickering once the buyer (father) decides. The seller (son) accepts a decision both because it would damage the relationship to argue and because he trusts the buyer (father) to care for his needs. In a study of US/Hong Kong negotiations, Tinsley (1998) observes that Chinese negotiators are more likely to subscribe to an equality norm, whereas US negotiators prioritise self-interest and joint problem solving.

Moe (2022) and Barnes (2007) illustrate how high masculinity (MAS), uncertainty avoidance index (UAI), and long-term orientation (LTO) scores in Japan might influence the negotiation strategy. An effective way for a western female CEO to prepare for negotiations with a relatively masculine-oriented culture such as is encountered in Japan would be for her to send ahead brochures and written documents indicating her position, authority, and experience to overcome the female disadvantage in high-level Asian business negotiations.

Lax and Sebenius (2006) propose the following checklist for reflecting on cultural expectations in negotiation as regards deeper expectations:

Negotiation objective: Is the ultimate goal of the negotiation more a signed contract or a relationship?

Fundamental view of the negotiation process: Is negotiation a process through which both sides can gain or one through which one side gains, and the other side loses?
Social unit: Is it an individualist or group-oriented culture?
Power/decision-making: Does the other side make decisions in an authoritarian fashion, with one key person? Is it a small-group process? Is there a formal or informal hierarchy involved? Is consensus required?
Implementation: How likely and expected is literal implementation of the agreement? Or is the deal merely a starting point for further negotiation?

On a process level, other variables will include levels of formality; style of communication, including relevant balance between appeal to status and objective reasoning; extent to which expressions of emotion are accepted as helpful or legitimate; and attitudes to time. As regards the nature of the agreement, is there an expectation that it will be based on principle (French preference) or built up on the basis of practice (English common law model)? Is the agreement to take the form an agreed contract (USA legalistic/egalitarian paradigm) or a memorandum of understanding setting out a framework for future relationships (collectivist/Eastern preference)?

Tinsley et al. (1999) summarise their advice as regards international negotiation as acknowledging the differences in individual and societal levels, trading off differences in preferences and abilities, asking questions to ensure understanding of the other party's perspective, understanding norms and the meanings underlying them, avoiding arguing about the inherent legitimacy of a social system, and being prepared to manage bureaucratic interactions with government.

The purposes of these models, as with psychological frameworks for thinking about personality, is not that they provide an invariable template for understanding a dispute and/or negotiation but that attentiveness to how these pre-conscious mindsets operate may improve the quality of inter- or intra-cultural dialogue. Painstaking research, listening attentively for underlying assumptions, and testing provisional assumptions are likely to improve both the quality and the effectiveness of a negotiation.

Augsburger (1992) states, 'Conflicts are universally similar, culturally distinct, and individually unique.' Processes of mediation as interventions that facilitate negotiation are themselves culturally specific. The CEDR and Fisher/Urry Western model of mediation with its focus on interests is itself the product of Western culture. Wehr and Lederach (1991) identified a different role for the mediator in the Central American context. They considered a Western mediator to be third-party 'outsider-neutral' (see Figure 3.4), who was 'external,' 'neutral,' and 'not connected' to the parties in dispute. However, in Central America, mediators are more 'insider-partial' (see Figure 3.5). They argued that an acceptable mediator in a traditional society was more likely to be 'internal' and 'partial' to the conflict and 'invested' in the outcome of the resolution whose acceptability to the disputants 'is rooted not in distance from the conflict or objectivity regarding the issues, but rather in connectedness and trusted relationships with the conflict parties' (Wehr and Lederach 1991).

Entry through functional role	----->	1. Distance 2. Anonymity 3. Connected through function 4. Connected through conflict	----->	Legitimacy Fairness Efficiency Effectiveness

Figure 3.4 Outsider-neutral model

Source: Wehr and Lederach 1991, Figure 3.1

Entry through trust	----->	1. Personal relationship 2. Closeness to 3. Knowledge of 4. Wholly connected	----->	Legitimacy Tradition Connections

Figure 3.5 Insider-partial (*confianza*) model

Source: Wehr and Lederach 1991, Figure 3.2

Cultural assumptions will underpin many of the choices regarding different mediation styles. Approaches to cross-cultural mediation that are responsive to context and to culture need to do more than interpret cultural differences and need to incorporate dimensions of cultural difference into the mediation model itself (Golbert 2009).

Loss Aversion

Loss aversion refers to the idea that we tend to disfavour a loss in relation to a given reference point more than we favor an equivalent gain. On a financial level, investors with an asset that has depreciated may be unwilling to sell it for an independent or market valuation, whereas those with an appreciating investment may be more willing to sell at the same price. On a symbolic level, this may influence the valuation attributed to a matrimonial home in family law, especially where it may represent the security of a relationship that one party may be reluctant to lose. In probate, the same process may apply to an heirloom in inheritance disputes. Different personality types may be more or less 'loss' or 'risk' averse.

Risk Aversion

Individual responses vary and may inform investment strategy and attitudes to assets, investments, and pensions. Research suggests people tend to avoid risk when choosing between options that are understood but prefer risk when they assess options they understand as losses. In the context of litigation, a claimant may accept a smaller settlement rather than go to trial and risk losing everything (risk aversion), whereas a respondent is more likely to go to trial, preferring to gamble rather than face a certain loss in settlement (loss aversion) (Strasser and Randolph 2004).

Practical Illustration of Negotiation

In a negotiation in relation to an employment dispute, for example, Party A may consider that they have a valid claim for unfair dismissal and discrimination valued at £120,000 if they succeed on all counts. Party B may initially consider that there is no merit in the claim but be willing to settle it for a nuisance value of £10,000. If Party A accepts there is a 25% risk that he won't succeed at all, then he will logically be willing to discount his claim by that amount and be willing to accept £90,000, leaving a gap between the two positions of £80,000. In learning more of Party B's case, Party A may accept that they have very little chance of succeeding on the discrimination claim, and even if they are successful, the value of the claim could be as low as £60,000. Party A may then revalue his discounted claim at £45,000. Party B may subsequently accept that they have a significantly greater risk of losing than they anticipated – say, 50% – and increase their initial offer by half their best estimate (£60,000) of what the case would cost if they failed at trial. At this point, the difference between the two parties – Party A, who would accept £45,000, and Party B, who would offer £40,000 – has been narrowed to £5,000. Where the transactional costs of going to tribunal are more than £10,000 for both parties, even in this positional type of negotiation, there is a ZOPA of £15,000. Logically, Party A would be better off accepting £35,000 than going to court, and Party B would be better off paying £50,000.

In a more collaborative form of negotiation, there may be many more issues at stake. In business contexts, 'reputational risk,' 'goodwill,' and 'transaction costs' are significant factors. Both parties may be interested in minimising their reputational risk with an amicable settlement.

An appropriate reference may be as valuable to Party A as vindication in an employment tribunal, and Party B may be concerned about the loss of goodwill resulting from a continued dispute. Where the falling-out has arisen because of personality clashes, there may nevertheless be room for 'arms-length' future collaboration. All these offer ways of creating value as much as dividing it. In practice, there may often be some ways of increasing the value of the cake. Even in highly adversarial cases, the value to the parties of no longer having to dedicate emotional energy to an intractable dispute may be a powerful incentive to settle. Businesses will also need to be aware of the 'opportunity costs' in terms of the loss to the business entertained by managers and other employees being tied up in preparing for an adjudicated outcome.

Conclusion

Negotiation involves the combination of the contrasting dispositions of 'competitive antagonism and co-operative coordination' (Gulliver 1988). In negotiating an agreement in the context of adversarial litigation, it is often assumed that one party's loss is necessarily the other party's gain. Fisher and Ury's model, with its emphasis on collaboration, provides a healthy antidote to the assumption of competitive antagonisms at the heart of distributive bargaining, but when pushed to extremes, it can distort the reality of business negotiations over finite resources. While excessive concentration on co-ordination can lead to neglect of a party's interests, excessive competition can undermine the need for co-ordination that is the prerequisite for effective progress towards agreement. Human evolution has favoured a combination of competitive and cooperative behaviour. Negotiation is most likely to be effective when it contains elements of both, collaborating but being willing to contend when collaboration is not reciprocated.

In practice, experienced negotiators will use a variety of techniques, being open to maximising the cake and increasing social advantage by collaborating while adopting a more adversarial approach when there is a breakdown of goodwill or lack of good faith. Negotiation is something we learn in families and communities, from earliest childhood, as a way of reconciling our needs and desires with others. As a mutual process is a way of creating, and maintaining, social harmony in which both, or all, parties benefit.

Questions

1. **What are some of the different kinds of power that are shown in negotiation?**
2. **How significant is timing in negotiation?**
3. **What are the advantages and disadvantages of the negotiating styles discussed?**
4. **How important is awareness of cultural difference in negotiation?**
5. **What do you consider the most effective techniques in responding to an adversarial negotiation style?**

Exercise 1

Discuss with your partner a negotiation that you have recently been involved in. This could be about the terms of the lease of a flat, the pay and conditions of a job you have been offered, the price of something that you have recently bought, the deadline for an essay, or the allocation of shared household tasks. The exercise will be most effective if you can discuss your perceptions of overcoming barriers or breaking deadlock.

Describe the style of negotiation that you adopted and your reasons for adopting it. What role did emotion play in the negotiation? Reflect on both your own feelings and those of the person you were negotiating with.

What were your objectives in the negotiation, and how well did you succeed in reaching them?
To what extent did you consider the needs and interests of the person you were negotiating with, and how did this impact on the substance of the negotiation?
How might you improve your negotiating style in similar circumstances in the future?

Exercise 2

Prepare a brief summary of your background culture and experience in terms of Hofstede's dimensions, noting where you feel your personal preferences differ from the stereotype of a group you belong to. Discuss with your neighbour an example of where you feel that you may have been judged or misjudged according to a cultural stereotype or such a misunderstanding that you may have observed.

Exercise 3

Prepare brief pre-negotiation notes for a job interview based on your current CV. How might you improve your BATNA in a way that will strengthen your hand in negotiation? What are the principle strengths you want to ensure that you convey, and how will you evidence these? Now consider the exercise from the perspective of a potential employer. What strengths will they be looking for in a potential recruit?

Further Reading

Fisher, R. & Ury, W. (1983) *Getting to Yes*. Penguin Books.
Gulliver, P. H. (1979) *Disputes and Negotiations: A Cross Cultural Perspective*. Academic Press.
Lax, D. & Sebenius, J. (2006) *3-D Negotiation: Powerful Tools to Change the Game in Your Most Important Deals*. Harvard Business Review Press.
Palmer, M. & Roberts, S. (2020) *Disputes Processes: ADR and the Primary Forms of Decision-Making*. Cambridge University Press.

4 Mediation Psychology

'The metaphor is the most powerful tool known to mankind' (Ortega Y. Gasset). ADR includes many different processes. In this chapter, we will concentrate on mediation that, at its core, is the 'capacity to re-orientate the parties towards each other, not by imposing rules on them, but by helping them achieve a new and shared perception of their relationship' (Fuller 1971). Mediation is inherently 'relational,' and understanding what is happening at a psychological level is a core skill of any mediator. For Randolph and Strasser and Randolph (2004), establishing the disputant's world view is 'the very essence of the mediator's task.'

Mediators increasingly come from psychotherapeutic as well as legal backgrounds, and psychotherapeutic skills form an important component of the training offered by some mediation trainers: for instance, in the UK, the School of Psychotherapy and Counselling at Regents College. In this chapter, I will set out some of the areas in which an understanding of psychology may help a mediator become psychologically literate and develop their skills. It also describes some of the psychological processes or 'heuristics' that may be happening in a facilitated negotiation and makes reference to some of the literature and processes that may be going on in mediation. The aim of the chapter is to identify some of the relationships between reason and emotion in fueling or sustaining conflict and achieving resolution.

Mediation is sometimes divided into two broad types: those in which people and relationships are prioritised over the 'substance' of a dispute and those in which the substance of a dispute eclipses the relationships. In facilitative mediation, the mediator takes responsibility for the process, relationships are seen as central, and the disputants are empowered to negotiate their own resolution. Transformative mediation (Bush et al. 2004) represents a developed form of facilitative mediation in which improving communication between the parties is the primary goal, and mediation is seen as having the potential to transform relationships with an emphasis 'recognition' and 'empowerment' that goes beyond resolution of a dispute and seeks to educate the parties and enable them to develop skills in empathy and listening. Narrative mediation (Winslade and Monk 2000) builds on this in a model that has been developed in the context of community and family mediation. A mediator works with disputants to help them better understand each other's 'narratives' or versions of events and potentially to create a shared meta-narrative to shape future relationships. Conflict often

DOI: 10.4324/9781003112617-4

arises when people 'fill in' gaps, infer motivations, or assume unwritten rules that govern behavior. Narrative mediation works by enabling parties to question assumptions, to better understand patterns of behavior, to be open to alternative interpretations of events, and to recalibrate expectations in light of developing cognitive empathy.

While more evaluative forms of mediation prioritise the substance of a dispute, and psychological skills may be less central, they nevertheless remain relevant. Even when the law casts a deep shadow over the mediation and an interpretation of legal facts domines the process, successful settlement can often be frustrated by powerful emotions of anger, envy, or greed.

Psychology is relevant to both forms of mediation in different ways. In the former group, psychological factors may the essence of a dispute while in the latter, an awareness of factors that may inhibit or enhance settlement may make the process of facilitating a negotiation more effective.

The 'Dance of Reason and Emotion'

Mediation often engages powerful emotions in the process of negotiation decision-making, in which a skilled third party can facilitate a reverse in the direction of a dispute and facilitate a move from antagonism to the re-engagement of the parties. How this happens is not always apparent to the mediator, but in mediations that have a successful outcome, at some point, there is a transition from competitive to collaborative decision-making.

Successful mediation often involves an adaptation of 'outlook' as a way of facilitating change. For Strasser and Randolph (2004), the establishment of parties' world views (*weltanschauung*) is 'the very essence of the mediator's task.' Our world outlook is an important source of our self-esteem; 'going with the grain of this' is likely to be significant in resolving conflict. Evolutionary psychology suggests that we are motivated by a hybrid of competitive and cooperative impulses. Evolutionary success has depended on an amalgam of cooperation (reciprocal altruism) and competition (social hierarchy). The task of the mediator is to understand why/how people see themselves and their adversaries as they do and how their awareness of the conflict may be impaired and can be improved (Curle 1971).

Psychotherapeutic Approaches

A theory of the unconscious permeates classical literature from the furies in classical mythology to the role of dreams. Many forms of pre-scientific healing (shamanism) and social control (oracular wisdom) adopt techniques that appear to deploy its power. The power of the unconscious is central to an understanding of psychotherapy and psychoanalysis in which 'intrapsychic' conflict is envisaged as central to human motivation and behaviour. In psychoanalytic psychotherapy, the presence of the therapist enables the patient to reintegrate aspects of their unconscious mind into their experience of the present. While mediation is not therapy, there are parallels between the mediatory 'other' and the psychotherapeutic 'other,' and the pressure of intense conflict may frequently unleash irrational and unconscious emotions and desires into the mediatory process.

Freud (1856–1939)

Sigmund Freud did not invent the idea of the unconscious but applied it clinically and made it operational (Storr 1989). For Freud, the unconscious mind was a source of feelings, thoughts, impulses, urges, and memories outside conscious awareness. The 'id' represents a repository of unconscious desires and repressed feelings. The 'ego' – our sense of self – is both driven by these motivations, including that of the 'libido' (fundamental desire of psychological drive) and in conflict with the 'super-ego,' an idealisation of self and what should and should not be done. Freud considered aggression to be innate and dangerous, and as a result of a 'primary mutual hostility of human beings, civilized society is perpetually threatened with disintegration' (Freud 1930). In many ways, the role of the mediator is in helping disputants access the pre-conscious or middle layer of the mind of which they are only dimly aware and which may enable them to better understand the trajectory of the conflict in which they are enmeshed.

Jung (1875–1961)

Other founders of psychoanalysis share the significance of the 'unconscious' but see it through a slightly different lens. Carl Gustav Jung adopted a more optimistic view of the unconscious, envisaging a 'collective unconscious,' which represented an inherited deposit of human experience manifesting itself in archetypes, images, and symbols. He envisaged the role of the therapist as enabling the analysand to hold tensions creatively in themselves so as to enable a new synthesis to emerge. Jung's work is significant for his characterisation of personality types in terms of introversion and extroversion. This work is often used by organisational and learning and development professionals in psychometric tests that explore individuals' preferences: for instance, in terms of work tasks and behaviours (MBTI, Insights Discovery, DISC, etc.). Such exercises assess personalities on the basis of multiple-choice questions on axes of extroversion/introversion, sensing/intuition, thinking/feeling, and organised/spontaneous. By becoming more aware of their own styles and preferences, a mediator is better able to both understand human differences and adapt their behavioral style to assist parties in resolving disputes.

Adler (1870–1937)

Alfred Adler, writing in pre-war Austria, hypothesised an innate 'will to power' as animating human behaviour. On an individual level, human beings are motivated by a conflict between feelings of low self-esteem and a desire for high self-esteem that are a potential source of human self-improvement. In managing power imbalances between parties, a skillful mediator can help disputants find 'ladders to climb down' and prevent blows to esteem through loss of face.

Klein (1882–1960)

Melanie Klein developed Freud's thinking in her work with children. She considered that 'ego' is present from birth and that a child experiences an innate conflict between hatred and love. The child moves between a 'depressive position,' in which there is an understanding that good and evil things are one, and a 'paranoid-schizoid defence,' in which separation leads to the projection of bad onto others as a defence against reality. In the depressive position, the complexity of circumstances may mean that a disputant is more willing to repair or reconstruct a relationship. In the stress of extreme or protracted conflict, parties are more likely to regress to an infantile position in which all that is good is attributed to themselves and all that is bad attributed to the person that they are in dispute with.

Frankl (1905–1997)

Viktor Frankl has proposed a source of integrative adaptation and a drive to create meaning that seeks to unify disparate aspects of our experience (Frankel 2006). All these theories may illuminate aspects of what is happening in a mediation.

Projection

Classical literature reveals the way that, when a protagonist cannot accept parts of their own experience, such negative emotions may become 'projected' outwards and attributed to some external person or agency. One reason for lack of self-knowledge is the fear of what that awareness might reveal. Unbearable emotions (whether of shame or guilt) are concealed by a process of repression and lead to the development of a 'mask': the personality they would like to be or be seen to be when they look in the mirror. To the extent to which we depend on the 'mask' for self-protection, we see a false image or 'mirage' of others as we see them in terms of their response to our psychic needs (Curle 1971). Through the psychic ruse of projection, we attribute to others the flaws we are dimly aware of in ourselves.

The Babylonian Talmud (500 BCE) recognises this in the exhortation 'Do not taunt your neighbour with the faults that you yourself.' Othello's morbid jealousy and Macbeth's guilty conscience, speaking through Banquo's ghost, reveal a universality to this process.

Freud developed this idea (*Projektion*) in his 'case studies' and letters to Fliess (Freud 1985). He recognised that the process may apply to both positive and negative aspects of oneself. We can often recognise in others attributes or qualities we cannot recognise in ourselves. For Klein, adopting the 'depressive position' is a way of countering this projection in a process of reparation.

In toxic disputes, all that is bad frequently becomes projected onto and experienced as the behavior of an antagonist. This 'defence mechanism' enables the party to understand themselves in positive terms without having to face less attractive aspects of their own personality.

A less extreme form of this takes place in 'projective identification,' in which an emotion is not totally denied but leads to strong identification with others who have this emotion, perhaps in a less extreme form. Where emotions run high and a mediator's intervention becomes a part of the system of a dispute, mediators may also be subject to such powerful projections and identifications and no less significantly need to become aware of the ways in which they form these projections themselves or respond with counter-transferences to those in their mediations.

Humanistic Psychology

French psychologist Mucchielli (1919–1981) draws attention to core principles of mediation shared with the 'humanistic' therapy of Carl Rogers (1902–1987), espousing 'unconditional positive regard': an attitude of open interest and availability, a non-censorious and non-directive attitude, a genuine interest in understanding the disputants in their own language, and the constant attention to remaining objective and aware of what is happening. Rogers developed this 'person-centred' approach to psychology in the 1940s. He considered that there was an inherent conflict between the primary positive nature of human beings and the social expectations imposed on them. For Strasser and Randolph (2004), there is a direct parallel between the process of time-limited 'non-directive counselling' taking place in therapy and the communication in individual sessions in which the mediator uses many of the therapeutic skills and concepts. While mediation is not therapy, both processes involve a potential change or adaptation of behaviour, in therapy so as to better to 'adapt' to what may appear to be a hostile social context and in mediation, a re-orientation of attitude to the other party in the particularity of a dispute situation.

Humanistic psychology and mediation share a set of core values that include:

Empathy: Contrast with sympathy, which may come across as patronising
Curiosity: Genuine but unintrusive curiosity aids understanding
Sincerity: Builds trust, goodwill, and understanding
Calmness: Models relationships for disputants
Objectivity: Important in creating trust and testing reality

Marshall Rosenberg (1934–2015)

Marshall Rosenberg, who worked as a mediator as well as a therapist, derived his practice from Carl Roger's cognitive therapy. Rosenberg understood humans as sharing the same universal needs and considered that acknowledging those needs could create a shared basis for mutuality, cooperation, and, more globally and idealistically, peace. Much of his work develops out of his PhD thesis on 'the relationship between (the) structure of social situations and two dimensions of self-evaluation; positive self-evaluation and certainty of self-evaluation' Rosenberg (2015), described 'connecting people' at a deep level as the 'core of mediation.' He developed his thinking on the West Coast of the USA at the same time as the San Francisco community mediation boards, and it in many ways represents a similar mindset.

Neuropsychology and Neurodiversity

Recent cross-discipline research in the areas of biochemistry, neuroscience, psychology, and psychoanalysis has illuminated the links between physiology and behaviour and the way in which biological systems are involved in the development of emotional responses (Gerhardt 2004). Regulatory patterns established early in life affect not only emotional development but also the development of the pre-frontal cortex. The basic brain is structured by evolution and can be thought of in a triune form, with the mammalian brain, cortex, on top of the reptilian brain, or amygdala, which stores and processes memories associated with strong emotional events. This is surrounded by a centre of emotions, the cerebral cortex, and above this, the pre-frontal cortex, or 'social brain,' where emotional experiences are rationalised and decisions made among alternative courses of action. Empathic responses are made possible by a well-developed pre-frontal cortex. Goleman (1995) writes of the relationship between different forms of knowing. The right hemisphere of the cerebellum processes information in an intuitive and integrative manner while the left hemisphere is more typically associated with logical and analytical thinking. The corpus callosum's intricate network of nerve fibres forms links between these two halves. The orbito-frontal and pre-frontal cortex are responsible for the development of empathy. Where cortisol or stress hormone is released, there is an impairment of empathic responses; contrastingly, the release of dopamine contributes to pleasure, the development of the pre-frontal cortex, and an empathic response. Intense negative emotions may trigger or hijack a person's amygdala and lead to extreme negative and aggressive emotion. Where heightened emotions threaten a breakdown of constructive communication, a mediator may need to call a break or separate parties into caucusing meetings.

Heuristics

Intuitions represent a form of understanding that is pre- or unconscious. Such mental shortcuts ease the load of decision-making. We all use heuristics in everyday life: e.g. rules of thumb, stereotyping, common sense. In mediation, awareness of these processes may enable the parties and mediators facilitating such a negotiation an opportunity to become more conscious of what is going on and the mediators to help challenge or unravel perceptions. Whether this involves the 'unconscious' or some other form of pattern recognition, being aware of the power and pitfalls of intuitions and consequently being able to check these against reasoned decision-making is an important aspect of the mediator's task.

Disputants often reveal significant clues during mediation, and mediators equally need to become aware of their own thought processes, prejudices, and pre-occupations if they are going to help others collaborate to reach settlement.

These processes include 'parapraxes'; these slips of the tongue or physical tumbling may give ideas of where there is a conflict in a person's thinking: e.g. arriving late, not signing cheques.

Body language offers an important source of insight. Mirroring another's body language can be a powerful way of developing rapport. Countering another's body language may be used to break a deadlock or to prevent a meeting from becoming torpid and overly comfortable.

Dissembling: 'During the lie, the subconscious mind sends out nervous energy that appears as a gesture that can contradict what the person said' (Pease 1984). In the expression 'tongue in cheek,' language mimics a physical tic that often accompanies deception.

Framing

The framework within which offers are presented may have significantly impact on how they are received. Even where this does not determine acceptance or rejection, it may influence the future quality of negotiations. For example, a small symbolic concession may mean that an unpalatable 'demand' is received more favourably. A success rate of 75% at trial is more likely to encourage litigation than a 25% risk of failure. At the exploration stage of mediation, mediators may ask questions or paraphrase statements to encourage parties to appreciate different perspectives, to widen or narrow their own perspective, or to focus on potential areas of agreement. This is almost always best done in individual meetings, and doing so in plenary sessions may easily be perceived as bias.

Anchoring

In bargaining, initial offers may establish the co-ordinates against which other offers are measured and determine the scope for resolution of a dispute. Contrastingly, many parties may conceive of making a 'first offer' as a weakness. Mediators may play a role in helping parties resist making an offer that might be perceived by the other as an assault or 'insult' and contextualising offers in ways that contribute to mutuality. Conventional wisdom in mediation holds that where there is even distribution of knowledge, 'anchoring' may be a powerful tool for determining the likely range of agreement, but where there is an asymmetry of information and the other party clearly has a better understanding of the context, it may be better not to make the first move.

Reciprocation

There is an almost universal social tendency to reciprocate: when given something, to give something in return. In distributive bargaining, agreement is typically met at a mid-point between opening offers. In these circumstances, making the second offer can provide the negotiator an opportunity to determine where the mid-point lies. Whether making the first to exploit anchoring or the second to gain the maximum benefit of concessions, conventional wisdom is that it is best to make as extreme initial offer as possible as long as this is not understood as negotiation in bad faith (Birke and Fox 1999).

Attribution error: Interpretation of others' behaviour without sufficient regard to context; an attempt at conciliation may be seen as a 'Trojan horse.' In these circumstances, a mediator can be an agent of reality by asking highly focused questions and, at the same time, being open to the possibility that the interpretation may indeed be correct. This may lead to interpreting another's behaviour as a result of an innate character trait without sufficient regard for context. Reactive devaluation may lead to proposals offered by an adversary being considered less favourably (Birke and Fox 1999).

Mistake of conjunctive probabilities: An example of attribution error, this is sometimes explained in terms of the Latin maxim *Post hoc ergo propter hoc* (After it therefore because of it). We tend to understand one event following another as a matter of causation, but this is not always the case, and parties may interpret unrelated actions as the result of a causal nexus.

Pattern recognition: Specialists, whether medical experts, engineers, accountants, or lawyers, are employed for a particular expertise and their capacity to recognise certain patterns. This recognition often takes place at an intuitive level. Junior barristers may consult Kings Counsel for this purpose: the capacity through their experience to value and pursue or defend a particular claim by appreciating its development and value at least, in part, on the basis of intuition.

Perceptual contrast: Contexts are often perceived in comparison to one another, instead of being assessed individually. This operates on a number of levels. Anchoring is an example of this process. Politicians and PR firms may 'bury' bad news by releasing it after some greater catastrophe.

Triggers: Psychological stimuli that prompt involuntary recall of a previous traumatic experience. While the stimulus need not be frightening or may be only superficially similar to an earlier traumatic incident (for instance, a thunderstorm could trigger memories of being in a bombing raid a generation previously), such triggers can prompt irrational or exaggerated responses. Although relevant to any form of mediation, this may be particularly unsettling in family mediation, where the dispute process may mirror or mimic the underlying reasons for the breakdown of a relationship.

Enemy images: Whether in family breakdowns or international politics, extreme forms of stereotyping involve our projection of negative images onto the 'other' and all that is positive onto the self in a process that Klein describes as 'splitting', which may reinforce intransigent behaviour and rigid belief systems that may become difficult to dismantle.

By contrast with the 'halo effect,' positive expectations can create a momentum leading to beneficial outcomes. Labelling a student as a 'scholar' or the 'fast track' in the civil service are examples where this may be at play.

Symbolism

The importance of active and empathic listening in mediation is hard to overemphasise. An important role of a mediator may be unmasking emotional content and context. Objects as well as words may fulfill a symbolic role: a separating couple may use solicitors and counsel to negotiate the division of the Elvis record collection. Brown and Marriot (2011) identify what they refer to as the 'ginger-jar' factor, in which a particular object may become symbolically saturated and take on a role – here, a jar given by a mother-in-law to a son – as a representation of the relationship that is ending in a divorce and assume an exaggerated role in a mediation. In a community mediation in Lambeth, an 'air-brick' in the wall between the garden of two neighbouring houses became a symbol of the complex relationship between two families and the combined 'opportunity' and 'threat' of breaking down barriers. Although the dispute was only partly resolved, a willingness by one party to move (although not replace the airbrick) was a turning point in the relationship and offered an opportunity for a fresh start. An effective resolution to a conflict may be premised on symbolic acts, whether the restitution of symbolic objects or the power of an apology. While an apology may not substitute for other forms of recompense, it may be a powerful indication of restoration and good faith. In the Ugandan Acholi ritual of *Mato Oput* (Bartlet 2009), a reconciliatory moment between disputants is marked by the shared ritual of drinking the 'bitter herb' and placing each other's foreheads against each other.

Tim Kelsall argues that in a post-conflict 'truth commission' in Sierra Leone, the truth was not revealed for a number of reasons, but a staged ceremony of repentance and forgiveness on the final day struck resonant chords with the participants and succeeded in 'forging a reconciliatory moment' (Kelsall 2005). In certain circumstances, ritual may be more important to reconciliation than truth: 'The unbearable truth of atrocities was partially eclipsed by the more palatable truth of remorse and desires for peace.'

Emotions

Fisher and Shapiro (2005) developed the Core Concerns Framework as a way of addressing the emotional dimension in negotiation and mediation and identifying common concerns that underpin human motivations. They suggest that these motives are hardwired into the human motivational system and, therefore, influence emotion and behavior, albeit moderated by culture and idiosyncratic neurobiological structures and tendencies. These human emotional needs may be far more significant than the facts in a negotiation or dispute.

Fisher suggests that there is a shared need across cultures for the following concerns: appreciation (recognition of value); autonomy (freedom to feel, think, take action, and decide, compromised when a person feels they will have a decision forced on them); affiliation (emotional connection to others); status (standing in relation to others); and role (whether in a job or other endeavour). The value of the Core Concerns Framework inheres in its capacity to illuminate the semantic landscape of a negotiation. Going with the grain of these needs may be an important part of facilitating a possible resolution to an intractable dispute (Shapiro 2010).

Effect of Litigation

Litigation as an inherently adversarial process is likely to release or trigger powerful emotions. This is reinforced by 'ritual' and the dignity of the law, where a judge is constituted in terms of dress and position as an archetypal authority figure, six feet above contradiction. Simply perceiving oneself as a 'plaintiff' (now, more commonly, 'claimant') is to position oneself as a victim looking for vindication. A claim for personal injury requires that someone owes you a 'duty of care,' that this has been breached, and that you have been injured as a result. In contrast, the 'defendant' is constructed as the perpetrator of harm. Defending a case naturally triggers 'defensiveness' and a formal process of self-justification. In a rights-based adversarial trial, success is dependent on conforming to an allotted role of competitive posturing; in contrast, the shift required in mediation involves a move from competitive to collaborative creation of a resolution. To make such a change in relationship possible in itself requires a change of self-understanding.

Groupthink

When competitive positions decay into antagonism, extreme positions can harden and become mutually reinforcing. In what has been categorised as a process of 'groupthink' (Janis 1982), any questioning of positions, even internally, can be seen as disloyal or even betrayal. In his study of USA foreign policy fiascoes, including the Bay of Pigs and the escalation of the Vietnam War, Janis demonstrates how the pressure of concurrent thinking can lead to poor decision-making and a refusal to consider facts and interpretations of them that do not conform to a powerfully normative consensus position. Such concurrent thinking is characterised by over-estimation of the power and morality of the group, closed-mindedness where there is a collective rationalisation of contrary information, and social pressure towards uniformity. The tyranny of consensus can occur in many settings other than foreign policy, where there are hardened positions and an assumption of moral or legal rightness. Where there is a strong group identity, shared culture, and moral assumptions, individuals will tend to self-censor criticism of an established position out of a desire to minimise the significance of their doubts, which would place them outside the comfort blanket of consensus. In these circumstances, silence can be wrongly interpreted as consent as members of a group feel that expression of dissent is somehow disloyal or unfriendly. In its extreme forms, 'mindguards' or guardians of orthodoxy filter information from other members of the group, which could challenge complacency.

This kind of defective collective decision-making can infect legal as much as military escalation. A part of the role of a mediator can be to challenge this thinking via encouraging vigilant reappraisal. An effective process of reality testing with both parties to a dispute can encourage disputants to return to a survey of alternatives; clarify objectives; examine the risks of preferred choices; reappraise previously rejected alternatives; and, crucially, recalibrate expectations in the light of contrary information: for instance, by getting experts from both parties together to analyse information.

Empathy

Empathy is perhaps at the heart of successful mediation. Bush et al.'s (2004) work on 'transformative mediation' envisages mediation as a process in which 'the third party works with parties in conflict to help them change the quality of their conflict interaction from negative and destructive to positive and constructive as they explore and discuss issues and possibilities for resolution.' Such an approach sees parties growing in awareness and moving from self-absorption and narcissism to responsiveness and emotional sensitivity. In essence, this process, which is also described in terms of 'moral growth,' is about developing a greater personal awareness in which mediation offers an opportunity for fostering empathy. An empathic relationship with mediators can help disputants empathise with each other. While transformation of a dispute may be the goal, mediation can be effective when parties are able to exercise 'cognitive empathy.' While this may fall short of emotional engagement, understanding the other's position is an indispensable stage in resolving a conflict.

Conclusion

Even where disputes appear to be about the facts, they involve disputes about different understandings of, attitudes to, and interpretation of those facts. A claimant will naturally be motivated by a sense that right is on their side, and a defendant will tend to be defensive in their response. Once a claim has been given a legal imprimatur and lodged with the court, it is likely to become more rigid as the investment of time and professional expertise constructs this in a way that appeals to the adversarial nature of court proceedings.

Repressed anger and other powerful emotions sabotage agreements. An understanding of what is going on in a dispute may facilitate a rational and empathic response and help construct a set of converging goals for the disputants. While a psychological approach to mediation is more likely to be congruent with facilitative mediation (especially in its 'transformative' and 'narrative' versions), it is nevertheless relevant to any form of third-party intervention.

A psychological approach to mediation is not without its challenges. Engagement with theories of a disputants' motivation, of which they may not be conscious, involves a departure from the conventional principles of a mediator's neutrality and detachment, but becoming more aware of our own triggers, motivations, and attitudes can help mediators model a rational and empathic response to those caught up in a dispute they are mediating.

Listening Exercise

In groups of three: Role A: Describe an occasion in which you are involved in a conflict that you are finding difficult or intractable to the other two people in your group. The situation should be neither so stressful as to provoke distress nor so trivial as to engage merely superficial emotions. The exercise will be most effective if you choose something on the edge of your comfort zone. Role B: Listen attentively to the person in Role A, and ask them questions you feel might enable them to better understand the conflict they are involved in and help them reflect on possible ways of resolving or ameliorating the situation. Role C: Record the questions asked by B, paying particular attention to the responses made by A, noting particularly those that seem most helpful to a breakthrough in understanding the situation from another person's perspective.

After you have each taken all three roles, reflect on the kinds of questions that you each found most helpful in understanding conflicts you are involved in.

Further Reading

Frankel, V. (1997) *Man's Search for Meaning*. Penguin.

Hanaway, M. (2021) *Psychologically Informed Mediation*. Routledge.

Shapiro, D. (2010) 'From Signal to Semantic: Uncovering the Emotional Dimension of Negotiation', *Nevada Law Journal* 10 (2), Article 8. https://scholars.law.unlv.edu/nlj/vol10/iss2/8

Strasser, F. & Randolph, P. (2004) *Mediation: A Psychological Insight into Conflict Resolution*. Bloomsbury Continuum.

5 Community Mediation

Community mediation offers a way of resolving disputes within a community setting. Mediation here is confidential, flexible, informal, and generally free at point of use. It is not generally attended by lawyers, and its outcomes are generally considered to be 'good-faith commitments' rather than directly legally enforceable. While, in some ways, the process is the simplest of all forms of mediation, the psychological dynamics can be more complicated than any other form.

Model

Community mediation in its initial conception follows the models of dispute resolution in many traditional societies e.g. Indian '*Panchayat*,' Norwegian 'village moots,' and African traditional dispute resolution. It works by affirming or repairing relationships in a way that is normative but non-coercive. The model is inherently non-commercial, and mediators are usually volunteers from the local community. Their experience and values give powerful normative force to the process. The San Francisco community boards in the 1970s offer an example of this revival of mediation in the developed North. The contemporary model has adapted the initial form of dispute resolution taking place within the community at a local level to incorporate the values of equality, diversity, and multi-culturalism. These would usually be ground rules to which all parties would agree to adhere to as a condition of taking part in the mediation.

Newham's 1983 Conflict and Change Project was one of the first examples in the UK. The earliest schemes often focused on victim-offender mediation (Marshall 1984). By 1984, there were 25 schemes in operation; by 1995, there were 36 schemes in operation and, by 1996, 65. Lambeth Mediation Service, set up after the Brixton riots in the late 1980s, provided a benchmark of good practice, not least in relation to inclusivity and racial diversity. Forum for Initiatives in Reparation and Mediation (FIRM) was set up in 1989 as an umbrella body and became Mediation UK in 1993. By 1997, Mediation UK reported there were 178 affiliated organisations, with 97 specialising in community mediation. By 2005, there were 250 community mediation organisations operating. Since 2008, there has been a significant decrease in community mediation closely related to funding pressures. In a more recent report, Harris estimates that from 200 organisations in the mid-2000s, they

DOI: 10.4324/9781003112617-5

dwindled to 40 in 2021 (Harris 2021). Harris suggests that there may be up to 70 organisations who offer community mediation today, but a number of these are homeless charities that offer mediation as an additional service to their primary activity. In the statistics provided by 13 out of 15 respondents, some 1,462 cases were mediated by around one third of the mediation organisations of which she was aware. Mediation UK was wound up in 2006 due to a lack of funds. There is currently (2024) no overarching association of community mediators although proposals that the Civil Mediation Council might take a co-ordinating role.

Philosophy

There is no single 'style' or philosophy of community mediation. While broadly facilitative, mediators from a community bring their own assumptions to their practice. Some adopt a problem-solving style and some more transformative (Bush et al. 2004) or narrative techniques (Monk and Winslade 2000).

Bush et al. (2004) presented four rationales or interpretations of what mediation can offer:

- The pragmatic 'satisfaction rationale,' in which mediation is used as a technique for satisfying human needs.
- The 'social justice rationale,' in which mediation is used as a tool for community building and can lead to political change.
- The 'transformation rationale,' enabling a change of relationship rooted in recognition and respect.
- The 'oppression story,' in which mediation is used as a means of social control.

In practice, these are not watertight compartments. There is a significant overlap between the 'satisfaction' and 'social justice' rationale. Many mediations fulfil both purposes. Social transformation focuses almost exclusively on the relationship to the exclusion of the factual context of the dispute and, in Bush and Folger's writing, can envisage a mediation as successful even when the underlying dispute remains. The oppression rationale is referenced in the writings of the critiques of informalism in the USA (Nader 1979; Abel 1982; De Sousa Santos 1980). It has been written about less in the UK. Examples of how this might operate in community mediation would be where housing associations require mediation as a procedural step in escalating investigations of tenants and insist that a mediation service share the outcome with them in cases in which a tenant has been accused of anti-social behaviour, with the result that mediation is neither entered into voluntarily nor fully confidential.

Liebmann (1998) has identified two strands of philosophy:

> The first of these was the 'grassroots' aim of providing self-help schemes for people to sort out their own problems rather than have them escalate into the hands of the law. This philosophy emphasises informality, volunteer help, benefits to the community as a whole, and community-based independent management of mediation services. The second strand is more 'agency-led,' a response

> by local authorities, Citizens Advice Bureaux and other statutory organisations to the ineffectiveness and expense of legal solutions to neighbour and community disputes. Moreover, if they provide the funding for the local mediation service, they want to see a degree of effectiveness in their terms. This philosophy emphasises clear procedures, a degree of formality and measurable outcomes.

Harris (2021) suggests that Liebmann's contrasting philosophies 'sit side by side with a recognition that what can help individuals can also benefit systems and vice versa.'

Mediation in the Shadow of the Law

Mediation is often understood as taking place in the 'shadow of the law.' If mediation fails, disputants still have recourse to court adjudication for a remedy. A significant factor in the resolution of mediated disputes is how parties consider that a case *might* be determined if it were adjudicated. Community mediations are less likely to have legal outcomes than other types of mediation. Claims for 'nuisance' regarding noise and noxious smells may be disproportionately costly and ineffective to adjudicate. Boundary disputes may be both expensive and difficult to resolve in a court where a judge cannot inspect the fence or hedges. Cases of poor communication and relationships between neighbours may have very little legal content. For these reasons, the shadow cast by the law may be less precise and more blurred than in other types of mediation. This makes community disputes more difficult to resolve, for there is little leverage to persuade parties to settle and makes community mediation particularly appropriate for imaginative resolution.

Types of Disputes

Community mediation deals with many kinds of disputes.

Dignan's (1995) survey for Mediation UK identified six broad categories of disputes among the 16 community mediation services surveyed:

- Disputes involving mildly anti-social behaviour
- Disputes resulting from lifestyle clashes
- Disputes involving minor harassment
- Disputes incidental to other more serious problems such as drug abuse
- Disputes involving serious harassment or criminal activity
- Disputes involving care in the community

Of these disputes, noise probably accounts for the majority, followed by abusive anti-social behaviour and children's behaviour problems. A subsequent report (Dignan et al. 1996) concluded that disputes over noise, boundaries, interpersonal conflict, and children account for over 70% of disputes.

In *Transforming Community Conflict* (Harris 2021), based on a survey of 15 community mediation services, all conducting mediation of neighbour disputes, 87% also conducted workplace and employment mediation, found 87% offered conflict coaching, 67% training to raise awareness of mediation in the community, 53% family mediation, and 20% restorative justice. While 27% of the organisations reported receiving referrals from health professionals, which she considers 'the most overlooked area where community mediation can benefit individuals and society is health.'

Other types of disputes frequently cited include boundary disputes, inter-generational conflict, parking disputes, disputes over animals, CCTV cameras, multi-party disputes including environmental planning disputes, and peer mediation in schools. Brown and Marriot (2011) write of mediating between gangs in the USA and give an example of mediation in a culture that is 'secretive, violent and criminal,' but there is less evidence of this kind of mediation in the UK. Dave Walker of CALM Mediation, formerly Southwark Mediation, has carried out gang-related work in London, and Yorkshire Mediation has become involved with conflict awareness and peer mediation training work in prisons to support relationships within and outside prison.

Around 20% of the services surveyed in *Transforming Community Conflict* (Harris 2021) offered peer mediation training for schools. This intervention involves training pupils, teachers, and ancillary staff in the skills of conflict resolution and encourages pupils to address issues in a supervised environment. It is often directed at redressing problems of bullying and helps students learn the important skills of handling and resolving conflict. Such initiatives may help develop a more democratic and inclusive culture in schools and become part of a school's philosophy, in which pupils are encouraged to take responsibility for tackling differences and diversity in ways that pre-empt violence and anti-social behaviour. It may also be a significant way of increasing awareness of mediation skills and helping children become skilled in conflict resolution. Quaker Peace and Service and Leap Confronting Conflict were among the pioneers of this initiative in the UK.

Process

Typically, the process in a community mediation would include a combination of separate meetings with individual disputants (caucus meetings in US parlance) and joint meetings with both – or all – sides of the disputes (round table meetings).

Gulliver (1979) discusses two distinct but simultaneous processes occurring in mediation: a cyclical process of exchange of information leading to modification of expectations and a developmental process involving distinct phases or sequences. This would be as applicable to mediation taking place in a community context as any other form.

Stages of Mediation

Stage 1: Pre-mediation
Stage 2: Preliminary communication
Stage 3: Clarifying the issues
Stage 4: Information gathering – exploring the issues
Stage 5: Substantive negotiations
Stage 6: Dealing with deadlock
Stage 7: Conclusion – drafting an agreement
Stage 8: Post-meeting follow-up

Pre-mediation

Cases are generally referred to the mediation office or those co-ordinating the mediation service by external agencies: CABs, housing offices, police, social workers, housing and environmental health departments. An increasing number of cases are also referred by health professionals, sometimes through social prescribing schemes. In an initial phase of mediation, administrators or volunteers in the office establish that both parties are willing to meet with mediators, assesses the suitability of the dispute for mediation, send out information, and speak to both parties. Where only one party is willing to engage with the process, some mediation services will offer 'conflict coaching.'

Preliminary Communication

After the initial contact with the office, whether disputants have been referred by external agencies or by themselves, the case is generally referred to volunteer community mediators. Mediators visit parties in their homes, remind them of the ground rules, and ensure agreement to mediation. At this stage, there is an emphasis on active listening in private meetings with all sides of the dispute, in which a mediator tries to explore the underlying issues at stake by exploring the interests of disputants beyond their stated positions and listening to what has been happening in the relationship between the parties.

Face-to-face meetings often lead to opening new issues and an asymmetrical understanding of the dispute. At this stage, mediators affirm the ground rules for mediation and explore the possibility of round table meetings. A significant part of this early discussion involves decisions regarding who attends meetings. The composition of a meeting should aim to address power imbalances between the parties so that all present feel comfortable and safe, and no party feels intimidated or coerced into settlement.

Ground rules for mediation include voluntariness, confidentiality, the non-binding nature of a negotiation until an agreement is reached, the significance of courtesy and respect in communication, and the importance of both sides listening and of the mediators being independent and not party to the dispute. Mediators may also invite the disputants to contribute to the formation of ground rules as part of the process of building consensus.

Clarifying the Issues

Following introductions, mediators work with both parties to establish an informal agenda. This if often done by way of a flip chart. Clarifying the issues generally takes place in joint meetings at a neutral venue. Both parties are asked to give an uninterrupted explanation of their understanding of the dispute. Parties are offered the opportunity for separate meetings for individual conversations if at any time the meetings risk 'boiling over' or either party feels the need for an individual meeting.

Bargaining

The bargaining stage often involves high levels of conflict and emotion. This exchange generally takes place in a plenary meeting. Mediation skills at this stage focus on facilitating communication and ensuring that the parties have heard each other. There may sometimes be situations of such entrenched hostility and antagonism that one or both parties are unwilling to meet. In these circumstances, some mediation organisations offer 'shuttle mediation': meeting separately with the parties and shuttling between the rooms. There is a danger, however, that shuttle mediation risks leading parties to avoid the issues, and even where this doesn't happen, an inexperienced mediator may get caught in the middle and become the scapegoat for the failure of a mediation. While shuttle mediation may result in an agreement, it very rarely leads to a significantly improved relationship.

Dealing With Deadlock

Very often, there may be a deadlock of mutual and entrenched intransigence at the stage of substantive negotiation. At the point a mediator may separate the parties into further separate meetings. Damage limitation may require deciding which issues cannot be resolved in the mediation and instead focusing on where common ground can be reached. Individual meetings may concentrate on the consequences of refusing to settle. Widening (or narrowing) the context of the meeting may sometimes help move towards resolution. At this stage, reality testing may involve asking challenging questions in a way that would not have been possible earlier in the meeting. There may be a more 'evaluative' style than at other stages of mediation. Such reality testing is always best explored in individual meetings and by way of questions rather statements that might be interpreted as partisan or biased.

Techniques deployed in overcoming impasse include:

- Diagnosing and seeking to circumvent barriers to settlement: e.g. people missing from the mediation.
- Identifying and retrieving missing information.
- Identifying and seeking to build on or mutualise common interests.
- Using the techniques of role reversal as a way of fostering empathy between the parties.
- Identifying possible openings that may occur after a sincere apology.
- Reminding parties that mediation is voluntary and that they are free to leave at any time.
- Identifying alternatives to settlement and the potential consequences of not settling.
- Returning to the ground rules and the importance of reciprocal uninterrupted listening.
- Even where it is not possible to reach full agreement, identifying a more limited agreement on ways of communicating in the future.
- Refreshments, often tea and biscuits, to fulfil a number of purposes: providing an opportunity for a break at the beginning, middle, or end of a mediation; helping the parties relax; and enabling them to reflect on what has happened so far.

Conclusion of Mediation

When substantive agreement is possible, a record of the meeting is generally drawn up. This should be in the parties' own words; it is generally signed by them at the meeting. If this is done on a flip chart, parties may take copies on their mobile phones. The agreement is then typed up by the office and sent to both parties as a memorandum of understanding. Mediators will often explain that this is a good-faith agreement and not intended to be legally binding. With both parties' agreement, a record may be shared with other bodies, such as housing officers. Clarifying the boundaries of confidentiality is a crucial aspect of a mediator's role at this stage. Where this is a condition of the agreement for funding the mediation, this requirement will need to be set out as an agreed ground rule before the parties in dispute consent to mediation. When a proposed agreement effectively changes legal relations, parties may agree to take the agreement to lawyers for formal drafting or defer agreement until they have gotten legal advice. Disputes tend to be cyclical in nature, and even a successful mediation may change the dynamics of a dispute rather than offering reconciliation or providing a definitive resolution of all the issues at hand. A 'mediation outcome statement' would typically include next steps to be taken. Dignan et al.'s (1996) survey found that the greatest proportion of mediations were terminated by withdrawal of one of the parties or referral of the case to another agency. The next largest category was either complete agreement on all issues presented or a better understanding between the parties of the other's positions, falling short of complete agreement.

Post-Meeting Follow-Up

In many mediation services, mediators will call parties shortly after the mediation to see how they are feeling. Mediation services often offer a review of how things have progressed after a number of weeks and report back to any referring agency, in general terms so as to not breach confidentiality, the outcome of the dispute. Mediation services may offer further sessions in intractable disputes.

Skills

Community mediation calls on a wide range of mediators' skills. During a mediation, mediators will need to focus, simultaneously, on what is going on in terms of the relationship between the parties, the process of the mediation, and what is happening in terms of the substance of the dispute. At the heart of a mediator's skill is empathic and active listening. Sometimes, even in mediations in which there has not been a substantive outcome, simply the experience of being listened to can be transformative. With any form of mediation, the parties to the mediation are responsible for any agreement arising. While the mediators may help the parties find the solution to a dispute, any suggestion of a solution could be seen as partial or biased. Part of the challenge of community mediation is holding open a non-judgmental and impartial space for disputants to negotiate their own settlement in a context in which tempers may flare and emotions run high. Active and empathic listening involves a willingness to step back and attend to all the detail, including body language, of what is being said and not said. It starts best from a place of genuine curiosity and involves reflecting back the substance and feelings of what is said and not said. By framing accounts in terms of the speaker's perspective or feelings, it may be possible to disarm judgment and to draw out the positive interests beneath what is being said.

The kinds of questions that may be asked depend on the context. A mediator may use open questions to build trust and understand the issues while using more focused questions to clarify and define issues. Summarising what has been said can ensure that the mediator has understood the issues and offer disputants an opportunity to clarify where a mediator has not understood the nuance of what is being said. Skilful paraphrasing can draw the venom out of what is being said in individual meetings. Reframing statements to open possible alternative ways of understanding a conflict may help parties find new perspectives and possible solutions to a dispute.

Examples of Reframing

Statement	Reframe	Purpose
She is lying about my children's behavior.	*Remove accusation and restore neutral language.*	*So you have different ideas about what has happened.*
She shouts at her children when they . . .	*Restore equilibrium.*	*So she minds about her children's behaviour.*
This is hopeless. I need to leave this mediation now.	*Lower temperature.*	*You are anxious about being able to come to an agreement*

Reality testing is best done in private and may encourage parties to modify their expectations. It is seldom possible to find a resolution to a dispute unless both parties move. Examples of reality testing include:

- How do you think your neighbour might respond to this suggestion?
- What will happen if you are unable to come to an agreement with your neighbour?

When parties have become cynical about their neighbours' motivations and intentions, a mediator's inextinguishable optimism may help them keep or attain a forward-looking and solution-centred focus.

Community Mediation Case Study

The initial contact with the mediation service was made by Freya (Party 1), a housing association tenant asking for mediation with her neighbour Molly (Party 2), who has shared ownership. Freya (aged 28) and her partner, Ron, have a son, Lucca, (aged 4). Her husband has a spent conviction for assault. Molly (aged 52) is a social worker with arthritis who lives by herself with her pet spaniel. The relationship between Molly and Freya has never been good, though Molly had been friendly when Lucca was born. Molly has since complained about the noise made by Lucca. Freya is now very upset at what she feels is the disrespectful way she has been treated by Molly. Molly is afraid of Ron, whom she finds intimidating.

The dispute came to a head on a hot summer afternoon. Molly parked her Ford Fiesta in a way that blocked Ron's car. When Ron asked her to move it, she shouted at him, and her dog jumped up, knocking Lucca over. Since then, there has been no communication between them. A representative of the mediation service has met with both parties, and the mediators were given the following brief description:

> 'P2 blocked P1 vehicle into a parking space. P2's dog then jumped up at P1. P2 has been sent a warning letter by the Housing Association with a copy of their pet policy. P1 has been given diary sheets to complete.'

Mediators met with parties individually and found out more about their feelings about and perspectives of the dispute.

Freya and Ron are both very angry. They think that Molly is unfriendly and looks down on them. Freya feels bitter that Molly complained about the noise that Lucca made in the garden. They spoke of Molly regularly smoking cannabis in her garden, saying it was unfair that Ron was imprisoned for drunken behaviour while Molly is getting away with smoking drugs. Ron felt inclined to call the police about the smoking until Molly persuaded him to try mediation.

Molly is upset and worried. She 'doesn't want to mix with her neighbours,' describing Lucca as unruly. She explains that she has severe rheumatoid arthritis and parked near the flat to unload groceries on a hot Saturday. Being tired and in some discomfort, she decided to have a cup of tea before unloading it. She claims Ron 'banged on her door' and raised his voice. When she went out to see what was happening, her 'affectionate' and excited spaniel jumped up and inadvertently knocked Lucca over. Molly is irritated that she has been sent a letter by the Housing Association setting out their pet policy and is livid that someone had called the RSPCA to complain that her dog had been left in the car on a hot day with the window closed and strongly suspects that Molly did this.

Mediators meet with the parties in two rounds of individual meetings prior to a round table. One of the issues that need resolving is who will attend the mediation. Molly fears Ron and Freya will 'gang up' on her, and Ron is not willing for Freya to go to the meeting without him. Ron agrees to be silent and to let Freya do the speaking in the first half of the meeting. It is agreed that Molly will bring a friend with her, and all are content for the round table to take place. Some progress is made in individual meetings when the mediators ask and are given permission to share the extent of Molly's disability, of which Freya and Ron were only partially aware.

Further progress is made in a roundtable meeting. Freya was unable to arrange a babysitter for Lucca, who therefor needs to come to the mediation. In the meeting, Freya visibly restrains Ron from losing his temper. Molly has expressed privately to the mediators that she is willing to apologise, largely because she is worried about possible damage to her professional reputation as a social worker. The mediators help create an opportunity for her to do this, and further progress is made when Molly explains that she has a GP prescription for cannabis as a means of pain relief. A turning point in the mediation occurs when Ron is invited to speak at the end of the meeting. Once Molly has apologised for blocking the car and explains that she will not park there again, he is willing to admit he had written to the council about the dog but is adamant that he did not write to the RSPCA. Molly accepts this. In the latter part of the meeting, there is a distinct thaw between Freya and Molly as Molly becomes more aware of the pressures that Freya is under in influencing the behaviour of both Lucca and Ron. The neighbours agree they will communicate more directly in the future and swap mobile telephone numbers. While they will probably never be friends, the mediation has opened the lines of communication and helped clarify boundaries between them. Ron ends the mediation by saying he would always be willing to help in an emergency.

Styles of Mediation

The style of community mediation correlates closely with the philosophy of the organisation. What Liebmann (1998) refers to as the 'grass roots strand' is probably more facilitative and closer to Bush et al. (2004) 'transformation story,' in which parties are encouraged to recognise and respect each other and perhaps involve aspects of 'narrative mediation' (Monk and Winslade 2000). The more top-down driven style likely to favour more evaluative and problem-solving styles of mediation and 'settlement' is captured in Bush and Folger's 'satisfaction' story.

Co-mediation

Most community mediation services involve two mediators both for safety reasons and to gather a more rounded and nuanced view of the dispute. It enables mediators to reflect among themselves regarding possible solutions and approaches and also to model cooperative behaviour. It is also used for training and mentoring and to reflect gender, age, race, and religious diversity when this is a live element in a dispute. Co-mediation can comprehend a variety of processes, and it is helpful to be clear about whether it is offered on the basis of mediators being of equal status (which requires an excellent working relationship, especially in toxic disputes) a senior/junior model, or a training relationship, in which one of the mediators may, in effect, be a participant observer who offers comments to the other.

Funding

Community mediation in the UK is underfunded. After its initial expansion to a high point of 250 in the mid-2000s, it has shrunk to 40 or 50 organisations today. The non-legal nature of many disputes has made it hard to find adequate funding to sustain community mediation organisations. Dignan et al.'s (1996) report found that borough, city, and county councils provided 42% of funding, national charities 17%, central government 17%, safer cities 6%, regional charities 5%, an industry 4%, with miscellaneous, unspecified, and self-funding accounting for a further 9% Most organisations have their roots in a community and depend on provision from the local authority for the bulk of their funding. Additional funding may be provided by housing associations, Police Commissions, and the provision of training. Funding is often tied to a service-level agreement, either of funding a specified number of mediations or providing service in a specific geographical area. Additional funding may be provided by fundraising within the community and charitable foundations, sometimes linked to a specific project or niche area of mediation. While community mediators try to provide services that are free at point of use, a number may earn income for particular types of mediation: for instance, either family or employment disputes, which may provide cross subsidy to neighbourhood disputes. Wandsworth Mediation has developed a model of support from commercial mediation. Commercial mediators offer their time on a pro bono basis, and the fee which they would normally earn then subsidises the mediation of neighbourhood disputes. In her 2021 report on community mediation, Harris (2021) estimated that the average cost of a community mediation case was £527.50, with family cases (£1,000) and intergenerational disputes (£800) being more expensive. The average income of ten mediation bodies surveyed was £75,771.80 and average expenditure £69,281.50. Although Harris (2021) does not include a detailed breakdown of funding sources, it appears that central government funding has been drastically reduced since the Dignan report, charitable funding is lower, and local authorities remain the primary source of funds. Of the 13 mediation organisations responding to a questionnaire on sources of funds, 8 included local authorities, 6 housing associations, 4 policing/police and crime commissioners, 2 grants, 1 commercial and workplace mediation, 1 training income, and 1 EU peace programme.

Harris (2023) estimates that the average cost of a community mediation is now £753.43. The report, which categorises the costs of some of the consequences that might be prevented by effective mediation, puts this in the context of Shelter Scotland figures that estimate an average cost of £14,924 to a local authority for a housing eviction in 2019–2020.

One possible model for future development is offered by Norway, where an initiative of the Ministry of Justice and Security has created a nationwide community mediation service, which is open to all residents and free at point of use. Konfliktradet has 550 community mediators, which, based on a population of 5.5 million, equates to one mediator for every 10,000 people.

Effectiveness

Dignan et al. (1996) reports that 23% of referrals resulted in complete agreement and 16% in partial agreement; 19% achieved some measure of reconciliation; 30% were terminated for some reason, usually on account of one party being unwilling to pursue matters further; 7% were unresolved; and 5% resolved without further intervention. The terminology of 'complete agreement' and 'partial agreement' would be more typically used in a philosophy informed by the 'satisfaction story' and 'reconciliation' than in a philosophy informed by a 'transformation story.' In this report, 40% of cases were dealt with by shuttle mediation, and only 27% involved face-to-face direct mediation. In an additional 27% of cases. it was only possible to work with one party, and in 6%, other (unspecified) methods were used. Of those cases in which it was possible to have a face-to-face meeting between parties, 80% resulted in agreement. Dignan's study estimated the number of neighbourhood disputes reported to local authority and housing departments was around 250,000 annually, of which around two thirds were noise related. In the six years leading up to 1996, there were 17 documented fatalities associated with neighbourhood noise complaints. One of the most persuasive reasons for adopting community mediation is that it prevents apparently minor disputes escalating into more serious criminal activity.

Critiques of Community Mediation

Few disputes are more visceral than the kind of toxic and smouldering conflict that neighbours may have lived with for years. At the same time, community mediation often reveals patterns of underlying structural and economic injustices. Inadequate provision of social housing, insecure private tenancies, high rates of youth unemployment, and poor provision of mental health services can manifest themselves as disputes between neighbours. While the relationship between the parties is the essence of a community dispute, there are often disparities of power and complex interlocking multi-party conflicts running beneath the surface. Differences of status, whether between owner-occupiers and tenants or those with different immigration status, add further complexities to disputes. Poor-quality local authority housing and inadequate sound insulation in post-war housing exacerbate or create problems between neighbours that would otherwise crystalise as disputes between landlords and tenants.

Mental health issues require particularly sensitive handling. Protracted conflict is invariably stressful, and this will be exacerbated when those in dispute are lonely or have pre-existing mental health vulnerabilities. In some cases of extreme mental distress or where parties may be incapable of making an informed consent to mediation, mediators may need to carefully consider whether mediation is going to be unhelpful or harmful. Occasionally, conflict may be driven by a desire for attention or to escape loneliness. In extreme cases, pursuit of a dispute may even become an individual's 'meaning of life' or a part of their identity, and they may find it impossible to envisage letting go of a dispute – even on advantageous terms. For all these reasons, handing relationships requires a sensitivity in helping parties develop the skills for resolving conflict. Mediators need to be aware of power imbalances, not only in the particularity of a dispute but also in relation to the role played by mediation in furthering or suppressing social justice.

While community mediation starts from an assumption of equality between the parties, there may be complexities if the local authority has 'taken a view' of allegations of anti-social behaviour, a view which may be partial and sometimes factually incorrect. This may equally be the case when a housing association has threatened one of the parties with a 'Notice to Quit' or compelled them to mediate as a term in the tenancy agreement. There is an overlap between restorative justice (QV) and community mediation. Some of the most complex issues (beyond the scope of this chapter) involve disparity of cultural expectations, including race, gender, and sexuality. Very often, mediators are from middle-class professional backgrounds, and those in dispute are working class or unemployed. It is here, as successfully developed by Lambeth Mediation Service in the 1980s, that inclusive recruiting of mediators from the community can have a powerful normative impact in shaping parties' expectations and disarming assumptions of bias.

Early advocates of community mediation communicated a utopian vision empowering participants to take control of their disputes, fostering participation, and educating citizens in resolving future conflicts without the need to rely on the state.

For Nader (1979) 'disputing without the force of the law' is a lost battle. De Sousa Santos (1980) developed a Marxist critique of informal justice, contrasting the informality of the community field 'dominated by a therapeutic model and a treatment ethic, with its emphasis on consensus' with the hardening of attitudes in penal policy. Abel (1982) drew parallels with the experience of colonial rule, in which indirect rule claimed to respect and empower indigenous authority, but its effect was to 'subordinate and undermine countervailing power.' For Abel (1982) the politics of 'informalism' was neither a force to be

> simplistically repudiated as an evil to be resisted, or dismissed as a marginal phenomenon that can safely be ignored. It is advocated by reformers and embraced by disputants precisely because it expresses values that deservedly elicit broad allegiance: the preference for harmony over conflict, for

> mechanisms that offer equal access to the many rather than unequal privilege to the few, that operate quickly and cheaply, that permit all citizens to participate in decision-making rather than limiting authority to 'professionals,' that are familiar rather than esoteric, and that strive to achieve substantive justice rather than frustrating it in the name of form.

Auerbach (1983) argued that when the legal establishment involves itself in ADR for reasons of efficiency, it limits access to the law for those who can't afford it. Fiss (1984) considered a propensity for settlement reinforces disparities in power and resources, compromises core legal values, and reduces the risk of political transformation. Grillo (1991) argues that informalism can encourage the suppression of disadvantages and reinforce existing inequalities.

More recent critics have applied some of the US critique of informalism to a UK context. Shah Kazemi (2000) suggests that 'mediation substitutes the mystification of the law and is more pernicious because its sources are less obvious and points of resistance concealed.' Pavlich (1996) has likened community mediation to a practice of 'secular confession' in which disputants narrate their stories of conflict in a 'rule bound' context to a delegated third party. Mulcahy (2000) considers the 'threat of coercive action by the state remains a shadow in many community sessions' but finds much of the debate about community mediation 'suggestive of intellectual nihilism.' She concludes a survey of community practice by suggesting that a new generation of thought offers a more cautious and 'incremental conception of challenge which suggests the possibility of a slower change in legal and political consciousness than was suggested by earlier generations of left-wing scholars who were hopeful of more rapid change.' Community mediation can take many forms, and while the more evaluative forms, especially when occurring in the 'shadow of the state,' can be oppressive, many community mediators will have their own stories of transformation. Mediators, however, do not always follow their own 'theory of practice.' There is sometimes a fine line between 'signposting' parties to appropriate agencies and giving them advice rather than offering information. Mulcahy comments that many 'participant observers' in her project were willing to 'step out of role' and give 'advice to disputants about the responsibilities of state agencies and other agencies which might be able to address their social problems.' Perhaps, as Merry (1993) observed, mediation can have a 'dialogic' relation with adjudication, both recognising 'the capacity for state control' and the ideological potency of 'popular justice' in its capacity to imagine a nonviolent ideology of managing conflict and commitment to consensual, amicable resolution of conflict.

Conclusion

In its pure and facilitative form, when mediators are recruited from the community, community mediation can offer something of a vision of popular justice, combining aspects of Bush and Folger's 'satisfaction' and 'social justice' rationale. When coopted by local bureaucracy or applied in a crudely instrumental form as a mandatory step by local authorities in repossession proceedings, mediation may be closer to the 'oppression' rationale. Community mediation may, on occasion, fulfil its transformative promise, but even when it falls short of this lofty ideal, it frequently provides a satisfactory and effective outcome which, by putting what is most important to the parties centre stage, provides a form of social justice which is quantitatively different to any available in a court.

Questions

1. **What style of mediation might be most appropriate to community disputes?**
2. **What are the implications of including mandatory mediation clauses in a dispute resolution process?**
3. **How might a mediator address criminal behavior as part of a dispute?**
4. **How might a mediator address racism when expressed between parties in community disputes?**
5. **What are some of the ethical dilemmas that may be faced in community mediation?**
6. **What are some of the critiques that might be offered of community mediation?**

Further Reading

Liebmann, M. (1998) *Community & Neighbourhood Mediation*. Routledge-Cavendish.

Merry, S. (1993) 'Sorting Out Popular Justice'. In S. Merry & N. Milner (Eds.), *The Possibility of Popular Justice: A Case Study of American Community Mediation*. University of Michigan Press.

Winslade, J. & Monk, G. (2000) *Narrative Mediation: A New Approach to Conflict Resolution*. Jossey Bass.

6 Civil Mediation

> Mediation is a flexible process conducted confidentially in which a neutral person actively assists the parties in working towards a negotiated agreement of a dispute or difference, with the parties in ultimate control of the decision to settle and the terms of resolution.
>
> (CEDR general definition of civil mediation)

Civil mediation may take place either in prospect of civil litigation or as an attempt to settle litigation. Parties may be represented by lawyers or other representatives. The outcome of the mediation is consensual and only legally binding when reduced to a written agreement and signed – a clear distinction from basic contract law. Lon Fuller's comments (1971) are as applicable to civil mediation as any other type:

> [T]he central quality of mediation [is] its capacity to re-orientate the parties towards each other, not by imposing rules on them, but by helping them achieve a new and shared perception of their relationship, a perception that will redirect their attitude towards one another.

Mediation is often described as taking place in the 'shadow of the law' (Mnookin and Kornhauser 1979), where the legal framework of a dispute is likely to be a dominant influence on how the matters between the parties are decided in negotiation. However, the mediation process as 'managed negotiation' does not require the existence of a dispute. It is extremely useful in transactional or non-contentious business, as a tool in contract renegotiation, and as a safety valve in preventing escalation: e.g. in the International Federation of Consulting Engineers dispute resolution boards. While a prediction of legal outcome is likely to be a significant factor shaping a civil mediation, the relationship between the parties is no less significant, even if that relationship is shaped by the knowledge that disputants can fall back on a legal determination of the issues if a negotiation stalls. In the UK, while mediators may evaluate, they will not give expression to their opinions and will remain firmly within the facilitative model. In cases nearing trial, the mediation will also take place in 'the shadow of the court,' where a prediction of how the court would determine a case, including the allocation of costs, will be included in

DOI: 10.4324/9781003112617-6

the determination of parties' best alternatives to a negotiated agreement (BATNA), although this will also take in far wider factors.

Civil mediation occurs in almost every legal context, including commercial contract, employment, professional negligence, intellectual property, construction, landlord and tenant, public procurement, information technology, banking, insurance, probate, and shipping and aviation. Many of these forms of mediation have developed their own distinctive specialist style, practices, and practitioners adapted to the specific legal and cultural context.

Employment mediation is generally applied to disputes between employers and employees when the employee is leaving or has left employment and will generally include lawyers. Workplace mediation usually involves working relationships in the context of an existing employment relationship, and parties are generally unrepresented, although unions and lawyers may be involved in some cases. When it is impossible to find a satisfactory resolution in the context of the employment contract, workplace mediation my subsequently change to become an employment mediation.

At a national level, there are several large mediation providers, including CEDR, ADR Group, ADR Chambers, ADR-ODR International, Academy of Experts, Chartered Institute of Arbitrators, Royal Institution of Chartered Surveyors, and independent panels of mediators. The Law Society maintains a panel of civil mediators, and the Bar Council has an ADR committee. While the Law Society has developed a code of practice for mediators, barristers who act as mediators are regarded as practicing outside their professional role since the provision of mediation is not regarded in law as the delivery of a legal service, is presently unregulated, and is not confined to the learned professions. Most subscribe to the European Code of Conduct for Mediators, which requires the taking out of professional indemnity coverage. Many barristers offer mediation through their chambers, and solicitors include mediation in the services they offer. Other mediators practice independently, often – but not always – with a subject specialism.

History and Development of Civil Mediation

The majority of legal disputes have always been resolved outside the courtroom, often without the facilitation of a third party. Civil mediation in its modern form, as a distinct process with its own structures and practices, initially developed in Canada and the USA. Curiously, the first civil mediation service provider in the UK, ADR Group, emerged in April 1989 as the result of an American lawyer, Richard Schiffer, purchasing a franchise from a Boston-based mediation organisation to develop the field in the British Isles. The Centre for Effective Dispute Resolution (CEDR) was set up by Eileen Carroll and a group of City of London solicitors as a charitable body supporting mediation in 1990 with the backing of the CBI. The value of CEDR mediation services in 2022 amounted to around 500 to 600 million GBP per year. CEDR's Ninth Mediation Audit (2021) detailed operational statistics taken from their own caseload; CEDR assesses the overall economic impact of the commercial mediation field in the UK delivered savings of £4.6 billion in 2021.

Civil mediation was given impetus by Lord Woolf's Access to Justice Reports (1995, 1996), aimed in part at challenging a culture of late settlement, which were formally introduced as the Civil Procedure Rules 1998, and Lord Justice Jackson's changes to the rules regarding civil costs and, in the case of cross-border disputes, given definition by the 2008 EU Mediation Directive, (now repealed by Brexit), written in part by Michel Kallipetis KC, who also assisted in drafting the Singapore Convention 2019.

The cumulative effect of these changes has meant that the culture of 'late settlement' that existed prior to the Woolf reforms to civil justice has largely been replaced by one in which parties are expected and required to engage with each other during the process of litigation, settlement conferences and mediation are the norm, and judges take an active role in promoting settlement. Arguably, the Woolf reforms paved the way for the development of mediation by making litigation in England and Wales so expensive that only the rich or foreign corporations could afford to litigate in London.

More recently, Road Traffic Accident Portal (since 2013) and Online Dispute Resolution (ODR) have taken this a stage further and require exchange of information online with limited costs recovery. Online dispute resolution, typically involving online interaction with parties replicating court pleadings, is now often the initial default option for consumer claims. The Civil Mediation Council was set up in 2003 by Jonathan Dingle to bring together the major civil mediation service providers and independent mediators to discuss matters of mutual concern. It is currently a not-for-profit registration body which speaks to government, although it represents fewer than 500 of the 18,000 or so trained mediators.

Stages of the Dispute

Mediation can take place at any stage of a civil dispute. It can be initiated pre-action, at source, as in consumer ADR schemes in which parties are bound to attempt ADR before beginning proceedings. ADR frequently takes place concurrently with proceedings, often with judicial encouragement. It may take place immediately pre-hearing, 'in the shadow of the court' as well as the law, when an impending legal decision and its concomitant costs focus minds. There is no perfect time procedurally, although some practitioners describe a 'sweet spot' when a case is sufficiently developed to have clarity over the issues but limited investment in the time and cost of preparation maximises the cost advantage to both parties of reaching a negotiated settlement. A cynic might suggest this occurs when defence solicitors have earned enough fees to permit their clients to engage once they have 'paid for the atrium.'

Process

Gulliver's research on negotiation (1979) has provided an analytical framework for understanding the process of mediation (Palmer and Roberts 2020; De Girolamo 2013) and been adapted to teaching the stages of mediation (FMA Teaching

Manual 2012; Parkinson 2020). While adaptations vary, Gulliver's theory illuminates a cognitive and strategic process in which a cyclical process, comprising the repetitive exchange of information between the parties, leads to a developmental process, in which parties adjust their expectations and preferences in moving towards an agreement.

Gulliver's Process of Negotiation

1. The search for an arena for the negotiations;
2. The formulation of an agenda and the working definitions of the issues in the dispute;
3. Preliminary statements of demands and offers and the exploration of the dimensions and limits of the issues, with an emphasis on the differences between the parties;
4. Narrowing the differences, agreement on some issues, and the identification of the more obdurate ones;
5. Preliminaries to final bargaining (which may include developing options for agreement);
6. Final bargaining;
7. Ritual confirmation of the outcome; and
8. Implementation.

Gulliver (1979)

Gulliver's process is accepted by Palmer and Roberts (2020) with the proviso that the initial identification of issues and the subsequent formulation of an agenda are 'analytically distinct,' and 'the phenomenon of agreement seems to lie uneasily between the phases of final bargaining and ritual affirmation.' In teaching, most mediation training organisations offering the facilitative model adopt a five-phase process: preparation, opening, exploration, bargaining, and concluding. Here, preparation would cover the first two stages of Gulliver, opening stage three, exploration stage four, bargaining five, and concluding stages six and seven.

De Girolamo (2013) offers an alternative formulation to the central portion of the process, which, excluding the search for an arena and implementation, becomes a six-stage process:

1. Unilateral articulation of positions;
2. Information exchange;
3. Testing of positions;
4. Shift in positions;
5. Bargaining proposals; and
6. Joint decision making for final agreement.

Underlying these models is a process by which initially competitive exchanges become more collaborative, and, at some elusive point, a change in posture leads to a change of substance in the negotiation. The structure is significant as, while the disputants remain in control of the substance of negotiation, the primary task of the mediator is to prevent the negotiation becoming 'stuck' by facilitating the shift between the phases. Palmer and Roberts's (2020) comments about the elusiveness of the 'phenomenon of agreement' may reflect the fact that the process is at once cognitive and strategic, and the shift between competitiveness and collaboration is both cumulative and asymmetrically reciprocal.

A civil mediation usually consists of a day with a mediator, during which the parties set out their cases in a joint session, followed by a series of individual confidential private (or, in the USA, 'caucus') and joint meetings in which offers and counteroffers will be developed and presented and the mediator will help the parties to create an agreement that will meet their needs. The mediator's energy and optimism can ensure that parties remain at the table even when negotiation flags.

Opening

Typically, civil mediation starts with a joint meeting in which all parties set out their positions. Prior to this, the mediator speaks with both parties' solicitors or mediation advocates before meeting to discuss practical arrangements and ensure that everyone fully understands the process. Both parties exchange 'mediation statements,' which set out the nature of claims and their initial negotiating positions. These preliminary arrangements comprise the process described in Gulliver's first two phases.

During the opening session, the mediator invites all parties to set out their perspectives without interruption. The opening meeting is often a time of high tension when mediation advocates are setting out a case with the intention of building trust and confidence with their principals, and any concessions are often minimal. Stage three of Gulliver's process overlaps aspects of opening and exploration.

The Process

- Managed or facilitated negotiation.
- Confidential.
- Voluntary.
- Flexible.
- Non-binding.
- Without prejudice.
- Future focused.

Depending on the nature of their case and expertise, either legal representatives or their principals dominate this session. In a complex mediation, subject to prior agreement with the mediator, this opening session may be attended by many more people than just the parties and their representatives. A company may be represented by several directors; accountants may be present. In a probate case, a party might be accompanied by tax lawyers as well as solicitors and counsel. In a procurement case, an NHS trust might be represented at several different levels. For successful mediation, everyone who will be part of the solution needs to be represented at the table and have authority to settle. When the approval of insurers may be needed for an expanded authority to settle, a mediator will need to check their availability to approve a settlement by an alternative method.

There has recently been a significant trend against having an opening plenary session. The mediator wants attendees to have specific assigned roles which need to be justified. Accountants or tax specialists are encouraged to be available by phone, contactable on Zoom, or present only towards the end of the day as the settlement begins to form.

Occasionally, an opening may involve 'setting out a stall' with little engagement between the parties. If a case involves the interpretation of a statute or recent case law, this stage may involve robust exchanges between lawyers as to their interpretation of the case law. This is becoming less usual and only happens when a mediator considers it helpful for settlement and the management of parties' expectations. If a mediator feels that further exchange is not helping the dynamic of a mediation, they initiate separate 'private' meetings with both parties. Frequently, mediators dispense with the opening session. While a joint meeting may involve some confrontation between the disputants, a mediator should never allow the lawyers of one party to cross-examine an unrepresented party.

Exploration

Exploration involves two different aspects: (1) information gathering and (2) reality testing which may occur over, two, three or more caucuses (US) or private meetings (UK). During this stage, a mediator will consolidate rapport, discover what matters to the parties, identify possible options for settlement, and expand their thinking by facilitating a structured exchange of information. The exploration stage comprises some of Gulliver's third and fourth phases of negotiation.

At this stage, it may often still be unclear whether the outcome of a mediation will involve the maintenance of a business relationship between the parties or a financial settlement with a separation of the ways. In initial meetings, a mediator may spend anywhere between half an hour and an hour exploring the factual and emotional context of a dispute. Typically, a mediator wants to establish how parties are feeling and get a sense of their priorities, their response to the initial meeting, and their expectations of the day including possible settlement options. While a mediator will already be aware of the attempts at settlement and should have explored details (such as the existence of Part 36 offers) in pre-mediation contact with the lawyers, further details, including the limits of authority of insurers, may become apparent at this stage.

One of the challenges of this stage with parties who have not had previous experience with mediation is maintaining the confidence of the party a mediator is not with at any time. If it becomes apparent there is missing information that is crucial to the negotiation, the party a mediator is not listening to may be encouraged to identify this material or further consider frameworks for settlement, even when there may be a very significant gulf in the figures this may involve. During this stage, a mediator discusses, separately, the strengths and weaknesses of both parties, generally doing so by asking probing questions. If parties are unwilling to consider the weaknesses of their own position, they may nevertheless be willing to consider the strengths of the other side's case. While occasionally, mediation may move immediately from an initial exploration to the bargaining stage, more often there will be more than one individual meeting with each party. As Gulliver identifies, during this process, the exchange of information may lead to both parties adapting and modifying their respective expectations as part of a developmental process.

Bargaining

While the whole of the mediation is concerned with a facilitated negotiation between the parties, bargaining is used to describe the exchange of offers which are – or could be if further detail is provided – acceptable (phase six of Gulliver's negotiation process) During the bargaining stage, a mediator works with the parties to identify a likely settlement framework and work on the specific terms for settlement by facilitating effective exchange of offers, helping parties test their positions prior to exchange, and overseeing the process of negotiation, moving between rooms and setting up conversations with different groupings of participants: e.g. a lawyer-only session.

In a typical civil mediation, there may be four or more rounds of negotiation during which parties first identify a framework for settlement (part of preceding phase five of Gulliver's process) and subsequently communicate these offers to each other. As part of the facilitation of the exchange of offers, a mediator may help parties package, present, and explain their offers and manage expectations. Parties are encouraged to explain the reasoning behind their positions prior to communicating them so that concessions will be most effective and the reasons for intransigence understood. In the predominant UK model, these offers will often be communicated by the mediator to the other party, but this is not invariably the case. A mediator will seek to offer reciprocal interpretation to parties as a way of helping them understand each other's perspectives and framework of understanding. If done effectively, this can facilitate the process of moving from a competitive approach to the more collaborative stage of joint decision making.

Although mediators (at least in the UK) are trained to avoid positional bargaining, initial exchanges of offers may be highly positional, with parties making a first extreme offer to 'anchor' the range of negotiation. A mediator will always encourage the parties to present the reasons and objective justification for their perspectives in a way that will facilitate further discussion and enable parties to understand the reasoning behind their perspectives to manage expectations. While some parties will seek to make the first offer as a way of signalling confidence and control, others, who are used to a positional style of bargaining, may be reluctant to make the first offer out of anxiety that this might be interpreted as a sign of weakness. Generally, if a party is confident of the factual nexus of the dispute and believes they know at least as much as the person they are negotiating with, they may consider there is an advantage in making the first offer. When there is a significant asymmetry of knowledge, it may be wiser to let the other party make the first offer. While some mediations follow an orderly progression of converging offers leading to a concluding negotiation, there may be many other patterns to a mediation. Lacunae in information, whether factual, legal or financial, are frequently identified at an early stage.

Latterly, seeking additional instructions may involve video conferences or telephone calls with parties who are not present at the mediation, side meetings with lawyers or accountants from both sides, or further negotiations with insurers regarding changes to the limits of authority in light of new knowledge. Just as civil litigation is often as much about costs as about the substantive merits of a case, so, in mediation, the allocation of costs is likely to be an important part of an agreement and a potential stumbling block. The balance of power between parties may change or develop during exploration. It is generally considered that mediators in civil litigation do not have an obligation to try to level the playing field.

Settlement

In the concluding phase of a mediation (Gulliver phase seven), a mediator will work with the parties to finalise the settlement terms and identify outstanding issues or implications of settlement that will require further work. They will ensure all matters in dispute are covered and agree on the next steps, whether or not agreement has been reached.

The mediation outcome statement will be drawn up by the lawyers for both sides when present. Drawing up a mediation outcome agreement can sometimes reveal further serious challenges. Even if there has been substantial agreement on the financial terms of the settlement, there may be significant further negotiation as to the precise terms under which the action is to be compromised. Generally, during this stage, lawyers for both (or all) parties will work together on drafting. Usually one party's legal representatives will write a first draft and circulate it to the other party's legal representatives for comment. While some outcome settlements may become effective as freestanding contractual agreements, more often, when litigation is in progress, they will be drafted as a 'consent' or 'Tomlin order,' which will become an order of the court setting out the terms under which the action has been stayed (phase seven of Gulliver's negotiation process). Either party is then at liberty to have the terms of the order enforced (phase eight – implementation – of Gulliver's process).

When an agreement is reached in a mediation, all parties are often brought together for some form of ritual affirmation. If a mediation has run overtime, it may not be possible to agree on all the details on the day of the mediation, but parties may draw up an agreement in principle that can subsequently be reduced to legal writing. The reason for this may be the absence of crucial in-house counsel or the need for an additional level of approval or ratification by insurers. If a mediation outcome statement does not finalise all the issues in dispute, it is important to identify outstanding issues and focus the minds of the parties on what steps may be taken to ensure that agreement is subsequently reached. Even when it is not possible to resolve the substance of a dispute, time spent in mediation may be valuable if it narrows the range of issues that have been raised, reduces the amount of time (and cost) necessary for subsequent litigation, or clarifies the nub of issues that need to be addressed.

Skills and Strategies in Mediation

The skills of a mediator are as much the interpersonal skills of a psychologist as the forensic skills of a lawyer. While knowledge of the legal framework of a dispute is helpful in facilitating negotiations to resolve it, parties remain in 'control of the decision to settle and the terms of resolution.' Psychological skills and knowledge of the subject area of the dispute are no less significant. A good mediator will be aware of what is going on during a mediation in terms of substantial and potential offers of settlement, the state of mind of each of the parties, and the process, including fairness in allocation of time. A mediator will support both parties by building rapport with each and, ideally, between the disputants. As part of this process of facilitation, they may prompt them on issues that are being swept under the carpet or denied.

Active Listening

As in other forms of mediation, active listening is one of the pivotal skills required in civil mediation. The mediators listen not just to the facts that are being related but also to the emotions with which they are being articulated and are sensitive to what is not being said. Active listening, which is also an element of psychotherapeutic counselling, starts from a place of genuine curiosity and operates by reflecting the substance and felt content of what is said while framing this from the speaker's perspective. Civil mediation will seek to draw out the values, mindsets, positive interests, and needs beneath what is ostensibly being said. Active listening includes deep psychological attentiveness, displayed by appropriate body language and verbal cues. It uses what Boulle and Nessic (2009) refer to as 'following skills' to indicate that the listener has heard what has been said by summarising, prompting, and asking clarifying questions but never giving advice. An empathic mediator verbalises both content and underlying feelings as a way of capturing the factual and emotional meaning of what has been said. A mediator may paraphrase what has been said by a party to emphasise or illustrate aspects of the experience.

Reframing

Reframing is closely related to active listening, but rather than simply reflecting back what has been heard, a mediator invites a party to interpret an issue in a different way by contextualising or presenting it in a different frame of reference. Inviting parties to consider a dispute from each other's or a superordinate perspective is a powerful intervention in facilitating the resolution of a dispute. The purposes of reframing include shifting focus from the past to the future, mutualising interests, detoxifying language by removing destructive personal accusations, emphasising the positive rather than the negative, and qualifying and relativising demands by redefining them as potential options for consideration.

Summarising

Throughout a mediation, a mediator will use summarising skills in different ways. At its simplest, summarising serves the important purpose of showing someone that they have been listened to and understood, offering them the opportunity to clarify and correct if they have not. In joint sessions, it serves a potentially more complex function in providing an account of where negotiations have reached in a way that is acceptable to both parties or providing an account of an agenda that meets both parties' needs and interests. Effective summarising builds on the skills of active listening by including both significant factual detail and emotional nuance. At key stages – for instance, when resuming after a break or coming together in a joint meeting – it can infuse optimism into a mediation by reminding parties of what they have achieved and help publicly affirm impartiality by providing an account that accurately states both sides of a dispute. When mediation comprises several disparate elements, acknowledging them openly ensures that those not currently the subject of negotiation have not been lost.

Reality Testing

Reality testing is one of the most challenging aspects of civil mediation. Without a shift in both parties' positions, it is unlikely that a settlement will be reached. Parties tend to give greater weight to facts that strengthen their position and less weight to those that diminish it. Reality testing seeks to redress this balance and get parties to reassess the strengths and weaknesses of both sides of the case. Where mediation is taking place 'in the shadow of the courts,' both sides' bargaining positions will be shaped by their assessment of the expected value of the case if it goes to adjudication. When both parties consider they will be better off than their best alternative to a negotiated agreement (BATNA) by reaching an agreement, a skillful mediator will be able to work without parties to help to identify this zone of potential agreement (ZOPA). Gaps in information held by the parties or an overly optimistic assessment of the strength of a party's case, sometimes reinforced by legal opinion, may make this difficult to identify. Even when principals have a realistic assessment of the legal strengths and weaknesses of their case, they may be less well informed about the level of costs they are likely to recover.

At its simplest, reality testing may involve asking a party to reassess the estimated value (EV) of a claim in light of new information. This may take several stages, involving recalibration of expectations on both sides of the dispute. Litigation risk, unrecoverable costs, recent case law, and possible counterclaims will all influence EV. The process will, of course, be conducted with both parties, leading – if effective – to a progressive convergence of expectations. Reality testing is best done by questions probing positions, assumptions, and options rather than directly giving assessment and advice.

A claim of personal injury taking place at work has been pleaded as worth £500,000 might be reduced in the following ways.

Claimant's initial PI claim pleaded as £500,000.
Litigation risk revised to 50%: EV £250,000.
Consideration of 20% risk of a defence of 'contributory negligence': EV £200,000.
Reduce estimate of quantum by 40% on basis of defendant's expert report: EV £120,000.
Estimated unrecoverable costs (25% of £80,000): EV £100,000.
Defendant's initial offer of £20,000 based on £100,000 maximum quantum and the defendant's 80% prospect of success.
Litigation risk revised to 50%: EV £50,000.
Revised quantum to £200,000 on basis of expert's reports: EV £100,000.
Irrecoverable costs of £20,000: EV £80,000.

In this example, as a result of exchange of information in relation to different aspects of the claim, an original unbridgeable gap has been eroded to create a ZOPA of between £80,000 and £100,000. While actual negotiations are much messier, the case illustrates the principle of progressive recalibration of expectations. In addition to irrecoverable legal costs, the friction of litigation, demands on management time, and reputational risk all provide internal incentives for settlement from the principals' perspective. While some claimants may relish the prospect of a 'day in court,' many dread the prospect of cross-examination, especially if there are allegations of 'exaggerating' the severity of the injury. A claim is often settled for significantly less than its EV on account of accelerated payment and the sheer emotional cost of having a contentious court case in prospect.

Generating Options

A significant core skill of the mediator is assisting the parties and their representatives in recognising as a vehicle for settlement an outcome not available to the court or beyond the scope of legal redress. The concept of the reintegration of a business relationship by renegotiating a contract; the giving of a formal, carefully crafted apology; or recognition of past conduct without liability is beyond the remedy of the court. In this way, the mediator can guide the parties to resolve disputes without reference to the dispute itself and enable the parties to move on without issues ever needing determination.

Mediation Case Study

The claimant, who worked in maritime insurance, had seen an opportunity to develop software to better align premiums with risk. He devised software based on season and a ship's satellite-derived location data to predict risk. Over two years, he developed software to create sophisticated and profitable algorithms, using historical data to identify significant pricing inefficiencies. The claimant resigned to develop the product with his wife, an actuary. They sold their house and took out a bank loan to fund the project while his wife continued to work until ill health intervened. Two years after he resigned, when the product was nearing completion, he approached his old employer seeking a test bed but was told that his idea had been developed in his absence and had now entered use. The claimant asserted rights over the software and sought damages of nearly £10 million; a bitter dispute ensued. Although the couple had limited means, they generated publicity, airing their case on television and in a Sunday newspaper and, as a small shareholder, created a scene at the company's AGM. The insurer asserted all rights in the intellectual property. They argued that the product was developed by the claimant while in their employment and with their commercial records. They denied all liability and rejected the quantum, which included a multi-million-pound loss of future profit.

The matter went to mediation pre-issue, where the claimant was unrepresented and the defendant represented by in-house counsel.

The mediation followed a conventional format with positional opening statements unmitigated by conciliatory remarks or any sign of movement. The claimants put their case assertively, focusing on the merits of the software design and how it would transform the market. They quoted industry-specific editorial commentary as evidence that the product had excellent commercial prospects. They pre-empted the defence, claiming the software was written at home during the evenings and on weekends. Counsel for the insurer asserted it would be a simple matter of IT forensics to prove that the development work was done in house. The prospects for success were remote and the quantum fanciful. The mediator adjourned the joint meeting and began a series of confidential meetings with each party.

In private, the insurers provided additional grounds for their belief that the software was developed while the claimant was working in their employ. They acknowledged that the claimant might 'theoretically' establish liability but characterised the claim for damages as 'entirely speculative, wildly ambitious and detached from reality.' Management, however, were exercised about the adverse publicity and the distraction to core responsibilities and business. They hinted that a nuisance offer might be forthcoming later in the day.

The claimant couple were repetitive in private session and went into greater detail about the impact of events on their lives. They had put 'life on hold' to develop their product and re-iterated the unfairness of what had happened. The husband had taken up other, not completely satisfactory employment – yet another sacrifice.

Relatively quickly, the insurer made a low six-figure offer, which was rejected without any meaningful response. The mediator continued to explore in both rooms. It transpired that the complainant's wife had been diagnosed with breast cancer and had given up her work. She told the mediator that, although she was now in remission, her diagnosis had made it difficult to secure a mortgage. The mediator asked for her consent to share this with the insurer, which she was happy to grant so they could understand how badly this episode had impacted their lives. The insurers were polite but unmoved, and all adjourned for lunch.

Progress was made in the afternoon as the claimants more fully understood that their lack of resources meant they could not realistically fund their case to trial. Although the range was narrowed to hundreds of thousands, a distinct gap remained.

The breakthrough to resolution occurred when counsel told the mediator that the insurer had spoken to a friend in another company and secured an offer of life insurance for the wife on terms as if she had not had cancer, and this was added to the financial offer. This was an offer that was almost costless to insurer yet of high value to the recipient and a beautiful example of how mediation can lead to outcomes which could never arise in litigation. The court could only consider material matters; there could be no mechanism to create such an unconventional remedy in the adversarial format of a hearing.

Costs

The allocation of costs is a significant part of any civil mediation. Civil cases may often be as much about costs as about the substantive merits of a case. By the time a case reaches court, the costs in issue may be significantly more than the value of a claim. Even successful claimants are unlikely to recover more than 70% of the relevant costs. There is an assumption in mediation that both sides will generally carry their own costs. Any variation would need to be specifically included in the mediation outcome statement.

Civil procedure rules apply to all cases in county courts and the High Court and provide powerful incentives to settle cases. This creates an additional reason for mediation. The function of Part 36 is to encourage sensible dispute resolution and provide clarity regarding litigation costs by prescribing what costs liability there will be after a judgement. Either side can make a Part 36 offer. Part 36 is prescriptive about how an offer can be made. The Part 36 code is procedural, not contractual. If a Part 36 offer does not comply with the CPR, then it will be a Part 44 – or Caldebank – offer, for which the costs remain at the court's discretion.

When a claimant makes a Part 36 offer which is not accepted and the claimant betters the offer at trial, the claimant is entitled to 'indemnity costs' from the date of expiry of the offer until trial, plus punitive interests and an additional amount.

When a defendant makes a Part 36 offer which is not accepted and the judgment is not more advantageous than the offer, the defendant is entitled to (1) their costs from the date when the relevant period expired and (2) interest on the costs. The defendant does not receive the enhanced benefits of indemnity costs and the higher rate of interest on costs awarded.

When both parties turn out to have been optimistic in their Part 36 offers and the claimant recovers more than the defendant previously offered to pay but less than the claimant previously offered to accept, the claimant is normally considered the successful party. Jackson LJ's judgment in *Fox v Foundation Piling Ltd* (2011) confirms that the claimant should normally be regarded as 'the successful party' within Rule 36/44.3 (2) because they have been forced to bring proceedings to recover the sum awarded, and their claim has been vindicated. As the successful party, they should recover their costs from the other side. But in *Multiplex v Clevaland Bridge UK Ltd* (2007), Jackson LJ took a different view of who the successful party was.

Mediation in the UK has become a critical procedural step in civil litigation. Parties who refuse offers to mediate risk adverse costs orders, even if they have made a successful Part 36 offer. Costs may be awarded on an indemnity basis – in which the successful party will recover a higher proportion of costs – if a party refuses a reasonable offer to mediate.

Dunnett v Railtrack plc (2002) establishes that parties are obliged by Civil Procedure Rules (1998) r 1. 3 to further the overriding objective of Part 1. If a party turns down the possibility of ADR when suggested by the court as part of its case management process, this may be taken in account in terms of costs.

Halsey v Milton Keynes (2004) as modified by *Churchill v Merthyr Tydfil* (2023) is the leading case on the scope of a court to order mediation while a dispute is being litigated and the implications of unreasonably refusing ADR. Halsey provided that a successful party whose Part 36 offer had been accepted could be deprived of some or all of their costs if they had previously refused or ignored an offer to mediate. The case sets out factors which are relevant to assessing whether a party has unreasonably refused ADR and is considered more fully in Chapter 10 on mandatory mediation.

Halsey acknowledged failure to mediate may be justified if a party has a watertight case, acknowledging that large organisations, especially public bodies, are vulnerable to pressure from claimants with weak cases inviting mediation as a tactical ploy.

In general, silence in the face of an invitation to participate in mediation/ADR is unreasonable, regardless of whether there was a good reason for a refusal to engage, unless you can show that your case falls into one of the exceptions listed in Halsey at paragraph 16ff.

In *PGF II SA v OMFS Company 1 Ltd* (2013), the Court of Appeal upheld the trial judge's refusal to order costs to the party whose Part 36 offer was accepted because the same party had previously ignored offers to mediate. Even though the parties' respective Part 36 offers were a long way apart, the court held that that did not mean mediation was bound to fail.

Garritt-Critchley v Ronnan (2013) identifies cases unsuitable for mediation as those in which the party wished to resolve a point of law, where a binding precedent might be useful, or where injunctive or other relief was essential to protect the parties. The court emphasised that cases in which there was distrust or emotion between the parties were perfect for mediation because the mediator's skills might be most useful in diffusing the conflict and enabling the parties to see the issues clearly.

Mediation can take many forms: in *R (Crawford) v Newcastle upon Tyne University* (2014), the court considered that a university's internal adjudication process, in which both parties had the opportunity to set out their respective positions, was a form of mediation, and in these circumstances, it was reasonable for the university to fail to respond to a further formal offer of mediation.

In *Thakkar v Patel* (2017), Jackson LJ provides that silence in the face of an offer to mediate, as a general rule, could constitute unreasonable conduct justifying a costs sanction. However, in *Gore v Naheed* (2017), Underhill LJ did not accept that the desire of a party to have their rights determined by a court of law in preference to mediation could be considered unreasonable conduct.

Role of Lawyers and Mediation Advocates

Lawyers play a significant role in mediation, and parties are generally legally represented. This may sometimes be by non–legally qualified 'mediation advocates.' The role of a lawyer in mediation is distinct from that of the lawyer in litigation. A good mediation advocate will be aware of the process of mediation and how it can be turned to a principal's advantage. The mediation advocate will need to have the skills both of advocacy and negotiation while helping the principal interpret the strategic moves of the other side. Crucially, whereas advocacy in court is addressed to persuading the judge, in a mediation, an advocate needs to persuade the other party in a dispute to recalibrate their expectations of a case and encourage them to settle. At the same time, the mediation advocate will seek to use the mediator to turn the process to their client's advantage. A skilled mediator will include the legal representatives in building trust and rapport to create a momentum for settlement. It may sometimes happen that the necessary 'shift' for settlement starts in meetings of the parties' legal teams before being more reluctantly accepted by the principals.

EU and Brexit Dimension

The Cross-Border Mediation Directive (2008) provided for the harmonisation of standards of cross-border mediation for the enforcement of agreements resulting from mediation but has now been repealed by Cross-Border Mediation (EU Directive) (EU Exit) Regulations 2019. Online Dispute Resolution Regulation (2013) led to the establishment of a free online platform (available in all languages of the EU) by which traders and consumers in member states could attempt to settle disputes relating to online sales or service contracts and access ADR providers in the EU. This has now been revoked by the Consumer Protection Regulations (EU Exit) (2018).

The ADR Regulations (2015) implemented the provisions of the ADR Directive (2013), which required traders to notify consumers about what options for ADR were available if they were unable to resolve a dispute, but that has now been amended by Consumer Protection (Amendment etc.) (EU Exit) Regulations (2018).

ADR is mandatory in certain regulated sectors where there is a high risk of consumer detriment (e.g. financial services, energy, aviation). In some sectors, the law requires traders to belong to an ADR scheme, but it gives them some choice about which scheme to join. This is the case, for example, for estate agents and telecommunication businesses. In non-regulatory sectors, ADR is usually voluntary.

International Enforcement of Mediated Outcomes

The United Nations Convention on International Settlement Agreements Resulting from Mediation (Singapore Convention 2018) provides an international framework for the recognition and enforcement of mediated settlement agreements that resolve international commercial disputes. It provides a parallel framework to the 1958 New York Convention for arbitral awards. While many countries have seen signing this convention as a way of signalling support for the principle of mediation as well as commerce and development, it does not have the same significance as the New York Convention in that mediated settlements depend on the consent of the parties rather than the decision of a third party such as a judgment or arbitral award.

Confidentiality and Mediation Privilege

Unlike most court proceedings, mediation is usually confidential. In a civil mediation, confidentiality applies in different ways. While in some jurisdictions, confidentiality is a statutory requirement, in the UK, it is generally a contractual obligation reinforced by mediators' code of conduct. In civil mediation, a mediator will generally explain that what takes place in joint meetings is confidential to the parties and should not be revealed outside the mediation. What takes place in individual meetings will not be revealed to the other party or at all without their consent. Some mediators highlight the existence of an exception if mediators suspect they may be required to make a disclosure under the Proceeds of Crime Act (2002) and the Economic Crime and Corporate Transparency Act (2023) in relation to money laundering, but this is still not invariably the case. For all practical purposes, the parties in a mediation are given a promise that their secrets cannot be revealed publicly unless specifically agreed between the parties.

The European Code of Conduct for Mediators (2018) has been adopted by nearly all major UK mediation service providers and makes reference to both the whole process and private meetings:

> The mediator shall keep confidential all information, arising out of or in connection with the mediation, including the fact that the mediation is to take place or has taken place, unless compelled by law or public policy grounds. Any information disclosed in confidence to mediators by one of the parties shall not be disclosed to the other.

Except in multilateral mediations involving public policy, confidentiality is almost always a specific contract term in a mediation agreement. CEDR's model agreement reinforces this with a term binding the parties not to call the mediator as a witness. (For a further discussion, see Chapter 9 on mediation secrets and Chapter 12 on mediation ethics.) All training organisations advise mediators to destroy papers after the event and to advise courts seeking to compel them to give evidence that they have no independent recollection.

Styles of Mediation

The overwhelmingly predominant style of civil mediation is facilitative. JAMS and some individual mediators offer a more evaluative form modelled on 'settlement conferences' in the USA, in which a mediator may adopt an approach of robust reality testing and even formal recommendations. While a skilled mediator takes responsibility for the process, they will also be prepared to draw on parties' suggestions in adapting the process to their needs and interests. Fisher and Ury's (1981) work on interest-based negotiation (see Chapter 3 on negotiation) has shaped the thinking behind contemporary models of mediation, interests are uniquely in the knowledge of the parties, and the task of the mediator is to facilitate a negotiation that enables those in dispute to mutualise those interests.

Some critics of evaluative mediation, such as Love (1997), consider it a contradiction in terms, arguing that any evaluation is at odds with a mediator's primary function. Love believes evaluation promotes polarisation, excludes non-lawyers from practice, can prevent negotiation, detracts from party responsibility, leads to the danger of loss of neutrality, and can turn a consensual process into one that becomes coercive. In practice, many mediators will, at times, adopt more subtly evaluative strategies: for instance, inviting the parties to test the reality of their positions; encouraging their lawyers to perform the sharper elements of evaluation, whether that be the party's own lawyer if they are being realistic; or ensuring a principal is made aware of both analysis and a narrower evaluation of their adversary's legal team when their own may be overly optimistic.

Other commentators, such as Riskin (1996), take a more pragmatic approach, recognising that mediators may use a diversity of strategies and interventions at various stages of a mediation and envisaging a grid of styles in which interventions vary along two continuums between facilitative and evaluative as well as broad and narrow frames of reference of problem definitions. A 'broad facilitative' style encourages parties to understand, create, and evaluate broad interest-based proposals. A 'narrow facilitative' approach invites parties to consider the costs and consequences of not settling and consider interests more specifically in the context of a court outcome. An 'broad evaluative' approach might urge parties to propose and accept broad, interest-based settlements while an 'narrow evaluative' approach predicts the specifics of an adjudicated trial outcome, including cost implications.

In practice, a skilled mediator might move across all four quadrants of Riskin's grid in the course of a single mediation. In an employment dispute, for instance, they might start with a broad facilitative approach, exploring how parties understand their interests and future relationships, narrowing this approach as it becomes clearer that the scope for resolution on the basis of a continued relationship seemed remote, adopting a broad evaluative approach in considering competing frameworks for settlement. The mediator might seek to break a deadlock by deploying a narrow evaluative style in assessing the prospects of various elements of a claim before an employment tribunal before returning to a narrow facilitative style in working with parties on agreeing on an appropriate reference. In adopting this kind of approach, a mediator may facilitate two interlocking conversations, one more narrowly legal, considering the likely outcome of the dispute were it to be adjudicated, and the other more creative and future focused about how relationships (whether business or personal) might be changed in the future by adopting a more collaborative approach.

Although more common in community forms, a civil mediation may also provide 'opportunities for transformation,' in which disputes can be viewed not as problems but as opportunities for learning and growth (Bush et al. 2004). In cases in which the preservation of a relationship is important to both (or all) parties, mediators may also work with disputants on understanding their narratives of the conflict (Winslade and Monk 2000), as well as underlying interpretive frameworks in seeking to replace antagonistic, conflict-saturated narratives with a more constructive alternative story which can work for both the parties. (See for instance *Termination Tempest* (2004), a Project on Negotiation open-access video resource.)

Conclusion

Civil mediation has seen the greatest growth of any area of ADR. While ideally, it can reorient the parties towards each other and provide for creative resolution of disputes, it would be wrong to see it as a panacea. If one party is genuinely not interested in settlement, there will be little point in a mediation that will only increase costs. Likewise, if one or more of the parties are not engaging with the process in good faith, the preconditions for negotiation are absent, and mediation may become a fishing expedition to trawl for evidence that will subsequently be used in ligation.

This, however, does not undermine the case for mediation in a high proportion of civil cases. At best, mediation may provide both recognition and empowerment and save the emotional cost of continued conflict. Even in the most intractable disputes, if mediation is unable to cut the Gordian knot of the dispute, it may narrow the issues to be adjudicated, facilitate the exchange of evidence, improve the working relationships between the parties, and save on both court time and costs.

Questions

1. **How does the process of civil mediation differ from community mediation?**
2. **What are some of the most significant skills in civil mediation?**
3. **Explain the distinction between 'negotiation' and 'bargaining' – how can a mediator facilitate transition between the two processes?**
4. **What are the responsibilities of a civil mediator?**
5. **In what way can mediation be said to take place 'in the shadow of the law'?**

Further Reading

Boulle, L. & Nesic, M. (2010) *Mediator Skills and Techniques: Triangle of Influence*. Bloomsbury Professional.

Mackie, K. et al. (2007) *The ADR Practical Guide: Commercial Dispute Resolution* (3rd ed). Bloomsbury Professional.

Menkel-Meadow, C., ed (2012) *Complex Dispute Resolution. Foundations of Dispute Resolution*, Vol I, Foundations of Dispute Resolution; Vol II, Multi-Party Dispute Resolution; Vol III, International Dispute Resolution. Ashgate.

Richbell, D. (2015) *How to Master Commercial Mediation*. Bloomsbury Professional.

Riskin, Leonard L. (1996) 'Understanding Mediators' Orientations, Strategies, and Techniques: A Grid for the Perplexed', *Harvard Negotiation Law Review* 1, 7–51.

7 Family Mediation

Definition

> Family Mediation a process in which those involved in family relationship breakdown, change, transitions or disputes, whether or not they are a couple or other family members, appoint an impartial third person, a Mediator, to assist them to communicate better with one another and reach their own agreed and informed decisions typically relating to some, or all, of the issues relating to separation, divorce, children, finance or property by negotiation.
>
> Family Mediation Council (2018)

Family mediation is a process of facilitated negotiation. While it has features in common with community and civil mediation, there is an added dimension of complexity and mediator responsibility, in that the mediation will primarily focus on issues regarding the future of the children, who will usually not be present in the mediation. These are likely to include residence, where, when, and with whom the children will live, and contact arrangements for spending time with a non-resident parent. Family mediation increasingly involves a cross-cultural and potentially international element. It may also engage public law child protection issues.

Most family mediation takes place in the context of divorce or other relationship breakdown. Such family disputes are uniquely suited to mediation. There is a high intensity of conflict; emotion runs high. There is inevitably an emotional dimension to any family dispute, and after a divorce, there is often a need to continue a relationship as parents if not as spouses. Although, in terms of jurisdiction, family law is a form of civil law, family mediation has its unique culture, history, and practices. It is more tightly regulated than other forms of mediation and raises a set of distinct issues regarding the relationship with the legal framework in which it takes place.

Principles

The core characteristics of family mediation are shared with other forms of civil mediation (McCrory 1981): confidentiality of the relationship with the mediator, impartiality of the mediator, voluntary nature of process, and procedural

DOI: 10.4324/9781003112617-7

flexibility, with parties remaining in control of the outcome. However, there is a significant and distinct variation in the role and type of interventions that may be required of a mediator. Issues of domestic violence and the well-being of children impart additional responsibilities, including protection of personal safety, respect for cultural diversity, considerations of the interests of children who will (generally) not be present in the mediation, and moral and legal boundaries on confidentiality.

The power and intimacy of the marital relationship and the potential for coercion within it sharpen the need for awareness of anything that could impair equality of bargaining. As Roberts (2014) writes, '[E]ven where there is a presumption of competence, mediation may be inappropriate in certain circumstances and especially where differences of power between the parties are substantial.' Although parties' lawyers will be consulted throughout the mediation process, it is unusual for them to be present at a mediation, as in other forms of civil mediation, and the mediator cannot simply delegate safeguarding issues or the responsibility to ensure the autonomy of parties to their lawyers. The issue is even more acute in the case of litigants in person, when proposals arising from mediation cannot be signed off by lawyers.

The principles of family mediation are premised on the complexity of negotiating the multiple layers of a process of separation that is at once legal, social, economic, and psychological. While such a process of change would be difficult even in the context of a strong continuing relationship, it is particularly demanding at a time when a relationship is impaired or has broken down. Whereas in court adjudication, children and property matters are addressed in separate proceedings, mediation allows the parties to negotiate a range of issues that address the emotional and psychological as well as the legal implications of a divorce.

Bohannan (1971), in *The Six Stations of Divorce*, identifies six dimensions of adjustment in separation and divorce:

1. The emotional divorce
2. The legal divorce
3. The economic divorce
4. The parental divorce
5. The community divorce
6. The psychological divorce

Complex issues such as where children will live and go to school and who will be primarily responsible for them during which parts of the week require difficult negotiation and adjustment in light of changing circumstances and are difficult to reduce to the clarity of a court order. No mediation agreement can cover all eventualities, and an important part of the mediation conversation is likely to be how differences over parenting will be resolved in the future. The psychological dimensions of an agreement are no less important than the legal framework in which they occur. While mediation may focus solely on finance or child-related issues, the two are often inextricably bounded up in that the fairness of financial measures will depend on who is looking after the children and where they live, etc. The model of family mediation considered next typically comprises all-issues mediation.

History of Family Mediation

Family mediation in the UK has been around since the 1970s. More liberal attitudes and the Divorce Law Reform Act 1969 led to an increase in divorces in the UK from around 50,000 per year in 1971 to 150,000 by 1979. Mediation began as a grassroots response to the need for a more human approach to relationship breakdown, as identified in the Finer report on 'One-Parent Families' (1974). The report recommended an approach to the breakdown of relationships, which it considered should be managed with the minimum of bitterness, with the parties taking primary responsibility for resolving their own disputes (Roberts 2014). The Booth Committee (1985 para 3.10) subsequently affirmed the principle that 'responsibility remains at all times with the parties themselves to identify and seek agreement on all the issues arising from the breakdown of their relationship.'

Early family mediation services were set up in Bristol (1978) and Bromley (1979) as projects in which independent out-of-court mediation was offered for child custody. During the 1990s, mediation extended its scope to financial matters, with an increasing involvement of lawyers as mediators. Family mediation now covers all issues amenable to negotiation in family law. While negotiating new ways of communication is not in itself a judicial issue, it will be at the heart of a successful mediation.

Process

Whereas other forms of civil mediation often take place in a single day, with disputants accompanied by their lawyers, family mediation usually takes place in three or more meetings over several weeks, which are not generally attended by lawyers. In the case of 'all-issues mediation,' this process allows for the in-depth exploration of issues regarding both children and financial matters in separate meetings while recognising that the issues are interrelated. After initial separate consultations to assess suitability for mediation, parties attend joint meetings, consulting lawyers and other professional advisors between meetings. While mediators may meet with parties separately during a mediation, and both should be offered this opportunity, mediators may be reluctant to do so too frequently out of a fear of being biased. Separate meetings are probably less frequent in family mediation than in other forms of civil mediation.

During mediation meetings, the parties work towards the completion of two separate documents: an open statement of financial information (OFS) and a memorandum of understanding (MOU). Whereas in most forms of civil mediation, the financial matters discussed remain confidential, in family mediation, the OFS should contain a complete statement of the assets of both parties and should be available to the court as a context for ancillary relief proceedings or a consent order.

In contrast, the MOU is a confidential document that records the outcome of the mediation, the reasoning behind decisions, and proposals for settlement. It is privileged and not in itself legally binding, but it provides a scaffolding or structure for agreement. Neither the MOU nor details of discussions taking place in mediation should be disclosed to the court, except with the consent of both parties.

Mediators in family mediation may be more willing to suggest options to parties than in other areas of mediation, (while never offering advice). The professional boundaries of what is acceptable are still contested. Whereas in many forms of civil mediation, the parties may have extensive experience of similar contexts, in divorce mediation, this is often, though not always, the only occasion when parties experience the legal dissolution of a marriage and mediation. Depending on the stage at which parties access mediation, mediators discuss all stages of the process of dissolution of a relationship, marriage, or civil partnership, including, for instance, how to inform children of the break-up. Where possible, a commitment to co-parenting and shared decision-making is the optimal solution. Complex and changing relationships between parents, children, and their siblings make it impractical for a court to determine all eventualities, and the best that can be hoped for in an order of the court is for a framework within which parenting decisions can be made.

Evidence suggests that family mediation is less costly and quicker than not using it in the case of a family breakdown. The National Audit Office report on 'Mediation in Family Breakdown' (2007) found that, on average, a mediated case took 110 days to resolve and cost £752, compared to 435 days and £1,682 in cases in which mediation wasn't used, and over 95% of cases settled through mediation were resolved within 9 months while only 7% of cases completed by non-mediation routes were settled within 18 months.

Mediation as Facilitated Negotiation

Mediation is essentially facilitated negotiation and takes place within the framework of what Gulliver (1979) (see Chapter Six on civil mediation) identified as eight distinct but overlapping phases. A cyclical process, comprising the repetitive exchange of information between the parties, leads to a developmental process in which parties adjust their expectations and preferences in moving towards an agreement.

The Family Mediator's Association elaborates on this model to identify 12 stages that follow the contours of Gulliver's process:

1. Explaining mediation and assessing suitability
2. Gaining voluntary and informed acceptance
3. Clarifying issues and needs
4. Prioritising and planning
5. Encouraging child and family focus
6. Gathering and sharing further information
7. Exploring options

8. Indirect and or direct involvement of children
9. Reality testing preferred options
10. Working out possible terms of agreement
11. Preparing summaries
12. Concluding mediation carefully

Parkinson (2020)

Legal Framework

As in other contexts, mediation operates in the shadow of the law. Until the Divorce, Dissolution and Separation Act (2020), implemented in 2022, divorce was allowed on a single ground: that a marriage has irretrievably broken down. This needed to be evidenced by one or more of five possible facts, as stated in the Matrimonial Causes Act (1973): adultery, unreasonable behaviour, desertion (two years), separation, agreed divorce (two years), and separation, contested divorce (five years). Case law developed in such a way that unreasonable behaviour became a subjective criterion. If one party considered that behaviour was so 'unreasonable' as to issue a divorce petition, it was clear that the marriage had irretrievably broken down, and it would be futile to try to prevent the divorce. The Family Law Act 1996, which initially included proposals for no-fault divorce, included a provision for mediation within its framework.

Proposals for no-fault divorce were abandoned in 2001 after vigorous lobbying and a change of government. Following a concerted campaign for public funding, the government finally recognised that mediation constituted a 'happy concatenation of economy and humanity' (Parkinson 2004). Although Parts I and II providing for no-fault divorce were abandoned, Part III provided legal aid for those eligible for family mediation.

The Divorce Dissolution and Separation Act (2020) now provides that divorce can be completed as a no-fault digital process. The mediation now no longer needs to deal with the question of marital fault and can focus on arrangements for the children and finances.

Children

In family mediation, the Children Act (1989), Section 1, provides that the court should regard the child's welfare as the paramount consideration when determining any question relating to the their upbringing. The first factor on the checklist is the 'ascertainable wishes and feelings of the child concerned (considered in the light of *his* age and understanding),' which will provide a particular focus for mediations when there are children. The Children Act replaces the previous concept of 'custody' with 'parental responsibility,' with a strong presumption that this will continue to be shared by both partners. Section 1 also sets out the principle of non-intervention of the court and starts from the presumption that parents should work out their own responsibility for children. This reinforces and reaffirms the importance of parents working together when making decisions regarding their children.

Section 1 (3): The welfare checklist includes:

- Child's physical, emotional, and educational needs.
- Likely effect of any change in circumstances.
- Age, sex, ethnicity, background, and other factors that the court considers relevant.
- Any harm suffered or of which there has been a risk.
- Ability of the parents to meet the children's needs.
- Range of powers available to the court.
- Court should only make an order with respect to a child when it considers that doing so would be better for the child than making no order at all.
- Five kinds of orders: residence orders, contact orders, specific issues orders, prohibited steps orders, and family assistance orders.

Section 1 (5) provides '[W]here a court is considering whether or not to make one of more orders under the Act with respect to a child, it shall not make the order or any other orders unless it considers doing so would better than making no order at all.'

In relation to family mediation, these provisions provide a statutory framework which will influence the structure and context of a mediation.

It is perhaps in relation to children that family mediation has the most to offer. Sensitive decisions regarding parenting can be challenging for many partners to handle, even in the context of a stable relationship and shared values. Expecting separating partners to make these decisions at a time of frequent anger, resentment, and guilt is incredibly demanding. At best, mediation can offer parties the opportunity to improve the quality of their communication and reflect on past experience in a way that may change their relationship from partners to co-parents. At times, this may lead to new understandings of personal 'narratives' (Winslade and Monk 2000) or the catharsis of being 'recognised' and 'respected' (Bush et al. 2004).

Financial Provision

Section 25 of the Matrimonial Causes Act (1973) provides the statutory framework for financial settlement to be made on divorce, although appellate courts have fundamentally altered the way that it is interpreted over the last 50 years. Section 25 (1) sets out the factors to be decided by a court in exercising its powers: 'First consideration to be welfare of any minor.' S 25 (2) sets out a list of relevant factors, including:

1. The income, earning capacity, property, and other financial resources of each party;
2. Their financial needs, obligations, and responsibilities;

3. The standard of living enjoyed by the family before the breakdown of the marriage;
4. The age of each party and the duration of the marriage;
5. Any physical or mental disability of the parties;
6. Contributions to the welfare of the family that each has made or is likely to make, including looking after the home and caring for the family;
7. The conduct of each of the parties 'if that conduct is such that it would be in the opinion of the court inequitable to disregard it'; and
8. The value to each of the parties of any benefit they may risk losing on account of the dissolution of the marriage.

In *Miller v Miller* (2006), the House of Lords set out a framework of how these principles apply. Baroness Hale set out three signposts to the correct approach:

1. 'The court is directed to give first priority to the welfare while a minor of any child of the family who has not attained the age of 18.'
2. 'The court is still concerned with the foreseeable future as well as with the past and the present.'
3. The court will 'encourage and enable a clean break settlement, in which the parties could go their separate ways without making further financial claims upon the other.'

MIAMS and Expectation of Mediation

Mediation information and assessment meetings (MIAMs) are meetings where parties are required to consider the suitability of mediation in the context of their separation or differences. While these are compulsory, mediation is not.

The Family Law Act (1996) made specific provisions for family mediation and for directions to be given requiring the consideration of mediation (Section 13 Resolution of Disputes) before the granting of legal aid. The Access to Justice Act (1999) specifies that all those applying for legal aid (with well-defined exceptions) need to first attend a mediation information and assessment meeting (MIAM). There has subsequently been strong state encouragement of family mediation, with the Family Justice Review (2011) recommending mediation and the Introduction of Legal Aid Bill and New Family Procedure and Pre-application protocol (2011) expecting both legally aided and privately funded parties to consider mediation before making an application for a court order. In 2013, legal aid cuts of £350 million removed legal aid from most divorcing couples. The Children and Families Act (2014) Section 10 (1) requires all separating couples to attend a MIAM prior to applying to the court to resolve parenting issues or for a financial order. There are a few specific circumstances, mainly relating to domestic abuse, in which this requirement does not apply. Recent legislation making specific reference to family mediation includes the Access to Justice Act 1999, the Children and Adoption Act (2006), the Legal Aid Sentencing and Punishment of Offenders Act (2012), and the Children and Families Act (2014).

The Civil Partnerships Act (2005) and Marriage (Same Sex Couples) Act (2013), with a few narrow exceptions, such as historic civil service pensions, now provide an equal framework of rights and responsibilities for same-sex and heterosexual couples.

While some family mediators saw compulsory MIAMs as a boon to mediation, lawyers are often the gatekeepers to mediation, and the process of family mediation is more of a complement than an alternative to mediation. The open financial summary becomes a document of the court, and while family mediation may facilitate the arrangements in the case of separating couples, the courts are responsible for giving this legal impress.

Features of Family Mediation

Co-mediation

Co-mediation is now rarely used in family mediation, largely on account of the cost. It can be used for a variety of purposes:

1. Mentoring and professional development in which a less experienced mediator learns from another or in which colleagues learn from each other's particular skills and expertise.
2. Enabling both parties to feel supported by someone of their own gender.
3. Fostering cultural balance and diversity when this is an important dimension of the relationship.
4. Uniting psychological and legal perspectives in all mediation issues. While psychological skills may be particularly important in decisions regarding co-parenting, the skills of a lawyer-mediator may be valuable in financial provision and in ensuring that the proposal will be endorsed by a judge.

Where two mediators work well together, co-mediation enables them to have a deeper awareness of what is happening in terms of process, psychology, and the dynamics of the negotiation. Co-mediation may make it possible to discuss particularly difficult issues within a mediation, to model constructive disagreement, and to offer multiple perspectives on options that the parties may be considering. Even experienced mediators may find it difficult to empathise with one of the parties; using a co-mediation model may provide balance and redress any partiality. Skilled co-mediators may be able to model the kind of constructive dialogue about contentious issues that they are hoping to encourage and add depth to conversations about co-parenting.

Except where conducted as part of a mentoring exercise, co-mediation leads to a significant increase in cost. There is a danger with inexperienced mediators that they may be drawn into a disagreement or that the divorcing parties may seek to encourage them to take sides. This may be particularly risky when mediators meet separately with the two parties, and there are gaps in the narratives that individual mediators are aware of. With divorcing couples, there may be complex transferences and projective identifications taking place with the mediators. When used well, co-mediation offers an opportunity for a 360-degree vision of what is happening in a way that is not possible with a single mediator.

Hearing the Children's Voices

Article 12 (1) of United Nations Conventions on the Rights of the Child 1989 provides that every child has the right to express their views, feelings, and wishes in all matters affecting them and to have their views considered and taken seriously. Section 1 (3) of the Children Act 1989 states that the court is required to have regard to 'the ascertainable wishes and feelings of the child concerned (considered in the light of his age and understanding).' The Family Justice Review (Norgrove report) considered: '[I]t is now generally accepted . . . that it must be right for children and young people to be given the opportunity to have their voices heard in cases that are about them.'

In the Family Justice Review Final Report (Ministry of Justice 2011), the UK government endorsed the view that there should be a 'non-legal presumption that all children and young people aged 10 and above should be offered the opportunity to have their views heard in dispute resolution processes, including mediation if they wish.'

The FMC Revised Code of Practice (2018) provides:

> 6.6.1 The Mediator must encourage the Participants to consider the children's wishes and feelings. All children and young people aged 10 and above should be offered the opportunity to have their voices heard directly during the Mediation, if they wish.

Although a few mediators from a family therapy background have included children in mediations since the early 1980s, historically, the interests of children have been represented though their parents. All FMC mediators now have an obligation to explain to parents that children aged ten and older should be offered the opportunity to talk to a mediator trained in child-inclusive mediation or another suitably qualified professional. Child-inclusive mediation, for which practitioners need to undertake additional training, is becoming much more common. FMC's 2019 survey reported that the number of child-inclusive mediations had more than doubled since 2017: 46% of mediations included in the survey concerned child-related matters, and 33% involved children ten or older. In 26% of the relevant cases, children had taken part in the mediation process (Parkinson 2020).

Research by the Department of Justice of Canada suggests that children and their parents have better relationships and there is less conflict between the parents when children are part of the process (Birnbaum 2009). While there is compelling evidence of the significance of listening to the voices of children in the process of separation (McIntosh et al. 2008), child-inclusive Mediation is not the only way to do this and needs to be considered alongside child legal representation, child custody assessments, brief interventions, voice of the child reports, judicial interviews, parenting co-ordination, and the use of child specialists.

Birnbaum (2009), in a report of the Canadian Ministry of Justice, adumbrated challenges that still need to be addressed:

> If children are heard, how much weight is given to the voice of the child? Should there be an age at which the child's views and wishes are determinative? At what age should children be interviewed and who decides whether they are competent to provide input into the decision-making process? What does children's participation really mean? How is children's safety being addressed in any of these processes? What methods can be used to ensure that there are mental health professionals, lawyers and/or judges skilled in interviewing children? What about issues of confidentiality and consent? What about children who have learning challenges and cannot express themselves verbally? What about follow-up with children and closure? What about children from different cultural backgrounds where talking about the family and feelings are not part of the culture? What about children and families with different levels of conflict (i.e., low, medium and high conflict families), in situations where domestic violence or child maltreatment is an issue? When should children be brought into the mediation process (i.e., before, during or after mediation has concluded)? Additionally, what should the focus on evaluation involve? – that is, evaluating outcomes that focus on the settlement of a family dispute is different from outcomes that focus on strengthening parent-child relationships post separation. How can adults empower children and facilitate a greater dialogue *with* children about their lives post separation and/or divorce? Finally, are children's voices being truly considered or are they being filtered through an adult lens about what is in their best interests?

Where child-inclusive mediation works well, children will feel respected, listened to, and potentially empowered. Some of their anxieties may be addressed, and there may be issues when a child's priority – for instance, where a family pet will live – is being ignored or where their ideas may help create a solution. Where there are differences of opinion among parents over schooling, the intervention of a mediator may help resolve them. The conversations that take place in mediation may help restore or improve the quality of relationships with one or both parents. Mediation may offer a safe opportunity for parents to explain the reasons for a separation in a compassionate way that may be difficult where communication has broken down. In some circumstances, it may be helpful to parents to offer an explanation or apology for an absence that may have been misinterpreted as a personal rejection. Parkinson (2020) envisages mediators as a 'reconnector of broken wires' of communication, and, when this is done skillfully, child-inclusive mediation may make children feel part of the process without being responsible for the outcome.

Child-inclusive mediation is time consuming and increases the cost of mediation. Some children may not want to be involved in decisions regarding their parents' separation, feeling they are being asked to grow up too fast. During the process of divorce, attitudes to children may have become a source of or exacerbated the friction between parents, and re-igniting these may make the separation harder to resolve. Children may feel fear or find it distressing to contribute to long-term decisions of their future, and the process, if inexpertly handled, may increase feelings of ambivalence and conflict of loyalties. Where children experience a deep conflict of loyalties, involvement in the process or expressing a choice may make it harder to relate to a parent who feels they have not been preferred. Participation in mediation may lead to children having a sense of being responsible for decisions that are not their own. When parents in the process are insecure or defensive, a mediator's confidential meetings with children may exacerbate distrust between the parents, especially if either feels that the other is coaching or persuading children on what they may say.

Child-inclusive mediation creates additional pressures in terms of explaining the role of the mediator. Children need to understand that they are not meeting a judge or a counsellor, and their wishes may not be met or fears resolved.

Development of Regulatory Framework

As a corollary of public funding and the statutory framework in which it operates, family mediation is more regulated than other forms. Family mediation has a complex regulatory history with a proliferation of organisations reflecting the different disciplines from which family mediators have been drawn. Organisations and practitioners in the not-for-profit sector were initially affiliated with the National Family Mediation Council (now National Family Mediation) (NFM). Family Mediators Association (FMA) was set up by a group of lawyers in 1988. These, together with the College of Mediators, Resolution (formerly Solicitors Family Law Association), and the Law Society were brought together under the auspices of the Family Mediation Council (FMC) (2007). The Family Mediation Council published a comprehensive code of practice for family mediators. The Family Mediation Standards Board (FMSB) operates independently of the FMC and supervises the FMC's registration and accreditation processes. It also operates a complaints and disciplinary appeals process on behalf of the FMC. Accreditation by one of the bodies affiliated to the FMC is essential to be eligible to take a legally aided case.

Court-Annexed Processes

There is currently no court-annexed family mediation in the UK, but financial dispute resolution (FDR) is offered by district judges as a form of facilitated evaluative negotiation. Parties are invited to share without-prejudice offers and the financial information on which they are based. If it is not possible to come to a resolution, the district judge may predict a possible outcome if a case comes to the point of adjudication. Parties in FDR do not have to accept this guidance and can have their cases adjudicated by a separate district judge.

Circumstances Where Mediation May Not Be Appropriate

To take place with integrity, mediation needs to provide a place of psychological safety which respects the values of party autonomy, informed consent, and voluntariness, and parties meet with a genuine desire to resolve matters between them in good faith. Anything that undermines these principles will put the integrity of the process at risk and may make it difficult or impossible to mediate.

Extreme power imbalances may lead to circumstances in which party autonomy is undermined. If, during a marriage, a pattern of dominance or coercion has developed, this is unlikely to be reversed simply by the presence of mediator. If one of the parties does not feel the mediation is 'psychologically safe,' it will generally not be appropriate. When there is extreme hostility and mistrust, the collaboration required of mediation may not be possible. If one or both parties lack a genuine willingness to compromise or shift position, there is probably little point in mediation.

Mental health issues such as severe depression, which may impair an individual's capacity to make decisions, or psychotic illnesses where it may be difficult for a mediators to be convinced that there is genuine 'informed consent' to a decision may make mediation impossible or inappropriate. Where parties lack insight into their mental health conditions, mediation may be impossible, but more severe problems, when accompanied by the insight of the party, may allow mediation with adequate safeguards: e.g. the presence of an advocate or family supporter. Where one partner has not accepted the fact that a relationship is finished, mediation will be premature until avenues of reconciliation have been explored and/or exhausted.

Domestic Violence

Mills (2008) has defined domestic violence as 'any incident of threatening behaviour, violence or abuse (psychological, physical, sexual, financial or emotional) between adults who are or have been intimate partners of family members, regardless of gender or sexuality.' Although the existence of domestic violence need not be an absolute bar to mediation, it is a complex issue, and it is difficult to ensure that the previous experiences of domestic violence do not influence the process of mediation, even when this is focused on future behaviour. Mediation assumes that parties have an equal voice in decision-making and are able to make decisions with autonomy, but this is not necessarily the case in the context of domestic violence, and raising issues in the context of mediation may both lead women (and, on occasion, men) to relive traumatic experience, thereby undermining accountability.

Mediators have a duty to ensure that mediation offers a place of psychological safety and that any agreement reached is not achieved as result of threats or coercive behaviour. A history of systematic domestic abuse is hard to reconcile with the equality necessary for a successful mediation. Roberts (2014) identifies a broad consensus that:

> cases involving serious abuse should not be mediated; that abuse itself (is) not negotiable, and that mediation (is) likely to be most effective where the parties (have) relative equality of bargaining power and (have) had the opportunity to make a free and informed choice about whether they wanted to engage in the process.

She distinguishes a UK policy that gives 'pre-eminence to the meanings and experiences of the individuals concerned' from a North American model which involves 'the making of a diagnostic judgment by the professional.' Where there is a history of abuse, Parkinson (2020) considers mediation may be appropriate if the violence took place a long time ago, and there is no fear of recurrence or if there was an isolated atypical incident, possibly involving both parties.

Victims of abuse can be seriously disadvantaged in mediation where power imbalances are unrecognised, and a family systems approach can hold victims partly responsible for abuse without offering enforceable protection (Lerman 1984). Abusers may prefer alternative dispute resolution because they feel able to determine the outcome through 'coercion, manipulation of mediators or other involved parties, intimidation, and even violence' while those who have suffered abuse may be unable to participate fully or freely in mediation and 'routinely assess the risks or costs of noncompliance with their abusive partner's demands, particularly related to disclosure of abuse' (National Advisory Council on Violence against Women 2004).

Screening for Domestic Abuse and Child Protection

Legal Services Commission Quality Mark Standard F4.1 requires mediation providers to offer a procedure that outlines the principles of child protection.

This is incorporated into FMC's Code of Practice (2018), which provides:

> 3.4.7 Mediators must have appropriate safeguarding policies and procedures in place.

This reinforces family mediators' responsibility for making sure they take appropriate measures to protect clients from harm or damage throughout the process. This applies to all family mediators, though mediators who see children as part of the process may have different policies and procedures in place to those who do not.

The policy of the College of Mediators (2018) considers:

1. Each participant must make a fully informed and voluntary decision to enter mediation. This requires that each participant is sufficiently informed and has sufficient time to make the decision to attempt mediation after all safety issues have been fully considered.

2. Safety issues must include not only the participants in mediation but also any children and any other significant member of the family of either party.
3. Assessment for domestic abuse and/or child protection is a continuing requirement which lasts throughout the whole of the mediation process.
4. Implementation of this policy requires a written procedure for safe and effective screening for domestic abuse.

Confidentiality

What happens in a family mediation is generally confidential and subject to privilege, but the exceptions go beyond those in other forms of civil mediation. In the agreement to mediate, mediators and parties undertake not to disclose information to any other person or body without first obtaining the written consent of all parties, except where there is an 'over-riding obligation of disclosure.'

Where a child or adult is said or believed to be at risk of significant harm, a mediator is under obligation to notify the appropriate agencies. Particularly sensitive issues may arise regarding children if parties make either disclosures or allegations when lawyers are absent. If a mediator considers there is a risk of a child suffering significant harm, they have a responsibility to notify the appropriate agency – generally police or social services. If the mediator considers there is a risk of an adult suffering significant harm, they have discretion to do so in that an adult has a capacity, which a child doesn't, to make such references themselves.

The FMC Code of Practice (2018) provides for an *obligation* to notify appropriate agencies in some circumstances and a *discretion* in others:

> 5.2.2 Where it appears necessary so that a specific allegation that a child has suffered significant harm may be properly investigated, or where the Mediator suspects that a child is suffering or is likely to suffer significant harm, the Mediator must ensure that the appropriate agency or authority is notified.
>
> 5.2.3 The Mediator may notify the appropriate agency if he or she considers that other public policy considerations prevail, such as an adult suffering or likely to suffer significant harm.

Therapeutic Mediation

Systemic family therapists in the 1980s adopted a therapeutic approach to treating family dysfunction. This has led to a model in which external experts are involved in proposing ways of addressing what they see as structural failure in family mediation. Therapeutic mediation is typically conducted by mental health professionals and takes place over a longer period than conventional mediation. The psychotherapeutic background of the mediators encourages focus on the interpersonal and psychological dynamics of a dispute, and their objective is to look beyond the 'manifest dispute' to the underlying causes of conflict. There is, therefore, a tension between party autonomy and the privileged advisory role of the therapeutic expert.

Whereas mediators facilitate, therapists, while not providing advice, may go beyond giving information and implicitly prioritise certain outcomes as healthier or more favourable. Roberts (1992, 2014) and Haynes (1992) have drawn attention to the danger of a porous boundary between therapy and mediation.

There is a risk that a functionalist view of the family may elevate professional expertise above family insight or the preferences of the parties (Roberts 1992). The presence of a third-party expert makes the negotiation in mediation more complex and raises issues of both party autonomy and informed consent. Are the choices those of the parties or of the therapist? Roberts (2014) draws attention to the dangers of 'distortion' where family therapeutic techniques are applied in court-annexed mediation and considers, '[T]his can result in the parties being subjected, unknowingly and involuntarily, both to the coercive pressures of the court and to the covert controls of "treatment."'

Cross-Cultural Mediation

Family mediation in the UK has its roots in a predominantly white neoliberal context, premised on the agency and equality of both parties and prioritises the individual over the community. There has, to date, been limited research into the cross-cultural dynamics of mediation. Shah-Kazemi (2000) critiques the dangers of 'hegemony' from the perspective of an ethnic minority member's experience of mediation. In practice, under the guise of neutrality, mediators become parties to the dispute. As Shah-Kazemi puts it,

> [T]the mediator's influence is instrumental in achieving the success of the negotiations, as in the minds of the disputants themselves the mediator can no longer be considered simply as a detached observer, but is a party to the process of mediation. A mediator ostensibly from the minority community who did not assert values that are commonly held, could also be seriously undermined and mistrusted, because the non-assertion of commonly identifiable values would indicate such a poor assimilation of the cultural norms by which the community abides.

Shah-Kazemi suggests that when those who do not share the same cultural identity as the disputants are involved, despite themselves, they lose their position of neutrality and fall prey to attempts made by interested parties to generate sympathy for their own cause: 'Without an appreciation of this cultural specificity, supposedly 'universal' principles run the risk of being hollow abstractions that are far removed from the concrete modalities of disputes in the real world' (Shah-Kazemi 2000). From her perspective. the ideal is that mediators be of the same ethnicity as the parties 'since no form of training can a priori, impart a fully comprehensive understanding of the 'universe of meaning' that shapes our responses to the whole gamut of situations that arise in the course of life' (Shah-Kazemi 2000).

One of the complexities of family mediation is the layering of different processes. In Asian societies, the mediator is traditionally depicted as a respected person of authority who takes leadership of the mediation, guides the disputants, and may prescribe solutions or evaluate the merits of the dispute. In the context of Asian Muslim communities, a religious marriage is at least as significant from the perspective of both personal experience and community recognition as legal civil marriage. Bano (2012) writes about the role played by Sharia councils in resolving marital disputes: 'The data reveal that the duality of law and unofficial law is misleading and fails to capture complex ways in which these "legal processes" shape the pattern of conflict resolution for Muslims in Britain.' In as many as 50% of the relationships studied, marriages would not be recognised by the English courts. This suggests a far more complex inter-relationship between law and alternative processes than where the role of the mediator is to facilitate negotiation, and adjudication, where an adjudicator's role is to make the decisions. In the process of a Sharia council, an imam, while fulfilling a mediatory function, is also bound to follow the Sharia in seeking to discern the will of God. Some divorcing couples may take part in a separate community mediation, a Sharia divorce, and a civil dissolution of a marriage as part of the marital breakdown. Bano and Webley (2024) consider that, in some contexts, the blurring of the distinction between 'conceptions of mediation and arbitration' make it difficult to be clear on 'who is determining the norms to be applied and who is the decision-maker.' Family mediation in the context of a Sharia council can offer something potentially emancipatory, provided it has been chosen as 'an informed expression of autonomy' rather than one 'deemed necessary for the grant of a religious divorce.'

Skills in Family Mediation

While the skills required of a mediator may be similar across different contexts, the centrality of relationships in family mediation requires particular experience and expertise in a number of areas, including a responsibility for the welfare of children (see statutory framework discussed earlier). Family mediators are more often women than in other areas of civil mediation, and there is particular emphasis on the transferability of the skills developed as therapists. Complex issues of parenting are uniquely difficult to reduce to writing in language that is enforceable by the courts. Since the implementation of the Children and Families Act (2014), there is a presumption that the separating parties will make a 'parenting plan' for the living arrangements of their children. Doing so requires tact, sensitivity, and sufficient flexibility to accommodate changing circumstances, including the development of the children.

Feminist Critiques

US critics of informalism (Felstiner et al. 1981; Abel 1982; Auerbach 1983; Fiss 1984) have drawn attention to the potential of mediation to legitimate inequality by concealing power relationships under a superficial consensus and the moral hazard inherent in preferring agreement over adjudicated outcomes. Grillo (1991), writing in the context of 'custody mediation' in California, developed a feminist critique of mediation building on previous criticism of informalism. Grillo suggests that while voluntary mediation has the potential to be empowering, when imposed it 'provides neither a just nor a more humane alternative to the adversarial system of adjudication' (Grillo 1991) and that

> forcing unwilling women to take part in a process which involves much personal exposure sends a powerful social message: it is permissible to discount the real experience of women in the service of someone else's idea of what will be good for them, good for their children, or good for the system.
>
> (Grillo 1991)

Even voluntary mediation, when dominated by an unrefined family systems perspective in which all family members are 'equally implicated in whatever happens within it' (Grillo 1991), may impose subtle and not-so-subtle messages about appropriate conduct and what may be said in mediation. A consensual process which discourages blaming and in which disputants may be encouraged to discount past experiences offers serious dangers that may lead to women acquiescing in their own oppression. Her argument, however, is as much about how the process of mediation may be conducted, and, at the same time, she affirms that 'few professional experiences can compare to the moment when the world of possibilities seem to expand for a couple, and hope and optimism coexist, at least temporarily, with pain and anger' (Grillo 1991).

It is contestable how far these arguments can apply in a context such as the UK, where mediation is a voluntary process. Some studies (Emery and Wyer 1987) suggest that mediation provides greater benefits for men rather than women and that while men clearly preferred mediation, women who went through litigation felt that they had 'won more and lost less,' relative those in mediation. Women in litigation reported fewer depressed feelings than did mothers in mediation or fathers in either group. Kelly and Duyree (1995) suggest, '[T]he data do not support the notion that women feel disadvantaged in the mediation process.' Davis (2000) records that women's responses are 'slightly more positive than those of men.' Irving and Benjamin (1995) maintain a range of academic sources offer 'a potent rejoinder to the feminist critique of mediation' and suggest 'that the majority of women most of the time prefer mediation over litigation because it offers a more equitable and sensitive process.'

Other authors examine the nature of lawyer intervention. Bryan (1994) considers that in a 'society of unequals, formalisation frequently proves necessary to protect weaker parties' and advocates a more proactive role for lawyers in mediation. Personal characteristics, emotional states (including need for closure, guilt, depression, low self-esteem, low expectations), and relationship patterns (dominance, dependency, physical and emotional abuse, ideology) all play a part, and 'Divorce lawyers must reclaim their professionalism and avoid the seductive call of informality.'

Conclusion

Family mediation began as a movement within the not-for-profit sector, reliant on the voluntary work of therapists and social workers and was primarily focused on the negotiation of children's matters as a fallout from divorce. As it expanded to include financial and property issues, it became increasingly dominated by lawyer-mediators. While all-issues mediation draws on both these understandings, the scope of the mediator is perhaps less clearly defined than in other forms of mediation. The family mediation profession still carries the signs of this tension between the traditional 'therapeutic mediator' (Blakey 2022) and the subsequent 'legal mediator.' This is reflected in its current regulatory framework, where the Family Mediation Council acts as an umbrella for its five constituent organisations while leaving regulation to its constituent bodies. While some consider that a role of hybrid mediator can combine the best of both traditions and lead to the development of a new profession, there is a wide spectrum of views at the level of professional self-understanding and what is achievable within the regulatory framework.

Family mediation, especially when dealing with financial matters, has many parallels with other forms of civil mediation. It exists in the 'shadow of the law' and the 'shadow of the court' where costs are concerned. When dealing with children, the skills demanded of a mediator are as much those of a psychologist as a lawyer and may require dealing with some of the acute hostility and defensiveness often found in community mediation. As Bohannan (1971) illuminates, there are many things going on in the process of a separation. Changes of relationships will have to be negotiated and accepted in a wider psychological, social, educational, and religious contexts. The wider claims of society may be at least as significant in shaping these changes as the formal legal framework.

Questions for Further Consideration

Family Mediation Scenarios for Discussion in Pairs

Would you consider mediation appropriate in the following contexts? If it is not, explain why not, and if it is, explain what procedural safeguards you would put in place.

1. Jane is an IT manager working at Brunel University. Her husband, with whom she lived for eighteen years, is unemployed and suffers from acute mental distress. He was initially unwilling to divorce but now apparently accepts the inevitability of this course. He has been given divergent diagnoses, including acute anxiety and paranoia.
2. Anthony is divorcing Chloe. During arguments over separation, Anthony was admitted to hospital with severe lacerations after Chloe hurled an Edwardian candlestick at him during a heated argument. This was not an isolated occurrence. Anthony is the editorial director of a publishing company, and Chloe is a well-known children's author.

3. Jenny has had a long marriage to Jerome, during which she has been systematically subject to domestic abuse. There have been several non-molestation orders in place, but none of these are now in force. Jenny would much prefer mediation to facing Jerome in court.
4. Peter is profoundly deaf. He is living in a property owned by his wife, Jessica, and is sleeping on the sofa. There is currently a residence order in place, permitting him to reside in the marital home, and a non-molestation order prohibiting him from entering her bedroom. The non-molestation order is silent as to whether or not he can enter the dressing room adjacent to his wife's bedroom, where their six-year-old son is sleeping. A *decree nisi* has been granted, and a decree absolute is expected in six weeks.
5. Sean and Simon are in a same-sex relationship and have a civil partnership, In the past, Simon has been extremely violent and has a criminal record for grievous bodily harm, although this does not relate to his former partner. During the process of separation, Simon twice assaulted Shaun, which led to Simon's arrest. Both parties are willing to mediate.
6. Andrew and Andrea had a stormy relationship, and Andrea suffers from endogenous depression. While there is no record of violence taking place during the relationship, Andrea feels profoundly ambivalent about mediation and the prospect of meeting with Andrew, especially if she is to be unaccompanied at round table meetings.

- From your discussion of these cases, what factors do you consider important in safeguarding the integrity of the mediation process?
- What are the opportunities and risks of mediation in the context of family disputes?
- What distinct ethical issues are raised by family mediation?
- What are the strengths and drawbacks of using qualified lawyers as mediators in the context of family mediation?
- In what, if any, ways should a mediator seek to influence the outcome of a family mediation?

Further Reading

Bryan, P. (1994) 'Reclaiming Professionalism: The Lawyers Role in Divorce Mediation', *Family Law Quarterly*, 177–222.

Grillo, T. (1991) 'The Mediation Alternative: Process Dangers for Women', *Yale Law Journal* 100 (6), 1545–1610.

Mnookin, R. H. & Kornhauser, L. (1979) 'Bargaining in the Shadow of the Law: The Case of Divorce', *The Yale Law Journal* 88 (5).

Parkinson, L. (2011) *Family Mediation: Appropriate Dispute Resolution a New Family Justice System* (2nd ed). Jordans Publishing.

Roberts, M. (2014) *Mediation in Family Disputes: Principle of Practice* (4th ed). Routledge.

8 Restorative Justice

Restorative justice (RJ) is used to describe that form of ADR applied in the context of the criminal justice system. It incorporates processes in which the active participation of the community is central. Weitekamp (1999) cites evidence from a range of sources, from the practices of ancient indigenous Australian and Inuit communities to the Code of Hammurabi and the Laws of Ethelbert of Kent, that restorative elements have always been part of the practice of criminal justice. Homer's *Iliad* offers elements of the importance of restorative actions in individuals taking responsibility for their behaviour. Various forms of restorative practice have been developed by religious communities in recognition of the interdependence of individuals and the communities of which they are a part.

The formal criminal justice system has always involved processes that require collaboration between the prosecution in the margins of a court and the penumbra of the law. CPS and prosecuting counsel frequently meet with defence barristers before a case to discuss whether the defendant might be willing to plead guilty to a lesser offence. Prosecutions can be dropped if they are not considered to be in the public interest. Credit can be given for a guilty plea and expressions of remorse, considered at the stage of sentence. The boundaries of youth justice are more flexible than the adult criminal justice system. Restorative justice is generally taken to refer to something beyond this, in which there is dialogue between the victim and the perpetrator of a crime and the community of which they are a part, taking place in the context of criminal charges. It may include any of the following: victim-offender mediation, whether direct or indirect; restorative group conferencing; healing and sentencing circles in Canada; and community restorative boards (CRBs) in the USA (Gavrielides 2007).

Restorative justice is, in essence, relational. It understands justice as 'what is right between people' rather than 'what the judges say.' It aims to heal relationships and approaches crime from the perspective that a criminal act is not only a failing of individuals, as defined by the criminal justice system, but also a symptom of failures and dysfunctions in human terms and the wider social system in which the individual exists. RJ offers

DOI: 10.4324/9781003112617-8

> an approach to achieving justice that involves, to the extent possible, those who have a stake in a specific offence or harm to collectively identify and address harms, needs, and obligations in order to heal and put things as right as possible.
>
> (Zehr 2015)

A core aspect of this approach is encouraging offenders to take responsibility for their behaviour. The process of reparation can be restorative.

Critics of restorative justice within the criminal justice system argue that it can erode the rule of law by trivialising wrongdoing and expanding the area of police discretionary power. For some advocates of mediation, the concept is inherently problematic. Boulle and Nesic (2009) do not include any reference to it in their *Mediator Skills and Techniques: Triangle of Influence*. Blake, Browne, and Sime (2016) do not refer to it in *A Practical Approach to Alternative Dispute Resolution* and Shipman, Waters, and Wood in Brown and Marriot's *ADR Principles and Practice* (2019) bracket it with community mediation in a single chapter.

Restorative justice scholarship is framed by a debate about 'institutionalisation.' On the one hand, radical purists associated with critical, radical, or abolitionist approaches to criminology would like to see RJ remain as an alternative to the criminal justice system that they see as harmful, stigmatising, and unfair. On the other hand, pragmatists or maximalists argue that RJ can do most good where it is embedded within the criminal justice system and can ameliorate the system by making it more restorative.

How far are criticisms justified? If ground rules of mediation include equality of the parties and voluntariness of the process, how can this be applied in the context of a criminal justice system in which one party is constituted as the victim and the other as the offender? How far can these processes be considered as mediation?

Definitions

For Marshall (1999), restorative justice is 'a process whereby parties with a stake in a specific offence collectively resolve how to deal with the aftermath of the offence and its implications for the future.' For Liebmann (2007),

> Restorative Justice works to resolve conflict and repair harm. It encourages those who have caused harm to acknowledge the impact of what they have done and gives them an opportunity for reparation. It offers those who have suffered harm the opportunity to have their harm or loss acknowledged and amends made.

For Zehr (2015), accountability is an intrinsic part of the process; it 'requires, at minimum that we address the harms and needs of those harmed, hold those causing harm accountable to "put right" those harms, and involve both of these parties as well as relevant communities in this process.' For Gavrielides (2007) restorative justice is 'an ethos with practical goals, among which to restore harm by including affected parties in a (direct or indirect) encounter and a process of understanding through voluntary and honest dialogue.' It 'adopts a fresh approach to conflicts and their control, retaining at the same time certain rehabilitative goals.' It is inherently contextual. 'Restorative justice cannot be delivered at national and abstract levels.' It needs to be delivered locally and within the specific suffering of individual cases (Gavrielides 2008).

Boyes-Watson (2000) offers a broader definition rooted in a theory of conflict resolution:

> a growing social movement to institutionalize peaceful approaches to harm, problem-solving and violations of legal and human rights. These range from international peacemaking tribunals such as the South Africa Truth and Reconciliation Commission to innovations within the criminal and juvenile justice systems, schools, social services and communities. Rather than privileging the law, professionals and the state, restorative resolutions engage those who are harmed, wrongdoers and their affected communities in search of solutions that promote repair, reconciliation and the rebuilding of relationships. Restorative justice seeks to build partnerships to reestablish mutual responsibility for constructive responses to wrongdoing within our communities. Restorative approaches seek a balanced approach to the needs of the victim, wrongdoer and community through processes that preserve the safety and dignity of all.

Common to all these approaches is the importance of relationship and paying attention to the feelings and the experiences of those involved in the incident giving rise to the intervention.

Values

Restorative justice is premised on a different scale of values and attitudes from those conventionally characterising the criminal justice system. A traditional legal approach considers the following: What laws have been broken? What evidence is there against the alleged perpetrator? Does this evidence reach a standard of proof 'beyond reasonable doubt'? If found guilty in accordance with statue and precedent, what is the appropriate punishment/sentence to be applied? According to Zehr (2005), restorative justice asks, 'Who has been hurt? What are their needs? Whose obligations are these? What are the causes? Who are the 'stakeholders'? What is the appropriate process?'

Practice

Restorative practice starts by considering an offence in the context of its impact on the victim rather than the state. It strives to affirm values of reciprocity and empathy and to facilitate often-uncomfortable communication and identifies dialogue (and sometimes reconciliation) as a specific aim in encouraging offenders to take responsibility for their actions.

Restorative justice can be viewed differently from the perspective of the community of which both victim and offender are a part and from those of the individual victim and offender. From the victim's perspective, objectives include achieving a resolution that reflects their definition of the incident. There may a desire for a cathartic exchange between parties involving apologies and sometimes expressions of remorse and for an element of restitution or reparation. From the offender's side, objectives include the encouragement and influence to accept responsibility and enable them to move on from the offending behaviour. The objectives of the wider community are met if a change of attitude is brought about that makes re-offending less likely. Although these approaches are not mutually exclusive, a victim-centred approach is characteristic of a more conservative ideology, and an approach that focuses on the social context of the perpetrator has predominated with those with a more liberal or radical perspective.

Some practitioners of RJ draw distinctions between 'restorative justice,' 'restorative practices,' and a 'restorative approach.' For the purposes of this chapter, I consider separately what are, in fact, overlapping categories. Restorative justice is generally

Figure 8.1 Restorative practices paradigm. McCold, P., & Wachtel, T. (2003, August 10–15). *In pursuit of paradigm: A theory of restorative justice* [Paper presentation]. XIII World Congress of Criminology, Rio de Janeiro, Brazil. https://www.iirp.edu/eforum-archive/in-pursuit-of-paradigm-a-theory-of-restorative-justice. Used with permission of International Institute for Restorative Practices.

used when the criminal justice system is involved, restorative practice for settings such as schools where to talk about 'justice' would be inappropriate, and 'restorative approach' as a portmanteau term including all interventions with a restorative element. Fully restorative practice involves the victim, the community, and the offender. When two of these elements are involved, practice is considered mostly restorative; it is only when all three are involved that practice is considered fully restorative.

The values informing restorative justice vary according to context. Restorative justice in the USA has been heavily influenced by an agenda of victims' rights, whereas the UK approach, especially in relation to youth justice, is more firmly focused on social support and directed towards rehabilitation. The criminal justice system has traditionally served the ends of retribution and deterrence, restitution, rehabilitation, incapacitation, and prevention. Restorative justice arguably contains elements of each of these. Restitution and rehabilitation are probably closer to the values of RJ than retribution and incapacitation, but taking responsibility for an offence may involve elements of punishment.

Restorative Justice Origins

Restorative justice is sometimes described as having its origins in indigenous justice practice with its roots in Māori tradition in New Zealand (Shapland et al. 2008). It has also been credited with a slightly different model as an initiative of two Mennonite probation officers in Ontario, Canada.

Since 1989, family group conferencing has been the dominant mode of dealing with youth offending in New Zealand. Probation officers in Kitchener, Ontario, developed a restorative approach in 1974–1975 in which they departed from the established treatment model and arranged for some young people to repair the damage they had caused. This became the Victim-Offender Reconciliation Project (VORP). VORP became the international model of one-to-one RJ encounters, whereas the Māori initiative paved the way for the equally valid family group conferencing.

Daly (2002) describes RJ as a mixed model of 'culturally appropriate' ways of dealing with young offenders.

> Intrinsic to both the family group conferencing model and Māori culture is the idea of 'whanau' (extended family) as a key channel of change and support. The New Zealand model emphasises inclusive participation and collective decision making and the achievement of 'social balance . . . by reintegrating young people in their family and community and by determining appropriate means of redress for victims.'
>
> (Maxwell and Morris in Shapland et al. 2008)

The Māori scholar Tauri (2018) has articulated a strong critique of how this narrative is deployed by governments and the criminal justice system to manage indigenous people who are disproportionately incarcerated in the criminal justice systems of Australia, NZ, and Canada.

Restorative Justice in the UK

The probation service in Sheffield set up the first victim-offender service in the UK in 1983. Between 1985 and 1987, the Home Office funded court-based project for adults in Leeds (Crown Court), Coventry, and Wolverhampton (Magistrate Courts) and a police-based scheme for young people in Cumbria.

During the first Blair Labour administration (1997 to 2001), RJ appealed to the Home Office's commitment to 'communitarian values' (Etzioni 1995) and its mantra, 'Tough on Crime, Tough on the Causes of Crime' as an effective means of diversion from the courts. The Crime and Disorder Act (1999) put an emphasis on offenders taking responsibility for their crimes (so-called responsibilisation) and adopted a form of risk-based early intervention. The Youth Justice and Criminal Evidence Act (1999) provided for a referral order from the court to a youth offender panel, consisting of practitioners from the police and the youth offending team.

Youth justice policy during this period (1997 to 2010) combined elements of support and punishment, prevention and criminalisation, diversionary and interventionist policies (Case 2021). During the Lib Dem/Conservative coalition adminstration (2005 to 2010), there was specific government funding for RJ projects, including for adults.

Stages in the Criminal Justice System

Restorative justice can take place at any stage in the criminal justice process but most frequently happens post-conviction as there may be particular dangers of its aims being compromised when sentencing is in prospect. In the case of youth justice – those on the margins of the criminal justice system, especially young and first-time offenders – it is more frequently used at a pre-sentence stage.

Section 57 (2) of the Criminal Justice Sentencing Act (2020) introduced the sentencing code (covering both adults and children) and identified the purposes of sentencing as: (1) the punishment of offenders, (2) the reduction of crime (including its reduction by deterrence), (3) the reform and rehabilitation of offenders, (4) the protection of the public, and (5) the making of reparation by offenders to persons affected by their offences.

Diversionary

At the earliest stage, police forces, at their discretion, use restorative skills to resolve conflict and do not refer cases to CPS if there are no formal proceedings (Level 1) or if a conference is arranged as an alternative to criminal justice process (Level 2). The work of the Thames Valley Police was groundbreaking in this area, with a particular emphasis on the use of restorative cautioning with youth offenders. A pilot scheme was introduced in 2008–2009 in England and Wales involving eight areas enabling trained police officers to resolve minor offences informally through a 'youth restorative disposal.' Some police and crime commissioners now commission RJ work as victims' services.

Out-of-Court Disposal

Out-of-court disposals were initially developed in the youth criminal justice system and may comprise 'youth cautions' (statutory out-of-court disposal for 10- to 17-year-olds) and 'youth conditional cautions, which may impose reparative conditions. A prosecutor can offer a conditional caution for certain offences which suspends a prosecution on condition that the offender complies with certain conditions. The Legal Aid Sentencing and Punishment of Offenders Act (2012) offers a pre-court process based on diversionary principles in which a community resolution provides for a police-administered non-criminal disposal that does not lead to the recipient receiving a criminal record and thereby suffering the risks associated with becoming identified as a first-time entrant into the youth justice system.

Pre-Sentence

The Crime and Courts Act (2013) provides for RJ to take place at the pre-sentence stage if the following conditions are met:

1. There is an identifiable victim or victims.
2. The offender accepts responsibility and has made a guilty plea (at any stage of the proceedings).
3. The victim, offender, and any other participants consent to take part in a restorative justice activity. Sentence may be deferred for a maximum of six months.

RJ at the pre-sentence stage may operate either as a deferred sentence or as a conditional caution, in which a defendant accepts their guilt of the offence for which the caution is imposed. A court may impose a RJ activity as a condition of a deferred sentence provided the victim consents. This could involve community gardening, litter picking, or other voluntary work. The revised Code of Practice for Conditional Cautions (2018) permits a prosecutor to offer a caution with conditions attached for minor offences.

The supervisor of deferred sentence reports to the court on the offender's compliance. If conditions are complied with, prosecution can be suspended.

The code of practice provides that the prosecutor should consider whether any of the following are applicable: opportunities to provide reparation or compensation to any victim or relevant neighbourhood or community; use of conditions to reflect and secure the interests of the victim and neighbourhood or community (for example, by requiring the offender to stay away from a specific area); use of restorative and reparative processes to have a positive impact on the community or individuals affected by the offending behaviour; opportunities to provide reparative unpaid work that benefits the community; or use of a financial penalty condition to punish the offender and deter future offending.

Whereas the current Victims' Code of Practice provides that all victims of crime are entitled to information about restorative justice, according the organisation 'Why Me?' only 5% of victims of a known offender recall being given this information ('Why Me?' 2024).

Sentence

The Youth and Criminal Evidence Act (1999) introduced referral orders for young offenders (ages 10 to 17) for first time. Referral orders can include victim-offender facilitated mediation; restorative conferencing, which may involve families/supporters and sometimes representatives of the community; or indirect mediation, in which victim and offender do not meet, and a mediator shuttles between the parties or communication takes place by letter. The Crime and Courts Act (2013) provides that courts can defer the passing of sentence to allow for restorative justice. Reparation orders consisted of a non-custodial sentence for 10 to 17 year-olds to make specific reparations to individuals or communities and were abolished by the Police, Crime, Sentencing and Courts Act (2022). In a community order or suspended sentence order, a judge or magistrate may make a specified action requirement under Section 201 Criminal Justice Act (2003). The Offender Rehabilitation Act (2014) Clause 15 provides for offenders to undertake reparative activities as part of a community order or suspended sentence order

Post-Sentence

Restorative justice with adults can take place in both a community and (more rarely) a prison context. It is offered by NGOs like 'Why Me?' as part of the services provided in prison service and community settings. While it may take the form of a victim-offender conference, there are many other forms of restorative activity in which the victim and offender may not meet face to face. Grendon Underwood offers a therapeutic community within the prison service in which every prisoner makes a commitment to reflect on their experience in expertly facilitated group meetings. Participation in RJ does not in itself lead to a reduction in sentence served or a successful parole hearing, but a successful restorative justice conference could form part of the context for a hearing of the Parole Board and might be considered both as to the attitude of the prisoner to their imprisonment and as an assessment of risk in terms of their likelihood of re-offending Newell and Edgar (2006). The parole board has issued advice on the circumstances under which it is appropriate to make reference to this in parole hearings.

Restorative Justice Case Study

Pete (not his real name) was a victim of a burglary. One day he woke up and noticed his car was no longer on his drive, and when he went downstairs, he saw that his front door had been tampered with and various items were missing from his home. Pete felt very confused, shocked, and angry about the crime that had been committed. He called the police, who came quickly and took the details. Pete also contacted a locksmith to help secure his property. The offender was caught soon after and given a prison sentence.

The police referred Pete to the local restorative justice team, who then contacted Pete to explain the service. Pete was keen to find out more about the offender and why he had targeted his property, and he also wanted to hear their story and try to help them not re-offend in the future. Pete also wanted to communicate to the offender the impact that the incident had on him and his family.

The service visited Pete twice to make sure he was well prepared to meet the offender in prison. The facilitators also visited the offender, Martin. At any point, Pete and Martin could have left the process, but they were both keen to go ahead. On the day of the meeting, Pete was accompanied by the facilitators and knew that Martin would also be accompanied by a prison officer, so he felt it would be safe. They had also agreed to pass on some information about each other so the meeting would not seem too strange – although Pete commented later that it was quite unusual to meet someone who had been inside his house and taken his property.

At the meeting, Pete told Martin how he and his family had been affected, and he could see that Martin was remorseful as he looked really upset when he heard about the impact. He was able to tell Pete why he had targeted his house and give him some advice about home security! In return, Pete was able to discuss with Martin ways in which he could avoid re-offending in the future and be a better person. Later, Pete said he felt really good about being able to help Martin on his way.

When interviewed after the meeting, Pete said he would recommend to others finding out more and engaging in the process. He said, 'It helped me get closure. It was good to hear Martin apologise and commit to being a better person going forward.'

With thanks to the participants and to Resolve West.

Other Jurisdictions in the UK

England and Wales are in many ways behind other parts of the UK in the provision of RJ. In Northern Ireland, legislation requires the court of prosecutor to consider RJ. The Criminal Justice Review (2000) and the subsequent Justice (Northern Ireland) Act (2002) provide that 'restorative approaches' should be introduced into youth justice legislation as a statutory restorative disposal and introduced restorative justice for almost all juvenile crimes. It is now firmly embedded in both pre-court and court-ordered disposals.

RJ has existed in some form in Scotland since the 1980s, in the form of small local projects run by the charity Safeguarding Communities-Reducing Offending (SACRO). Although there have been efforts to develop RJ for dealing with cases of serious crime, including SACRO's Talk After Severe Crime (TASC) project and the subsequent Restoration in Serious Crime (RISC). The Victims and Witnesses (Scotland) Act (2014) was introduced as the Scottish implementation of the EU Directive on Victims' Rights (2012). In many jurisdictions, the directive was seen as a way of putting RJ on a firmer foundation, but the Scottish Act makes very limited reference to RJ. Despite the Scottish government's manifesto (2021) reiterating a goal outlined in the Restorative Justice Action Plan (2019) to have RJ services 'available across Scotland by 2023,' delivery is still patchy. Scottish RJ is largely concentrated in youth justice under the diversionary whole-system approach. For there to be a statutory requirement, services (and particularly referral pathways) need to be more developed across Scotland's relatively small but complex justice system.

'Thriving Survivors' is a charitable organisation established in 2016 in Glasgow (UK) to support survivors of sexual and domestic violence along a four-stage recovery pathway, including restorative work involving perpetrators, if appropriate. Their services, though controversial to some, have been welcomed by victims of sexual harm.

Canadian Context

Victim-Offender Reconciliation Program (VORP)

One of the early experiments in RJ in Kitchener, Ontario (1974), involved victims of vandalism meeting with offenders. This provided a framework that enabled the courts to offer a restorative approach without undermining the more formal values of the rule of law. This became a model for other victim-offender reconciliation programs in Canada and the USA.

Sentencing Circle

A sentencing circle is a restorative justice hearing derived from a First Nations concept conducted in collaboration with members of the community and the criminal justice system. It is a process some judges adopt as an alternative to hearing formal sentencing submissions from the defence and Crown lawyers. It combines the relational aspect of RJ with the maintenance of judicial accountability and the right of appeal. The first use of a sentencing circle as part of a criminal justice trial was by Yukon Territorial Court Judge Barry Stuart in *R v Moses* (1991). By participating directly in the hearing rather than speaking through lawyers the offender assumes greater responsibility for both their prior actions and their sentence.

Safeguards within the process include:

1. Any criminal record reports are received and marked as exhibits in the circle hearing process.
2. A record is made of the proceedings.
3. Any disputed facts are judicially determined through evidence heard under oath.
4. The circle hearing is open to the public.
5. The offender must participate voluntarily.

6. The offender is entitled to representation by counsel and to address the circle.
7. A Crown attorney is present to speak to the public interest, to ensure the victim's issues are canvassed, and to make recommendations regarding sentence.
8. Media can attend to report on the proceedings. (Restrictions may be made on attributing statements to specific individuals.)
9. Participants have access to pre-sentence reports.
10. The judge remains responsible for the sentence.
11. The decision is subject to appeal or review

The judgment of *R v Morin* (1996) sets out the practical workings of these safeguards.

Restorative Processes

Restorative processes are used in relation to non-criminal harm: for instance, anti-bullying processes in schools or redressing anti-social behaviour in a mental health setting, including secure offender units. They can also be used as internal disciplinary processes in a prison or young offender institution, where a concern for personal development is prioritised over punishment.

One frequently used model was developed by Terry O'Connell, an Australian police officer in New South Wales, who adapted New Zealand's family group conferencing to develop a distinct conferencing style for restorative justice in Australia. He subsequently worked with Charles Pollard, chief constable of the Thames Valley Police, to develop a Socratic method for restorative practices in the UK.

This model provides for a rigorous conversation following five themes: a 'unique perspective' on what has happened; 'thoughts and feelings' about what parties were thinking and feeling during the dispute; 'harm and affect,' discussing who has been affected and how; 'needs' – what do participants need to feel better? and 'ownership of solutions' – what needs to happen to move the process forward? Adopting a deliberate conversation ensures that details that might otherwise be missed are attended to, and thoughts are distinguished from feelings in a way that enables the parties to focus on the future without denying the past.

This system was initially developed in the criminal justice system. It has since been applied by the Mint House in Higher Education and become a model for use in other settings, including mental health and disciplinary and grievance procedures in the private sector.

Restorative Approach

Restorative approaches are used to describe the culture of organisations seeking to adopt restorative processes. Schools, colleges, universities, and, less commonly, private institutions may seek to adopt a philosophy that prioritises the values of relationships rather than punishment. Such institutions might include mediation as part of disciplinary and grievance processes and encourage self-awareness, mutuality, and learning rather than punishment among employees.

Restorative Justice in a Political Context

Although beyond the immediate scope of this chapter, practitioners have seen processes such as truth and reconciliation commissions incorporate principles of restorative justice into the handling of grievous transgressions of human rights at a national and collective level. The Gacaca process in Rwanda has also been presented as incorporating restorative elements. In Northern Uganda, traditional processes such as *Mat Oput* and reconciliation supervised by community elders have been adapted to meet modern contexts.

Evidence of Success

Early qualitative analysis records high rates of satisfaction but demonstrates a need for more government-funded research. The Young Offenders Mediation Project established in Scotland (1996) by SACRO, in its 2009–2010 report, records an almost 90% success rate with 1,100 young people dealt with over the year. The government commissioned Sheffield University to research the effectiveness of RJ in 2001. Reports evidenced in the writing of Shapland and Sherman and Strang (2001) have indicated the effectiveness of RJ at a national and global level (Shapland 2011; Sherman and Strang 2007), but the Home Office and Ministry of Justice have been reluctant to adopt and implement programs with statutory force at a national level.

There is some evidence that the Ministry of Justice sees the primary criteria for RJ as re-offender rates rather than participant satisfaction. It is less willing to resort to some specific RJ measures. Reparation orders (non-custodial sentences for 10- to 17-year-olds to make specific reparation to an individual or community) declined from approximately 3,300 in 2009–2010 to 51 in 2019–2020. The Police Crime, Sentencing and Courts Act 2022 abolished youth reparation orders and youth conditional cautions. The current sentencing framework offers other avenues for reparation, including referral orders and youth rehabilitation orders (YROs), both of which, according to the MOJ, offer more flexibility than the reparation order. Reparation orders cannot be given in conjunction with a referral order or a YRO, thereby significantly restricting the situations in which they can be used.

Critics of the 'institutionalisation' of RJ highlight a danger of RJ becoming 'instrumentalised' if improving re-offending rates and efficiency in processing cases undermines its essentially voluntary nature.

The Office of National Statistics has recorded data on restorative justice as part of the Comprehensive National Crime Survey since 2010. In March 2013, victims of crime were offered the opportunity to meet the offender in 8.7% of incidents. Between April 2016 and March 2017, victims of crime were given this opportunity in 4.1% of incidents, representing the fourth annual decline.

Restorative Justice Council

The Restorative Justice Council (RJC) is the national, independent membership body for the field of restorative practice in the UK. It acts as the national voice for its membership, advocating the widespread use of all forms of restorative practice, including restorative justice. Its main concern in recent years has been the development of standards and accreditation for RJ. It also runs conferences on new initiatives in RJ.

RJ APPG

To provide more impetus to the RJ movement, the 'Restorative Justice All-Party Parliamentary Group' (RJ APPG) was formed in April 2021 to drive forward cross-party conversations on restorative justice and raise awareness of its principles. Its goals are:

- To examine the use of restorative justice principles within the UK justice system and beyond.
- To raise the profile of restorative justice principles in Parliament.
- To provide opportunities for policy discussion and consultation.

Conclusion

In the criminal justice system, restorative justice is unlike other forms of ADR in that from the start, one party is deemed to be the party responsible for the offending behaviour and one the victim or injured party. Many of the skills required in facilitating the process, however, are those of an experienced mediator, and formal inequality of the parties – when the process is entered into voluntarily – need not inhibit the kind of authentic dialogue from which both offender and victim can learn and understand their experiences. At best, RJ can validate the experience of all parties in a way that complements the abstraction and typological categorisation of the criminal justice system.

Many of the restorative justice projects referred to relate to the early 21st century, and there is evidence of a hardening of attitudes within a criminal justice system in which many of the more liberal element have been eroded by reduction of funding and which is increasingly shaped by a populist bias favouring harshly punitive attitudes and against considering the social context in which the criminal justice system operates.

Defending RJ within the MOJ has meant justifying its existence in terms of the overriding objective of preventing re-offending. This creates a danger of compromising the integrity of the process by prioritising that which is measurable over that which is significant and discounting the learning experience that restorative justice can offer to both victim and offender.

'Victim' and 'offender' are seldom hermetically sealed categories. The experience of those enmeshed in the criminal justice system is more complex than this binary characterisation. On the one hand, focusing exclusively on the interests of victims may distract attention from the inequalities which form the nexus of offending behaviour. On the other, overemphasising the interests of offenders may trivialise offending behaviour in ways that undermine support for restorative justice programmes and erode the principles of equality and consistency on which the rule of law depends.

Restorative justice, at best, offers victims and offenders the opportunity to learn from and take responsibility for their experience. While formal equality of the parties may be compromised, if victim and offender participate voluntarily, many of the techniques and strategies of skilled mediators can create a dialogue that is otherwise denied in the criminal justice system. Experience from New Zealand, Canada, and Australia suggests that this can be done so that an offender is held accountable for their actions in a way that is more meaningful to the participants, makes them less likely to re-offend, and is consonant with the rule of law.

Restorative processes have traditionally operated on the margins of the criminal justice system, whether in minor offending or youth justice, by diverting first-time offenders from the courts, or in the overlap with mental health. In more serious cases, restorative processes may nevertheless be powerful and even cathartic when operating independently of the formal criminal justice system acting as an arm of the state.

Restorative processes in educational and health (especially mental health) settings can contribute to a culture that encourages mutuality and institutional self-reflection. Restorative approaches at an institutional level may be helpful in resolving institutional conflict in a way that can contribute to a culture of collegiality.

Like other forms of ADR, RJ is more a complement than an alternative to the formal legal system of adjudication. As an inherently relational process, it functions best when tailored to local contexts. Properly implemented, it need not threaten the values of objectivity and fairness in the criminal justice system or prioritise the rights of victims over the awareness of vulnerability as a human characteristic we all share.

Questions

1. **What do you consider the core components of restorative justice?**
2. **Working in pairs, summarise the arguments for and against restorative justice.**
3. **Imagine that you are the victim of a criminal offence and are considering taking part in a restorative justice process. What might be your needs to make this a safe process, and what might the needs of the perpetrator be if they are to take part in this process?**
4. **Are there categories of offence to which restorative justice should not apply?**
5. **Who should decide whether restorative justice is appropriate in the case of criminal offences?**
6. **In what, if any, circumstances might restorative justice retraumatise a person who has suffered serious harm?**

Further Reading

Liebmann, M. (2007) *Restorative Justice: How It Works*. Jessica Kingsley.

Weitekamp, E. G. M. (1999) 'The History of Restorative Justice'. In L. Walgrave & G. Bazemore (Eds.), *Restorative Juvenile Justice: Repairing the Harm of Youth Crime*. Criminal Justice Press.

Zehr, H. (2015) *The Little Book of Restorative Justice*. Good Books.

9 'Mediation Secrets'

Mediation depends on a relationship of trust and integrity between the parties and the parties and the mediator. This, in turn, requires the opportunity for parties to explore opinions, ideas, and potential solutions in confidence, without being bound by them if a mediation subsequently falls apart. This chapter examines how far those 'secrets' should be protected and sets out some of the relevant case law and international parallels. The issue is important as it crystalises the legal status of the mediator, the accountability of the mediator and parties for any agreement reached, and the complex relationship of the mediation process and litigation. The nub of the problem is that while protection of confidentiality is important for the mediation process, it cannot be without limits. If it is allowed to become a cloak for inappropriate behaviour, it will undermine the integrity of the process it is intended to serve.

Definitions

'Confidentiality' relates to the withholding of evidence from all parties. The right to confidentiality is grounded in values of human dignity and autonomy (*Douglas v Hello* 2001) and attaches to private communications taking place in professional or other relationships of trust, whether the confidentiality derives from an express term of contract or is implied by the fiduciary nature of the relationship. For a private individual to bring an action for breach of confidence, it was previously necessary to show that they had suffered some actual or potential detriment (*Attorney General v Observer Ltd* 1990), but it is now clear that any disclosure may engage Article 8 of ECHR (*Campbell v Mirror Group Newspapers Ltd* 2004). A threatened breach of confidence may entitle the person to seek an injunction, and an actual breach may entitle them to damages or other equitable remedies.

'Privilege' relates to the right to withhold evidence from a court and comprises specific rules of evidence, the most relevant in relation to mediation being 'legal professional privilege' and 'without-prejudice privilege.' While privilege admits exceptions, it offers far stronger protection against disclosure than confidentiality. 'Confidentiality' does not, in itself, exclude evidence from being admissible in court, and a court may compel disclosure when it considers it to be in the interests of justice and necessary for the fair disposal of a case.

DOI: 10.4324/9781003112617-9

In considering mediation, current case law illustrates that different rules may apply to the fact of settlement, the terms of settlement, statements made by parties during settlement, documents and evidence disclosed during mediation, statements, notes, opinions, and impressions voiced by a mediator.

Mediation Practice

'Confidentiality' is an inherent and definitional feature of mediation and, for many parties to a dispute, one of its most attractive promises.

For Alexander (2014), it is an 'essential quality'; for Andrews (2018), it is one of 'six foundations of mediation'; for Agapiou and Clark (2018), if 'confidentiality cannot be achieved, then mediation properly so-called cannot be exercised.'

Reasons given for confidentiality in mediation include the following:

1. Support for the integrity of the process in encouraging parties to be frank in disclosing their needs, interests and concerns;
2. Preventing parties from using mediation as a fishing expedition to discover details that could subsequently be used at trial;
3. Encouraging parties to enter mediation when they have legitimate interests to protect; and
4. Encouraging mediators to take on the role knowing that they will not be compellable as witnesses.

Confidentiality operates in two ways in mediation: confidentiality of the whole process as against the rest of the world and the confidentiality of information shared by one party with the mediator and withheld from the other.

In community mediation, parties are often told that what takes place in mediation is confidential. In civil mediation, a mediator will generally explain to the parties that what takes place in joint meetings is confidential to the parties, and what takes place in individual meetings will not be revealed to the other side or at all without their consent. Mediators will also highlight the existence of an exception if mediators suspect that they may be required to make a disclosure under the Proceeds of Crime Act 2002 in relation to money laundering, but this is not invariably the case.

The mediation agreement often refers specifically to confidentiality as a contract term. CEDR's model mediation agreement (2023) contains exceptions where:

- 'The mediator or any party or their representative is required by law to make disclosure';
- 'The mediator reasonably considers that there is a serious risk of significant harm to the life or safety of any person if the information in question is not disclosed'; and
- 'The mediator reasonably considers that there is a serious risk of being personally subject to criminal proceedings unless the information in question is disclosed.'

The commitment to confidentiality is reinforced by a contract term binding the parties not to call the mediator as a witness. For practical purposes, the parties to a mediation are promised that their secrets cannot be disclosed to other parties or the courts.

In family mediation, the situation is more complex. It will generally be explained at the outset of the mediation that confidentiality is not absolute. Mediators undertake in the agreement to mediate signed by both parties that they will not disclose information to any other person or body without obtaining the written consent of all participants, except where there is an overriding obligation of disclosure. They will also explain to participants that when financial issues need to be settled, the court will require full financial information to achieve a final settlement in divorce, and this information is provided on an open basis and is therefore not legally privileged. There is an obligation on the parties to disclose this information, and once completed, the open financial statement will be available to the court as the context for any consent order. It will be made clear to participants that the confidentiality of mediation is not absolute, and a mediator is under an obligation to notify the appropriate child protection agencies if a child or adult is said or believed to be at risk of significant harm.

Confidentiality

Keane and McKeown (2014) define the scope of confidentiality in mediation as follows: '[P]roceedings are confidential as between the parties and as between the parties and the mediator and therefore even if the parties agree that the matters can be referred to outside the mediation, the mediator can enforce the confidentiality provision.' But not everything that is confidential is privileged, and privilege itself cannot be an absolute bar to the admissibility of evidence.

Privilege

Legal professional privilege is the strongest form of privilege. Material shared with a legal advisor will be accompanied by legal professional privilege, but that will not necessarily cover materials shared with a mediator. Privilege in mediation is basically an extension of 'without prejudice' privilege and is there to protect the parties rather than the mediator.

The rationale of the 'without prejudice' rule is to facilitate the settlement of disputes without litigation and to uphold the expectation of parties that material shared with this expectation is immune from disclosure. Courts have long identified the existence of a legal privilege attaching to statements and communications when parties enter into negotiation with the aim of achieving reconciliation. As a process of assisted negotiation, secrets shared in a mediation, provided they are made with the intention of settling a case, will benefit from the common law principle of 'without prejudice' privilege. May LJ in *Aird v Prime Meridian Ltd* (2006) defined mediation judicially as taking the 'form of assisted "without prejudice" negotiation' and opined that 'what goes on in mediation is privileged so that it cannot be referred to in subsequent court proceedings if the mediation is unsuccessful.' The privilege is that of the parties rather than the mediator and may therefore be waived by them, even if the mediator objects. It is also not clear that the 'without prejudice' rule covers material shared individually with the mediator and not with the other disputant.

In *Rush & Tompkins Ltd v the Greater London Council* (1989), Lord Griffiths summarised the rule governing the admissibility of evidence as:

> founded upon the public policy of encouraging litigants to settle their differences rather than litigate them to a finish. Parties should be encouraged so far as possible to settle their disputes without resort to litigation and should not be discouraged by the knowledge that anything that is said in the course of such negotiations (and that includes, of course, as much the failure to reply to an offer as an actual reply) may be used to their prejudice in the course of the proceedings.

There are two related rationales for the rule. First is a policy reason: parties should be encouraged to settle their disputes without litigation. Secondly, once parties have agreed to enter 'without prejudice' negotiations in awareness of the convention, their expectations should be upheld. These related justifications shape the reach and scope of the rule (Zuckerman 2013).

In *Unilever plc v Procter & Gamble* (1999), Walker LJ sets out exceptions for the inadmissibility of evidence. Following *Oceanbulk Shipping & Trading SA v TMT Asia Ltd & Ors* (2010), in which the Supreme Court determined that privileged material should be admitted to aid interpretation of a settlement, this amounts to ten exceptions to the general principle:

1. Evidence of settlement, where there is an issue as to whether an agreement has been concluded.
2. Where evidence of the negotiations is admissible to show that an apparent agreement should be set aside on the ground of misrepresentation, fraud, or undue influence.
3. Where a clear statement made by one party and on which the other party is intended to act, and does so, may give rise to an estoppel.
4. Where exclusion of the evidence would act as a cloak for perjury, blackmail, or other 'unambiguous' impropriety.
5. In order to explain delay or apparent acquiescence.
6. To prove that the claimant has satisfied a duty to mitigate his loss.
7. Where there is an express or implied agreement that an offer is expressly made without prejudice except as to costs.
8. In matrimonial cases, there has developed what is now a distinct privilege extending to communications received in confidence with a view to matrimonial and parental conciliation.
9. Where there is a dispute as to the interpretation of the settlement.
10. Where a party can rely on anything said to show that settlement should be rectified.

In *Reed Executive plc v Reed Business Information Ltd* (Costs Alternative Dispute Resolution) (2004), the Court of Appeal decided it did not have the power to order disclosure of negotiations taking place in a mediation for the purposes of determining costs. The claimant had argued that it should be awarded substantial costs on the basis of the defendant's unreasonable refusal of ADR and, for that purpose, unsuccessfully sought disclosure of the details of the without-prejudice negotiations that had taken place between them. Jacob LJ confirmed that there are exceptions to the general rule of non-admissibility of without-prejudice negotiations and declined to order disclosure.

In *Cumbria Waste Management* (2008), a case involving a three-party mediation between the company, DEFRA, and the company's legal advisors, the deputy High Court judge found the evidence from the mediator was inadmissible on account of contractual confidentiality or as not falling within one of the exceptions to the without-prejudice rule. In *Aird v Prime Meridian* (2007), the Court of Appeal considered that what goes on in a mediation is privileged and cannot be relied on in subsequent proceedings. But in *Brown v Rice* (2007), in which the ADR group intervened to argue for 'mediation privilege,' Stuart Isaacs QC, sitting as a deputy High Court judge, went behind the confidentiality of the mediation to investigate what happened in an unsuccessful mediation to determine whether an agreement had been reached, although one of the parties and the mediator objected.

In *Farm Assist Limited v Secretary of State for the Environment, Food and Rural Affairs (No 2)* (2009), in which a contractual clause bound the parties not to call the mediator in any litigation or arbitration 'in relation to the dispute,' the issue arose as to whether the agreement was entered into under duress. Ramsay J dismissed an assertion of mediation privilege. He identified the source of confidentiality as 'without prejudice privilege,' belonging to the parties and not the mediator, and stated the exceptions 'which permit use or disclosure of privileged communications or information outside the conciliation where, after balancing the various interests, it is in the interests of justice that the information should be disclosed.'

Briggs (2009) argued, extra-judicially, that *Brown v Rice* was wrongly decided and advocated a common law privilege tailored to dispute resolution. He distinguished between the treatment of two aspects of confidentiality in mediation – 'the shared secrets' being those taking place in round table discussion and therefore brought within the scope of the without-prejudice rule – and the 'mediator secrets' being those arising from individual meetings between the parties and the mediator enabling the parties 'separately to unburden themselves to the mediator' and arguably falling outside the without-prejudice rule.

More recently, in *Ferster v Ferster* (2016), the Court of Appeal found an email sent by a mediator within the context of a mediation fell within the 'unambiguous propriety exception' to the 'without prejudice' rule. The case concerned acrimonious litigation between three brothers who were equal shareholders in a gaming company.

The Court considered the policy behind the 'without prejudice' privilege was to encourage frank discussions and negotiations, but the respondents' threat, as an attempt at blackmail, fell firmly within the exception to the without-prejudice privilege rule. The impropriety consisted of threatening to pursue contempt proceedings unless the applicant paid the respondents a much higher price for their shares than had previously been discussed.

The Court held that although it was possible for the parties to extend the ambit of without prejudice contractually, the relevant clause in the mediation agreement was not to be construed as overriding the public policy exception for blackmail.

Specific Provisions in Family Mediation

In *McTaggart v McTaggart* (1949), the Court of Appeal found that communications with a probation officer in the course of negotiations for marital reconciliation are privileged and cannot generally be admitted in evidence without the parties' consent. *Henley v Henley* (1955) affirmed that this privilege applies whether the initiative for reconciliation comes from the parties or the conciliator. The Royal Commission on Marriage and Divorce (The Morton Commission 1956) recommended the 'conferment of a privilege of marriage guidance counsellors,' but the recommendations were not implemented.

In *Re D* (1993), Bingham MR, sitting with Butler-Sloss LJ, found a distinct form of mediation privilege applying to communications made for the purpose of conciliation. The 'mediator' here was a psychologist, and the privilege derived from the public interest in preserving the confidentiality of attempted conciliation. Conciliation was considered to 'embrace reconciliation, mediation, and conciliation.' Counsel for the claimant argued that 'the privilege that applies to communications made for purposes of attempted conciliation is now an independent head of conciliation.' Bingham MR followed Lord Hailsham and Lord Simon in *D v NSPCC* (1978) in affirming a category of privilege 'based on the public interest in the stability of marriage.' He opined that the privilege was not absolute, but evidence would only be admitted if 'the public interest in protecting the interests of the child outweighs the public interest in preserving the confidentiality of attempted conciliation.' The privilege he considered attaches to the *bona fides* of a conciliator rather than any specific professional status. Bingham MR considered that a conciliation privilege had developed by analogy to without-prejudice privilege, referring to an

> unquestioned line of authority establishes that where a third party (whether official or unofficial, professional or lay) receives information in confidence with a view to conciliation, the courts will not compel him to disclose what was said without the parties' agreement.

The case of *Re D (A Child) (Hague Convention: Mediation)* (2017) decided the availability of mediation in post-abduction family relations was vital in remedying the damage caused by abductions. If experienced mediators were given the impression that expressly confidential mediation might be subject to disclosure in court, that was likely to have a detrimental effect on the mediation process. It determined there was a strong argument for holding that mediation in the context of proceedings under the Convention, where immunity arose from express terms, would be immune from disclosure in all circumstances, save where, as in *Re D (Minors) (Conciliation: Disclosure of Information)* (1993), disclosure might be justified by a risk of significant harm to a child. In *Re E (A Child) (Mediation Privilege)* (2020), Samuels QC (sitting as a High Court judge) granted an application to prevent a party from relying on matters that took place in a mediation.

Other Jurisdictions

Scotland

TheScottish Law Commission (1991) has offered support for 'confidentiality' of family mediation. There is an explicit provision in Sections 1 and 2 of the Civil Evidence (Family Mediation) (Scotland) Act 1995 that information about what occurs during family mediation assisted by accredited mediators is not usually admissible in evidence.

Ireland

In Ireland, Section 10 (1) of Mediation Act 2017 provides for a duty of confidentiality subject to the exceptions in Section 10(2) where disclosure:

(a) is necessary in order to implement or enforce a mediation settlement,
(b) is necessary to prevent physical or psychological injury to a party,
(c) is required by law,
(d) is necessary in the interests of preventing or revealing –

 (i) the commission of a crime (including an attempt to commit a crime),
 (ii) the concealment of a crime, or
 (iii) a threat to a party, or

(e) is sought or offered to prove or disprove a civil claim concerning the negligence or misconduct of the mediator occurring during the mediation or a complaint to a professional body concerning such negligence or misconduct.

USA

In the USA, the National Conference of Commissions on Uniform State Laws approved and recommended for enactment the Uniform Mediation Act in 2001. At least ten states (including the District of Colombia, Idaho, Illinois, Iowa, Nebraska, New Jersey, Ohio, South Dakota, Utah, Vermont, and Washington) have adopted this in placing mediation privilege on a statutory basis. The Uniform Mediation Act, (41) s. 4 p. 7 provides:

> (a) Except as otherwise provided in Section 6, a mediation communication is privileged as provided in subsection (b) and is not subject to discovery or admissible in evidence in a proceeding unless waived or precluded as provided by

> Section 5. (b) In a proceeding, the following privileges apply: (1) A mediation party may refuse to disclose, and may prevent any other person from disclosing, a mediation communication. (2) A mediator may refuse to disclose a mediation communication, and may prevent any other person from disclosing a mediation communication of the mediator. (3) A non-party participant may refuse to disclose, and may prevent any other person from disclosing, a mediation communication of the non-party participant. (c) Evidence or information that is otherwise admissible or subject to discovery does not become inadmissible or protected from discovery solely by reason of its disclosure or use in a mediation.

The Central District of California adopted a federal common law mediation privilege in *Folb. v Motion Picture Industry Pension and Health Plans* (1998).

Australia

In Australia, s.24A of the Supreme Court Act 1986 of the State of Victoria provides:

> Where the Court refers a proceeding or any part of a proceeding to mediation, unless all the parties who attended the mediation otherwise agree in writing, no evidence shall be admitted at the hearing of the proceeding of anything said or done by any person at the mediation.

Hong Kong

In Hong Kong, the Mediation Ordinance (entered into force in 2013) contains confidentiality provisions, and the law societies' mediation rules provide a detailed account of the types of communications inadmissible in subsequent proceedings:

> [T]he parties shall not rely on or introduce in any subsequent judicial or arbitral proceedings: (i) any oral or written exchanges within the mediation made in connection with any mediation conducted under these Rules between a party and the mediator or between any party; (ii) any views expressed or suggestions made within the mediation either by the mediator or a party in respect of possible settlement of the dispute; (iii) any admission made by a party in connection with any mediation conducted under these Rules; (iv) the fact that a party had or had not indicated a willingness to accept any suggestion or proposal for settlement by the mediator or by any party; and (v) any documents brought into existence for the purpose of the mediation including any notes or records made in connection with any mediation conducted under these Rules by a mediator or a party.
>
> (Koo 2011)

European Union

The European Directive on Mediation provides protection for 'mediation evidence' that goes beyond the scope of English without-prejudice protection. Article 7 sets out minimum standards for the protection of confidentiality; the UK implemented this in relation to cross-border mediation by the Cross-Border Mediation (EU Directive) Regulations SI 2011/1133 but revoked on 31 December 2020.

The directive provides 'for a minimum degree of compatibility of civil procedural rules with regard to how to protect the confidentiality of mediation in any subsequent civil and commercial judicial proceedings or arbitration,' subject to two narrow exceptions to the principle:

> (1) Given that mediation is intended to take place in a manner which respects confidentiality, Member States shall ensure that, unless the parties agree otherwise, neither mediators nor those involved in the administration of the mediation process shall be compelled to give evidence in civil and commercial judicial proceedings or arbitration regarding information arising out of or in connection with a mediation process, except:
>
> (a) where this is necessary for overriding considerations of public policy of the Member State concerned, in particular when required to ensure the protection of the best interests of children or to prevent harm to the physical or psychological integrity of a person; or
>
> (b) where disclosure of the content of the agreement resulting from mediation is necessary in order to implement or enforce that agreement.

Prior to leaving the European Union, Britain implemented the directive to apply only to cross-border mediations, but several European nations implemented the EU Mediation Directive in more ample ways than the UK to include within-country mediations.

France and Germany adopted a unitary system covering both domestic and cross-border mediations. France implemented the directive via decree (2011 and 2012). Mediation proceedings are confidential unless the parties agree otherwise. Germany implemented the Directive as the Mediation Act (Mediationsgesetz 2012). The act requires strict confidentiality (s.4) but admits of several exceptions, including where necessary for the mediator to disclose the content of the mediation proceeding to enable the implementation or enforcement of the settlement agreement and overriding considerations of public policy, such as ensuring the protection of the best interests of children or to prevent harm to the physical or psychological integrity of a person.

In Austria, the Act on Mediation in Civil Matters (2003) creates an absolute duty of confidentiality for registered mediators. A registered mediator may be subject to prosecution if this duty is breached. The duty cannot be waived by the parties. The European Mediation Act (2011) transposes Directive 2008/52/EC to establish that mediators cannot be compelled to give evidence regarding information arising out of or in connection with a mediation process in either civil and commercial judicial proceedings or in arbitration.

In Italy, Article 9 of Legislative Decree 28 (2010) creates a duty of confidentiality for each individual involved in the mediation process, including parties, counsel, and the mediator. This obligation applies to documented statements and information acquired during the proceedings. However, if the parties consent to the disclosure of information, the mediator is exempt from the obligation of confidentiality. The mediator is also exempt if keeping the information confidential would be in violation of the law. Article 10 of Legislative Decree 28 provides that mediators cannot be called as witnesses in any subsequent judicial proceedings and Article 200 of the Italian Code of Criminal Procedure that a mediator cannot be compelled to testify about information obtained during mediation.

India

Section 22 of the Mediation Act (2023) provides that the mediator, mediation service provider, and parties to mediation proceedings are obliged to keep confidential statements, proposals, documents, and any other communication exchanged during the mediation. Recording mediation proceedings through audio or video is prohibited.

The information discussed during mediation cannot be used as evidence in court, arbitration, or any legal proceedings. The Delhi High Court Mediation and Conciliation Rules (2004) require confidentiality of events transpiring during mediation. The Supreme Court, in the case of *Moti Ram (D) Tr. LRs and Anr. v Ashok Kumar and Anr* (2010), confirmed that mediation proceedings are confidential in nature, and only an executed settlement agreement or, alternatively, a statement that the mediation proceedings were unsuccessful should be provided to the court by the mediator.

Case for a Specific Mediation Privilege

Advocates

In the current law, despite some conflicting authority, there is no independent mediation privilege going beyond the scope of without-prejudice privilege. Mediation privilege, which is sometimes regarded by mediators as a litmus test that the process of mediation is taken seriously, would shield mediators and mediations from the scrutiny of the Court. CEDR and the ADR group have argued for a specific mediation privilege. Cornes (2008) argues for a 'statutory special privilege for mediators' that 'admits of mediation is more than assisted negotiation' but does not specify in what this 'extra element' inheres. Agapiou and Clark (2018) argue for 'legislation underpinning confidentiality in mediation as the best way to bridge the gap between theory and practice' but recognise the complexity of the 'potential conflict between encouraging mediation through promises of confidentiality, providing certainty of the confidentiality regime and also ensuring that unconscionable conduct which too stringent controls on disclosure would facilitate is not permitted.' Brown and Marriot (2011) highlight the 'scope and need for clarification of the law relating to privilege in mediation.'

Critics

Reich (2001) considers, 'There is no empirical evidence establishing that the mediation process requires confidentiality' and that creating a new category of privilege is contrary to the 'public policy interest.' Green (1986) discerns no difference between a mediator's desire to avoid calls to give evidence and 'the normal desire of any person, whether percipient witness or professional consultant, to avoid being involuntarily drawn into a court battle.' Genn (2012b) argues that, 'without scrutiny, it is impossible to know whether the processes or the outcomes for parties are fair in the context of the legal rights and responsibilities that gave rise to the dispute'. Shapira (2012) identifies a conflict between the mediator's role in ensuring the fairness of the process and the duty of confidentiality and argues that the parties' 'informed consent' is essential to this fairness. Meggitt (2020) considers these objections are addressed in practical terms in the codes of conduct of the Centre for Effective Dispute Resolution (CEDR) and the Chartered Institute of Arbitrators (CIArb).

As a heterogeneous process, there may be contexts in which mediation confidentiality is undesirable. The same principles do not necessarily apply in the same way to family, civil, community, and restorative justice cases. In the case of public interest mediations, there are strong reasons why deliberations should not be confidential.

Susskind as cited in (Goldberg et al. 1985), has argued in the context of public interest mediation,

> Environmental mediators ought to accept responsibility for ensuring 1) that the interests of the parties not directly involved in the negotiations, but with a stake in the outcome are adequately represented and protected; 2) that agreements are as fair and stable as possible and 3) that agreements are interpreted as intended by the community at large and set constructive precedents.

Elsewhere he argues that environmental mediators need to be 'held accountable for the fairness of the processes in which they engage as well as the quality of the agreements they help to reach' and that they need to be accountable to judges who appoint them as well as the parties involved in a mediation (Susskind 1981).

Conclusion

While current law offers less protection than some mediators would like to see, the combination of private law rights to confidentiality and without-prejudice privilege provides a high degree of protection to mediation secrets, except where public policy and the protection of the integrity of the process require.

Courts will generally admit the fact of a mediation agreement as an exception to the without-prejudice rule, and, in cases of fraud, unambiguous impropriety, or duress, confidentiality can be overridden when it is in the interests of justice to do so (*Farm Assist Ltd*). The provisions of the Proceeds of Crime Act 2002 and evidence of serious harm in family mediations provide clear examples of when mediation secrets will not be upheld. Proponents of a statutory mediation privilege have not been able to provide compelling evidence that doubts over confidentiality are impeding the take-up of mediation.

Questions

1. **What are reasons for the protection of confidentiality in mediation, and why should there be limits to it?**
2. **What are some of the exceptions to the without-prejudice rule as regards mediation?**
3. **What are your reasons for supporting or not supporting a statutory mediation privilege?**

Further Reading

Bartlet, M. (2015) 'Mediation Secrets "In the Shadow of the Law"', *Civil Justice Quarterly* 35 (1).
Briggs, M. (2009) 'Mediation Privilege', *New Law Journal*, 3rd and 10th April.
Koo (2011) 'The Development of Legal Protection for Mediation Confidentiality in Hong Kong', *Common Law World Review*. 40 (3), 263.
Shipman, S. et al. (2019) *Brown and Marriot 'ADR Principles and Practice* (4th ed). Sweet & Maxwell.

10 Mandatory Mediation

Mediation and other forms of ADR have been progressively integrated into the administration of civil justice. While the provision of mediation has become more professionalised and formalised, at the same time, courts in both North America and the UK have become directly involved in the promotion and management of settlement. This chapter will discuss various forms of mandatory mediation and consider the arguments for and against a degree of compulsion. It will provide a brief summary of relevant civil procedure and an examination of relevant case law.

Mandatory mediation is a contentious issue for several distinct reasons:

1. If mediation becomes mandatory, it may lose its identity as a voluntary process that provides an alternative to adjudication.
2. Automatic court reference to mediation could lead to the enmeshing of public and private processes with the consequent problems of public accountability.
3. Mandation has profound implications for the regulation of the mediation profession since the court as public provider of justice will be responsible for the quality of those to whom it refers litigants.
4. The consequent regulation of the profession may lead to its increasing 'legalisaton' and make it harder for non-lawyer mediators to make their distinctive contribution.
5. Reference to mandatory mediation where unsuccessful may lead to additional cost.

Models of Compulsion

Sander (2007) distinguishes between two types of mandatory mediation: 'discretionary' judicial referral and a self-enforcing 'categorical' referral, in which all cases of a certain type are referred. He considered that compulsion might be acceptable as a 'kind of temporary expedient, a la affirmative action' when combined with (1) judicial oversight and (2) the maintenance of a pathway to adjudication without disproportionate costs penalties.

DOI: 10.4324/9781003112617-10

2021 Civil Justice Council Report

The Civil Justice Council, in its Interim Report (2017), distinguished between three types of compulsion, the first two of which would correspond to Sander's 'categorical' format:

Type 1: Parties are required to attempt ADR as a pre-condition of access to the court, with the claimant unable to issue proceedings until evidence of the appropriate efforts is produced.
Type 2: Parties are required to engage in or attempt ADR at some later stage, such as any case management hearing.
Type 3: Power of the court to require unwilling parties in a particular case to engage in ADR on an *ad hoc* basis in the course of case management.

To these types should be added effective mandation by way of adverse costs orders.

The Civil Justice Council Final Report (2021) considered compulsory ADR could be a 'desirable and effective development' when a return to normal adjudicative processes is possible and concluded:

1. Where participation in a suitable and effective form of ADR occasions no expense of time or money by the parties, making it compulsory will not usually be controversial.
2. Greater use of compulsory judge-led ADR processes will prove acceptable, given they are free and appear effective in the contexts in which they are already compulsory.
3. Compulsory mediation may be considered, provided it is sufficiently regulated and made available where appropriate in short, affordable formats.

Arguments for Compulsion

Arguments for mandatory mediation are primarily utilitarian and predicated on the efficiency and efficacy of mediation as a dispute resolution process:

1. Compulsion would lead to higher settlement rates.
2. It would reduce the burden on the courts.
3. It would overcome unfamiliarity with the process and enable better outcomes for the parties who would understand the benefits that mediation offers and claim them for themselves.
4. *Churchill* (2023) in its revision of *Halsey* (2004) considers that some forms of mandation are not per se incompatible with Article 6 ECHR.

Arguments Against Compulsion

Arguments against compulsion have distinct legal, pragmatic, and philosophical strands to them. They are predicated on a recognition of the distinctness of the parallel processes of third-party-facilitated negotiation and judicial adjudication:

1. The legal argument that to 'oblige truly unwilling parties to refer their disputes to mediation would be to impose an unacceptable obstruction on their right of access to the court' (*Halsey* 2004). It follows from this that as a fetter on the constitutional right of access to the courts, staying proceedings to compel mediation would be a breach of Article 6 of the ECHR.
2. The practical argument: it might not work, either because the parties are intransigent or because they do not know enough about it and are therefore unlikely to engage in the process. It may lead to an increase in costs where disputants fail to settle in mediation.
3. A qualitative argument relating to adjudication: pushing more disputes into ADR would undermine the value of the adjudicative system, which is the foundation on which the effectiveness of any form of ADR ultimately relies. It privatises the provision of justice as a public good and reduces the body of precedent-bearing cases on which common law depends.
4. A qualitative argument relating to mediation: compelling parties to mediate undermines the autonomy of the parties and the inherent voluntariness of the process, which are foundational values of mediation.
5. A political (and justice) argument that compulsion is paternalistic: forcing unwilling disputants to engage with their adversaries in a way they do not want to.

Civil Procedure Rules 1998

Rules of civil procedure in England and Wales have already developed to involve compulsory participation in ADR. CPR 1998 1.4(1) provides that the court must 'further the overriding objective by actively managing cases.' CPR 1.4(2)(e) explains that active case management includes 'encouraging the parties to use an alternative dispute resolution procedure if the court considers that appropriate and facilitating the use of such procedure.' CPR 3.1 provides for the court's general powers of management including the 'giving of directions' when a party has not complied with any relevant pre-action protocol. CPR 26.4(2B) enables a court to 'direct that the proceedings, either in whole or in part, be stayed for one month, or for such other period as it considers appropriate' for the parties to attempt ADR.

Support for ADR is a feature running through pre-action protocols. Practice Direction Paragraph 8.1 stipulates:

> Starting proceedings should usually be a step of last resort, and proceedings should not normally be started when a settlement is still actively being explored. Although ADR is not compulsory, the parties should consider whether some form of ADR procedure might enable them to settle the matter without starting proceedings. The Court may require evidence that the parties considered some form of ADR.

The Civil Procedure Rules Committee (2024) has made proposals for changes to CPR in light of *Churchill v Merthyr Tudfil.* Proposed changes including reference to ADR in the overriding objective.

Changes to 1.1 would add that dealing with a case justly and at proportionate cost includes, so far as practicable, using and promoting ADR methods. Reference to ADR in the overriding objective would underline that considering the use of ADR should be a key part of the court process.

Changes to 1.4 and 3.1 would clarify the position established in *Churchill v Merthyr Tydfil* (2023) that judges may order as well as encourage parties to participate in ADR.

Changes to Parts 28 and 29 would add that courts must consider whether to order or encourage parties to participate in ADR for fast-track, intermediate-track, and multi-track claims.

Changes to Part 44 would add that failure to comply with an order for ADR or unreasonable failure to participate in ADR proposed by another party would come under the consideration of the conduct of parties when deciding to make any order about costs.

Case Law

Until recently, case law had considered that, although judges could encourage mediation, they could not compel engagement. The primary remedy for an unreasonable refusal to engage with mediation was an adverse costs order.

In *Halsey v Milton Keynes NHS Trust* (2004), Dyson LJ in the Court of Appeal considered the question of whether the allocation of costs should be made against a party who had refused to mediate. To order costs against a successful party for refusing to mediate, although not barring the litigant from the court, could nevertheless be seen as providing a degree of implied compulsory mediation. Dyson said six factors that needed to be considered regarding the reasonableness of a refusal to mediate:

1. The nature of the dispute;
2. The merits of the case;
3. The extent to which other settlements have been attempted;
4. Whether the costs of mediation would have been disproportionately high;
5. Whether any delay in setting up or attending mediation would have been prejudicial; and
6. Whether the mediation had a reasonable prospect of success.

He considers that 'to oblige truly unwilling parties to refer their disputes to mediation would be to impose an unacceptable obstruction on their access to the court' and that compulsory mediation could infringe Article 6 of ECHR.

In the recent case of *Churchill v Merthyr Tydfil Borough Council* (2023), the Court of Appeal, comprising Lady Chief Justice Kerr, Sir Geoffrey Voss MR, and Birss LJ, reconsidered Dyson's dicta in *Halsey* in the context of a case in which the claimant had refused to take part in a council's internal complaints procedure. Deputy District Judge Kempton Rees at first instance considered the claimant's lawyers had unreasonably refused to engage with the procedure but that he was bound to follow Dyson LJ's statement in *Halsey*. Although the dispute resolution process here involved an internal complaints procedure in a claim for invasive Japanese knotweed brought against the council, the court heard submissions from the Bar Council, the Law Society, CEDR, the Civil Mediation Council, and the Chartered Institute of Arbitrators about the court's capacity to lawfully order the parties to court proceedings to engage in a non-court-based dispute resolution process.

Voss LJ decided in the Court of Appeal that Dyson LJ's comments in *Halsey* were not part of the 'essential reasoning' in that case and did not bind the judge to dismiss the council's application for the stay of these proceedings. The court can now lawfully stay proceedings or order the parties to engage in a non-court-based dispute resolution process, provided that the order made does not impair the essence of the claimant's right to a judicial hearing and is proportionate to achieving the legitimate aim of settling the dispute fairly, quickly, and at reasonable cost. In considering the exercise of a court's discretion, the Court of Appeal considered the Bar Council's list of relevant factors. While refusing to lay down fixed principles, the court considered the matters mentioned by the Bar Council, Mr Churchill, and the Court of Appeal in *Halsey* that were likely to have some relevance:

1. The form of ADR being considered;
2. Whether the parties were legally advised or represented;
3. Whether ADR was likely to be effective or appropriate without such advice or representation,
4. Whether it was made clear to the parties that, if they did not settle, they were free to pursue their claim or defence;
5. The urgency of the case and the reasonableness of the delay caused by ADR;
6. Whether that delay would vitiate the claim or give rise to or exacerbate any limitation issue;
7. The costs of ADR, both in absolute terms and relative to the parties' resources;
8. Whether there was any realistic prospect of the claim being resolved through ADR;
9. Whether there was a significant imbalance in the parties' levels of resource, bargaining power, or sophistication;
10. The reasons given by a party for not wishing to mediate: for example, if there had already been a recent unsuccessful attempt at ADR; and
11. The reasonableness and proportionality of the sanction if a party declined ADR in the face of an order of the court.

Churchill v Merthyr Tydfil Borough Council (2023) provides that the court now has the power to order not only ADR involving a third-party neutral but also, potentially, an internal complaint procedure. This reinforces a set of cases in which judges have been willing to stay proceedings for mediation or made costs orders against parties refusing to mediate.

In Hussain v Chowdhury (2020), a claim seeking permission from the court for the claimants to pursue charity proceedings under s.115(5) of the Charities Act 2011, the judge ordered a stay for mediation against the wishes of at least one party. In *Hamon v UCL* (2023), a case in which hundreds of students applied for a group litigation order in proceedings against UCL for failure to provide face-to-face teaching, UCL successfully argued for a stay to enable these student complaints to be handled through the Office of the Independent Adjudicator (OIA).

In *Burchell v Bullard* (2005), a party who ignored an offer to mediate at a pre-action stage was deemed to have unreasonably refused to mediate. In *R (Cowl) and Others v Plymouth City Council* (2001), Lord Woolf LCJ held that parties must consider mediation before starting legal proceedings, particularly where public money is involved.

In *Dunnet v Railtrack* (2002) the Court dismissed Mrs Dunnet's appeal against Railtrack, refusing to order costs against her, on account of Railtrack's refusal to contemplate mediation prior to appeal. Brooke LJ offered a vigorous exhortation of the value of mediation and of the reality of a costs sanction if a party rejects 'the chance of alternative dispute resolution when it is suggested by the court.'

In *Hurst v Leeming* (2001), Lightman J considered that 'mediation is not in law compulsory, but alternative dispute resolution is at the heart of today's civil justice system.'

In *Mann v Mann* (2014), Mostyn J considered that a costs sanction for refusing to participate in ADR did not amount to unlawful compulsion. Norris J applied the same logic to boundary disputes in *Bradley v Heslin* (2014).

PGF II v OMFS Company Limited (2013) provides further detail to the Halsey criteria requiring parties to engage with a 'serious invitation' to participate in alternative dispute resolution, even if they have reasons which might justify a refusal. Briggs LJ held in the Court of Appeal that 'the court's task in encouraging the more proportionate conduct of civil litigation is so important in current economic circumstances that it is appropriate to emphasise that message by a sanction which operates pour encourager les autres.'

Gore v Naheed and Ahmed (2017) represents an apparent outlier in the shift towards compulsion. The case concerned the existence of a right of way and involved complex issues of law; his solicitor thought 'mediation had no realistic prospect of succeeding.' Patten LJ opined:

> I have some difficulty in accepting that the desire of a party to have his rights determined by a court of law in preference to mediation can be said to be unreasonable conduct particularly when, as here, those rights are ultimately vindicated.

In *Thakkar v Patel* (2017), in which the defendant did not refuse to mediate but 'dragged his feet,' Jackson LJ ordered the defendants to pay to the claimants 75% of the costs of the claim whilst recovering their costs of the counterclaim.

International Parallels

In Italy, judges have the power to order parties to attempt mediation in any civil dispute, requiring them to file a request for mediation with an accredited mediator within a set time frame. In some kinds of civil disputes, parties are required to attend an initial mediation session as a pre-condition for pursuing their claim. This consists of a meeting in which a mediator explains the process and its benefits and is similar to MIAMs in English family proceedings, although under the Italian system, both parties are required to attend, and the court may impose financial sanctions for non-attendance.

In ECJ case law, *Rosalba Alassini* (2010) considered whether a compulsory mediation process was a breach of EU law. In a preliminary reference to the ECJ, the court asked whether the provisions complied with Article 6 ECHR and the Universal Service Directive (2002) (a directive on universal service and users' rights relating to electronic communications networks). The scheme introduced by the Italian government obliged a customer to go through a process of mediation before bringing a claim against a service provider. Advocate General Kokott concluded that the Italian compulsory out-of-court dispute resolution provisions were pursuing 'legitimate objectives in the general interest': i.e. a quicker, less expensive method of dispute settlement which also lightened the burden on the court system and was likely to produce a more satisfactory long term solution to the dispute. The court considered that the procedure was proportionate, given the legitimate cost- and time-saving aims.

In *Menini v Banco Popolare Società Cooperativ* (2018), the ECJ clarified what it considered to be the necessary features of a scheme which renders access to the courts conditional on attempting ADR:

> [T]he requirement for a mediation procedure as a condition for the admissibility of proceedings before the courts may prove compatible with the principle of effective judicial protection, provided that that procedure does not result in a decision which is binding on the parties, that it does not cause a substantial delay for the purposes of bringing legal proceedings, that it suspends the period for the time-barring of claims and that it does not give rise to costs – or gives rise to very low costs – for the parties, and only if electronic means are not the only means by which the settlement procedure may be accessed and interim measures are possible in exceptional cases where the urgency of the situation so requires.

In India, the Supreme Court has upheld mandatory pre-litigation mediation for all commercial suits under the Commercial Court's Act 2015. Mediation Act 2023 mandates individuals to attempt resolution of civil or commercial disputes through mediation before considering legal action in a court or tribunal. After two mediation sessions, a litigant has the option to withdraw from the process. The mediation proceedings themselves should be concluded within 180 days, with the possibility of extending this period by an additional 180 days if all parties consent.

In Canada, the Ontario Mandatory Mediation Program applies to most civil disputes initiated in the state. Parties are required to attempt a mediation, convened by an approved mediator, within 90 days of the filing of the first defence. If a party refuses to participate, they may be subject to the wasted costs of the mediation and further sanctions by the court.

In the USA, Florida has undertaken mandatory court directed mediation since 1987. Under the Floridan civil procedure rules, parties can request that mediation be dispensed with, but such applications are comparatively rare, and around 100,000 cases are diverted from court adjudication to mediation every year (Quek 2010). The Alternative Dispute Resolution Act 1998 requires all federal trial courts to implement ADR and grants judges authority to send a case to mandatory ADR procedures. Mandation may takes many forms (Welsh 2011). Some courts order all cases into mediation; others use a substantive screen, identifying specific lawsuits to be referred to mediation. Some require all civil lawsuits to go to mediation but exempt particular types of cases.

Australia has adopted 'categorical' mandatory schemes and uses both discretionary referral and court-mandated mediation (Hanks 2012). The Civil Dispute Resolution Act 2011 requires parties to take 'genuine steps' to resolve their dispute before commencing proceedings. Courts in all Australian jurisdictions have the power to refer parties to mediation without their consent, and in some states, parties to certain kinds of disputes are required to attempt ADR before they are permitted to commence proceedings. The Queensland District Courts Act 1967 Section 97 provides that parties to civil litigation may be required to attend a mediation orientation session.

Academic Commentary

Ahmed (2012) considers there is already 'implied compulsory mediation' in the courts in England and Wales, and there now needs to be a formal recognition that the courts can compel mediation backed by appropriate costs sanctions. De Girolamo (2016) criticises the 'opt out' in a previous pilot of mandatory mediation such as the London County Court Scheme and argues for express legislative provisions supported by a pilot in which mediation is truly mandatory. Quek (2010) postulates a 'continuum of mandatoriness' and argues that while 'categorical' referral is 'synonymous with arbitrariness,' 'discretionary' referral can retain a clear distinction between coercion 'into' and 'within' mediation. Bartlet (2019) believes that compulsory mediation, in its harder forms, should be resisted, to protect both the values of adjudication and the integrity of mediation, a process that is distinct from litigation. Meggitt (2014) characterises the courts as 'pushing parties towards mediation without expressly admitting that they are doing so and with the apparent sole intention of saving money.'

Schaffer (2018) raises the spectre of the 'floodgates,' referring to the growth of litigious disputes and 'the judiciaries' diminishing capacity to deal with them, inefficiency and high costs,' emphasising that mediation has played a significant role in contributing to access to justice and the saving of resources. He concludes the 'mandatory' aspect of court-based schemes is not per se incompatible with the nature of mediation.

Koo (2015) adopts a comparative approach with the case law in Hong Kong to propose a reformulation of the Halsey guidelines to include situations in which failure to mediate resulted from unreasonable conduct of all the parties, and a party acted unreasonably in mediation. Shipman (2006) emphasises that ADR can increase costs and argues that to 'encourage ADR routinely fails to take sufficient account of the needs of the individual case' but accepts that, provided costs sanctions are proportionate, there should be no breach of ECtHR Article 6 regarding an individual's right of access to court. Clark (2022) identifies 'the slow growth of voluntary mediation' and anticipates 'the benefits for the parties and state that may accrue from mandating.' He follows Schaffer in arguing that mandatory mediation is not *per se* objectionable on legal or policy grounds but needs to be implemented in a way that balances competing interests of efficiency, preserving the qualitative goals of mediation, and filling the justice gap that mediating in the shadow of the law can leave.

Critical Evaluation of Mandatory Mediation

Churchill v Merthyr Tydfil Borough Council (2023) seems to have adopted the reasoning of the Civil Justice Council Final Report (2021) that 'mandatory ADR' represents 'a proportionate response to the need to ration delivery to civil justice.'

The least strong form of compulsion might require parties to 'consider' mediation before litigating and seems unproblematic in terms of access to justice. This could either be in the form of attending a mediation information and advice meeting, which an applicant is obliged by Children and Families Act (2014) to attend, subject to statutory exceptions in some family proceedings or engaging with ACAS prior to bringing a case before an employment tribunal. ACAS conciliation is mandatory in the sense that ACAS must offer it rather than the parties being obliged to set it up.

Cost-led forms of compulsion (as pre-*Churchill*), while involving a penalty for unreasonably refusing to engage with mediation, are not an absolute bar to litigation. However, impecunious parties might feel coerced into mediation by the risk of adverse cost orders.

Mandatory ADR in its categorical forms, whether as a result of pre-action protocols or orders at an interlocutory stage, raises significant problems about the constitutional right of access to the courts.

While there will clearly be many cases that settle because of mediation with significant costs benefits, there will also be cases that do not and thereby lead to a greater cost burden. In the case of small-value claims, which may benefit from a telephone mediation scheme without significant increase in costs, the burden of participating, as with compulsory consulting with ACAS prior to bringing an employment tribunal claim under the Employment Tribunal Act (1996), may be outweighed by the potential benefit of settlement. For high-value cases, in which costs may be in the realm of £100,000, the archetypal mediation, usually conducted over the course of a day by a neutral individual, will often be a proportionate step to be taken at an interlocutory stage. In mid-value cases, however, there are likely to be occasions when impecunious litigants cannot afford both a day of mediation and a day in court. In such cases, compulsory mediation may be a significant fetter on access to the court.

Whereas adjudication is a public process of applying the law to the facts in a reasoned and public forum, mediation is a private and confidential process of facilitation appealing to the different values of equal participation, respect, and autonomy in which both parties need to be willing to engage in good faith to reach a negotiated outcome. As Neuberger (2010, 2015) asserts, court adjudication is

> not just a public service but an inherent 'aspect of government' itself. . . .
>
> (Neuberger 2010)

> [M]ediation must not be invoked and promoted as if it was always an improved substitute for litigation. People plainly should have the constitutional right to refuse to agree terms because they want their day in court: by the same token, they have the same constitutional right to refuse to mediate if they want their day in court.
>
> (Neuberger 2015)

Mediation – Just about Settlement?

Academic commentary has drawn attention to the way that the informalism of mediation may undermine the interests of the vulnerable litigant. Historically, critics such as Fiss (1984), Abel (1982), and Nader (1979) have identified this in relation to poorer litigants. Grillo (1991) has extended the analysis to women in compulsory mediation in cases of divorce. While it is true that structural inequalities are inherent in bilateral negotiation, the compulsory nature of mediation fuels inequality in increasing costs. It promises a form of 'resolution' but cannot provide redress in the case of intransigence.

Genn (2012) has applied the spirit of these critics to highlight the dangers of civil justice reform in the context of cuts to legal aid, opining 'the outcome of mediation, therefore, is not about *just* settlement it is *just about settlement.*' Informality can mask power differentials that are brought into sharper focus with the more formal procedural requirements of adjudication. It is in the nature of this informality that the distinction between a coercion into mediation by a judge and within mediation by a mediator who, in the case of compulsion, derives their authority from a judicial or court order, can be eroded. While a party may theoretically be free to leave a mediation, in the hands of an inexperienced mediator, a judicial direction to mediate compounded by fear of an adverse costs order may make parties feel pressure to settle. Where mediation is linked with the court process, parties may find it difficult to associate coercion from the judge with a reduction of the autonomy they feel within a mediation (Quek 2010). The greater the level of participation required, the more coercive the requirement to mediate becomes as a party is compelled to present a case in a manner not of their own choosing (Sherman 1993).

The case of *Churchill v Merthyr Tydfil* (2023) involved a broad interpretation of ADR to include a council's internal complaints procedure. It is arguable that a tenant could be required to exhaust a social landlord's internal complaints procedure before bringing a case for disrepair. In such circumstances, an unrepresented tenant could be profoundly disadvantaged against a social landlord who themselves created and managed an ICP process or could use it to delay a tenant's access to the courts until an assured shorthold tenancy had expired. As CEDR acknowledged in its intervention in *Churchill v Methyr Tydfil* (2023), mediation has been an adjunct to civil justice for over 35 years and actively encouraged by the judiciary since the Woolf reforms to civil justice. It is difficult to understand what a good process which has voluntariness as its hallmark gains by being compelled.

There may be cogent reasons for compelling parties who may be unaware of mediation to attend a mediation information and advice meeting as in Family Law or engage with ACAS as in employment law, but neither of these processes requires meeting with the person a party is litigating against outside the protection of the courts or has significant costs implications.

There is a strong case for engaging with a telephone mediation service in relation to small claims cases, especially where it is free, relatively non-onerous, and does not require meeting with an adversarial opponent, but compelling litigants to mediate, for instance, in cases of the recovery of a debt or litigation in which there is an allegation of bad faith is harder to justify.

An analogy is sometimes made with enforcing an arbitration clause, but whereas an arbitration agreement has a determinative outcome – the arbitration award – mediation does not. You may compel a party to meet with those they are litigating against but you cannot in conscience require them to settle. A compulsion to settle would fall foul of the principle articulated by Lord Justice Ackner in *Walford v Miles* (1992) that an 'agreement to agree' is unenforceable, and 'the concept of a duty to carry out negotiations in good faith in inherently repugnant to the adversarial position of [negotiating] parties.'

Change in the Nature of Mediation

The Civil Justice Council Final Report (2021) accepts that compelling mediation may require the safeguards of 'regulation,' but this is more than an incidental problem. With the current exception of family law, in which regulation has been necessitated by MIAMs, mediation in the UK is still largely unregulated, and membership of the Civil Mediation Council is voluntary. There is no requirement to be legally or professionally qualified.

Mandatory mediation would inevitably compromise confidentiality. Courts would need to have the power to inquire as to whether parties have attended mediation, if they have come to an agreement, and whether participation in mediation had been perfunctory or substantive. Not only would a closer and more coercive relationship with the courts require a change in the boundaries of 'confidentiality,' but it would be likely to favour mediation in its more evaluative forms.

In judicial ENE or FDR hearings, unrepresented litigants have the protection of a legally qualified judge, which would not be the case in court-annexed mediation. While mediators can, in appropriate circumstances, impart legal 'information,' they cannot give legal advice. In the case of mandatory mediation, especially where unaccompanied by legal advisors, this rule would prejudice the interests of litigants in person, who would no longer have the long stop of judicial determination of rights. Compulsion would either require a fundamental change to the nature of mediation to safeguard the interests of litigants in person or unfairly prejudice the right of an impecunious litigant to bring a case to court. The regulation necessary as an adjunct of compulsion would require a greater judicial scrutiny of the process of mediation, increase the dominance of the role of lawyers in mediation, and require a form of regulation and registration that might sit uncomfortably with the skills of non–legally qualified mediators. The language of 'rationing civil justice' is at odds with the constitutional right of access to the courts.

The arguments in favour of compulsion are deeply problematical when applied to litigants who have a reasoned objection to engaging in the process of dialogue with their adversaries, whether because of vulnerability, out of a belief that such an engagement may be used against them, or because they may require an authoritative and precedent-bearing declaration of their rights.

Argument becomes far more persuasive when applied to parties holding a brief mediation information and advice meeting at an interlocutory stage. Such a meeting could act as a filter to triage those cases suitable for mediation, those in which parties might like to try another form of ADR, and those which will need to proceed to trial.

Questions

1. **What criteria should be applied in deciding whether to compel a party to a) attempt to mediate and b) take part in an internal complaints procedure before issuing proceedings?**
2. **What effect does the case of *Churchill v Merthyr Tydfil* have on the *Halsey* criteria?**
3. **What do you think might be the advantages and disadvantages of requiring tenants to exhaust an internal complaints procedure before undertaking court proceedings for disrepair?**

Further Reading

Bartlet, M. (2019) 'Mandatory and the Rule of Law', *Amicus Curiae*, Series 2, 1 (1), 52–83.

De Girolomo, D. (2016) 'Rhetoric and Civil Justice: A Commentary on the Promotion of Mediation Without Conviction in England and Wales', *Civil Justice Quarterly* 35 (2), 162–185.

Masood, A. (2012) 'Implied Compulsory Mediation', *Civil Justice Quarterly* 31 (2), 1–8.

Quek Anderson, D. (2010) 'Mandatory Mediation: An Oxymoron – Examining the Feasibility if Implementing a Court-Mandated Mediation Programme', *Cardozo Journal Conflict Resolution* 11 (2), 479–510.

11 ADR Spectrum and Hybridity

This chapter considers the spectrum of dispute resolution mechanisms, the situations in which they may be appropriate, and some of the possibilities for varying them according to context.

Sander (1985), in the Pound conference, introduced the concept of the 'multi-door court house,' where disputants' settlement processes would be tailored to the dispute, with court adjudication, mediation, and arbitration as possible alternatives. One way of understanding the spectrum of processes is as a conflict ladder with which ADR can be used as a technique for the de-escalation of conflict. The first rung of the ladder would be unassisted negotiation, and authoritative court adjudication would be at the top.

Many of the steps in between might enable parties to de-escalate the conflict and take a step down the ladder. Early neutral evaluation or expert determination of an issue between two parties might persuade them to return to bilateral negotiation and enable them to settle the dispute on more advantageous terms than those resulting from litigation. But intransigence in the face of a proposal for settlement may have many sources. It may be possible to identify specific legal or factual barriers to settlement, even where parties are eager to find a resolution to their dispute. Specific processes may be designed or invoked to enable the parties to address these barriers and reach a successful resolution of the dispute.

Sander and Goldberg's (1994) suggest that the choice of dispute resolution process would be led by two lines of enquiry:

1. What are the disputants' goals in making a choice of forum?
2. If disputants are amenable to settlement what are the obstacles to settlement and how may they be overcome?

Non-adjudicative options

Negotiation

Bilateral negotiation is the simplest and most direct form of resolving conflict (see Chapter 3). By engaging directly with each other rather than appealing to an authoritative tribunal, parties are unencumbered by the constraints of adjudication and can

DOI: 10.4324/9781003112617-11

make their own decisions about what is important to them and the resolution of their dispute. Once litigation has been initiated, it may be settled by a formal process of offer and acceptance made between the parties and covering all relevant issues in the dispute. The result of negotiation may be brought before the court as a compromise agreement or the litigation discontinued. Approximately 90% to 95% of cases filed for court hearing will end by a process of negotiation or mediation (Sander 1985).

Collaborative Law

Collaborative law is a development of negotiation in English family law in which lawyers agree to meet and, if possible, negotiate an agreement and make a commitment that they will not represent parties at trial if they are unsuccessful. In essence, it involves a limited and voluntary curtailment of party autonomy. Because the curtailment is of a voluntary and limited nature, it does not curtail the constitutional right of access to the courts. This has the advantage of building a commitment to settlement among both parties and their legal teams but does not close the door to adversarial litigation if the process breaks down. In that case, both parties would need to hire fresh lawyers. In addition to lawyers, parties might appoint independent financial advisors, a family consultant, a child specialist, or an accountant who will together make up a collaborative team. In some cases, there may be a neutral facilitator or process manager appointed on behalf of both parties. Whilst relatively expensive on account of its extensive use of professional expertise, collaborative law is probably the closest to a gold standard in family law, combining the benefits of legal advice and maximising the mutual benefit while not depleting resources or undermining relationships by unnecessarily adversarial processes.

Collaborative law is be suitable for high-value cases in family law in which both parties have maintained some form of contact and recognise that they have more to lose than gain by litigation. It increases the likelihood of parties being able to keep some sort of relationship, maximises benefits in terms of tax and inheritance planning, and can help the separating couple make the transition from partners to co-parents.

Conciliation

Conciliation has, in the past, been used to cover much of the area for which mediation is now used. It has sometimes been used specifically to describe mediation in family matters (see, for instance, *Re D (Minors)* (1993)) and often used interchangeably with mediation. Brown and Marriot (2011) treat mediation as synonymous with conciliation. For the purposes of this chapter, 'conciliation' refers to a particular form of mediation, often conducted in more spartan terms, in which the mediator takes a more pro-active and evaluative role in settling the dispute. For CEDR (2023),

> Conciliation is a flexible process conducted confidentially in which a neutral person actively assists the parties in working towards a negotiated agreement of a dispute or difference, with the parties in ultimate control of the decision to settle and the terms of resolution.

Conciliation has a high success rate in consumer disputes and is, in essence, facilitative, taking place in individual (telephone or video conference) meetings with consequent savings in cost and time. Like mediation, it is flexible, voluntary, confidential, and without prejudice. The conciliator arranges to meet the parties individually, and, unlike a mediation, there is typically no joint session. The conciliation process comprises several phone calls over an agreed period of time. (CEDR cases must be completed in 90 days, but in most instances, the process takes around 50 days.) With some schemes, such as that offered to members of the National Association of Funeral Directors and their customers, if a solution is not agreed between the parties, the conciliator can offer a 'recommendation for settlement,' which becomes binding if accepted by both parties. Where there is no agreement between the parties, the customer may choose to proceed either to adjudication or to another forum for the resolution of the dispute, such as court.

In the UK, in workplace and employment matters, the Advisory Conciliation and Arbitration Service (ACAS) has had a statutory role to provide services to both sides of industry since 1976. ACAS is involved in all applications to the employment tribunal. An applicant may not institute employment tribunal proceedings without first obtaining an early conciliation certificate from ACAS. Although contact with ACAS is compulsory, participation in the process, usually by way of a telephone conversation with a conciliator, is voluntary. ACAS remains available throughout the life of any proceedings, and its good offices can be used for finalising an agreement. ACAS also offers advice on employment regulations, publishes codes of practice for fairness in the workplace, and supports the resolving of collective employment disputes.

Conciliation may be effective in many employment disputes, and the intervention of ACAS may be especially helpful when litigants in person bring cases against small employers, and neither party has legal expertise.

Early Neutral Evaluation

In early neutral evaluation (ENE), parties and their legal teams put their cases to a neutral or neutrals to obtain an evaluation of what might happen if a case comes to trial. This is generally a non-binding and without-prejudice process. This can take place as a private process in which parties agree to employ a neutral expert, or, in the USA, it may involve a specially constituted jury. ENE is frequently offered by dispute resolution organisations such as CEDR, the Chartered Institute of Arbitrators, and Barristers' Chambers.

Judicial Early Neutral Evaluation

Early neutral evaluation developed in the northern district of California (USA) out of the role of the special settlement master as a way of enabling parties to gain an objective insight into the strengths and weaknesses of their respective positions.

ENE may be used to determine or predict findings on matters of both fact and law. When both parties are committed to accepting the findings of an expert, it may be less expensive than a mediation. While the process may be an antidote to unrealistic expectations of disputants, lawyers are also the gatekeepers to it. The advantage of a court-directed ENE is that parties will have the opportunity to assess the strength of their cases, including the likely costs of taking the case to trial, even if their lawyers have not specifically requested this. By structured questioning inviting parties to a dispute to evaluate the strengths of their respective legal arguments and evidence and, where appropriate, giving an indication of how a case might be decided, ENE may encourage a return to bilateral negotiation and lead to the settlement of a case.

In England and Wales, Early Neutral Evaluation can take place as a result of the court's general powers of management under Civil Procedure Rules (CPR) 1998 Rule 3.1(2)(m), which make provision for the court to order ENE: the court may 'take any other step or make any other order for the purpose of managing the case and furthering the overriding objective, including hearing an Early Neutral Evaluation with the aim of helping the parties settle the case.'

In the Chancery Division, the opinion of the judge will be provided informally, and it may be necessary for a hearing of half a day. In the Queen's Bench Division, the judge can decide the form of the opinion given and consider an appropriate time estimate for the hearing, which may be more than half a day.

Regional Employment Tribunal Judge Burgher has incorporated 'Dispute Resolution Appointments' into employment tribunals as a way of seeking to resolve disputes prior to a contested hearing. These appointments are non-consensual, confidential, and evaluative; if these are unsuccessful, the case will be heard by a different judge.

Since 2006, employment tribunals have also offered judicial mediation. Around 65% of these cases have achieved successful settlement on the day of the mediation.

The outcome of judicial ENE is without prejudice unless privilege is waived and non-binding unless the parties agree. It is possible that agreed terms of ENE may be binding upon certain events or binding for a defined period, such as when an issue is dealt with on an interim basis.

There are currently pilot schemes in some county courts, and ENE has become established practice in the Chancery Division, commercial court, and technology and construction court but, with the exception of employment tribunals, has not been integrated into the civil justice system.

In *Lomax v Lomax* (2019), the Court of Appeal affirmed the court's power to order ENE, even when one party did not consent to the procedure. This offers an opportunity to understand the legal reasoning and attitude to evidence of their adversary. The process is most effective when deployed at an early stage and, even when it does not create an immediate settlement, may create a persuasive case for resolving a dispute. ENE may be particularly beneficial when the alternative is a more evaluative form of mediation, and there is little scope for a facilitator to help parties expand the size of the cake.

Dispute Resolution Hearings

These are small claims hearings taking place in the county court. The Civil Justice Council report (2021) records an experimental process in Hampshire,

Dorset, Wiltshire, and Romford involving a process in which cases in the small claims track are called in for a compulsory dispute resolution hearings (DRH). The process is led by a district judge, backed by the sanction that non-attending parties may have their claims struck out. These so-called DRH hearings appear to have enjoyed success, at least in certain hearing centres, and are within the scope of a review by a working party of the Civil Justice Council chaired by HH Judge Cotter.

Financial Dispute Resolution in the Family Court

Financial dispute resolution (FDR) is a form of court-assisted evaluation that can lead to a negotiated settlement in family proceedings. Family Practice Direction (2022) provides that parties and their legal advisors appear before a district judge after an initial directions hearing, offering an opportunity to 'reduce the tension that inevitably arises in family disputes.' In applications for financial relief in divorce proceedings, cases will be listed for a FDR as a compulsory stage if there is an application for a financial remedy. Parties are required to make full financial disclosure and exchange documents before the hearing. Meetings are generally attended by legal advisors who will address the judge. Separating parties will not be compelled to meet each other, although they may be given time for informal negotiations outside the court. The judge may question parties and will offer a non-binding indication of how they would approach the issues at trial. The FDR provides an opportunity to narrow the financial issues between the parties and to seek guidance from the judge on the legal context. Discussions taking place are without prejudice, and if the case settles, a financial agreement is drawn up between the parties that will become a consent order. If the discussions do not resolve the dispute, the case will be listed for hearing before a different judge.

Special Settlement Master

The role of settlement master has its roots in English Chancery practice and has been adopted and adapted in the USA in the case of complex civil cases, where Federal Rules of Civil Procedure provide for an appointment under Order 53.

The role includes recommending findings of fact on issues without a jury if appointment is warranted by:

1. Some special condition;
2. The need to perform an accounting or resolve a difficult computation of damages; or
3. Pre-trial and post-trial matters that cannot be effectively and timely addressed by an available district judge or magistrate judge of the district.

Civil procedure in England and Wales is increasingly proactive in encouraging parties to settle and may appoint a settlement master who has a dedicated role to facilitate settlement in complex civil cases.

Executive Tribunal

Modified settlement conferences have been devised in the USA to negotiate complex areas of law since the Telecredit and TRW patent infringement case in 1977. They are addressed to senior executives of the companies involved in a dispute. Whereas traditional negotiation takes place between the parties, in an executive tribunal, a neutral evaluator presents an assessment of a case and offers advice as to the likely outcome at trial to a team of those responsible for settling it. The presence of the neutral expert can modify the expectations of senior management teams and encourage them to move back into bilateral negotiation by considering a dispute within a pragmatic financial framework rather than predominantly legal one. In an executive tribunal, the parties and their lawyers negotiate the procedural rules. There is a much shorter time for preparation and limited discovery than in a court hearing. A short hearing (maximum of two days) is conducted in the presence of the neutral advisor. The case is presented to those with authority to settle. Lawyers, therefore, are encouraged to focus on their central or best issue, and parties then meet to subsequently negotiate a settlement. If they cannot settle, a neutral advisor may offer an opinion (Liebermann and Henry 1986). This process, conceptually akin to an evaluative form of mediation, is sometimes referred to as a mini-trial.

Executive tribunals are private, voluntary, and without prejudice and can be flexible and tailored to facilitate settlement. They are, however, expensive and involve lengthy preparation and dedicated time from senior staff. They generally involve a legal and rational analysis of a dispute and are suitable for complex and costly commercial court cases.

Summary Trial

In the USA, ADR practitioners, in particular Judicial Arbitration and Mediation Services (JAMS), have adopted procedures which mimic or model court processes but offer a non-binding or predictive outcome of what a court might decide. The process may provide a sober but costly analysis of issues that encourages parties to settle. Where civil law issues would be determined by jury trial in personal injury cases, parties may conduct a non-binding jury version of a mini trial. This procedure gives parties insight into probable trial outcomes while potentially saving on costs (or increasing them, if the parties do not settle) by reducing discovery and time for trial. Jurors, who are unaware that their verdict is non-binding, may be questioned about how they have come to a decision.

Adjudicative Forms of ADR

Ombudsman Process

Originally, the scope of ombudsmen (Old Norse *umboðsmaðr*, meaning 'representative' or 'proxy') was confined to public bodies. In Sweden, the parliamentary ombudsman was established by the Swedish Riksdag in 1809. The first UK ombudsman was appointed under the Parliamentary Commissioner Act 1967, and the jurisdiction of an ombudsman initially depended on an MP to refer a case of 'maladministration,' with the consent of the complainant. The role of ombuds has now been extended by analogy to include businesses and private sector organisations; the cost of investigation is met by the industry to reduce litigation and maintain public confidence.

The advent of the Parliamentary Commissioner for Administration can be traced back to Crichel Down and the recommendations of the Whyatt report (1961). The specific problem was that there was no mechanism for the in-depth investigation of maladministration. The challenge was how to provide this without undermining the role of MPs in following up complaints on behalf of their constituents by asking PQs and writing to ministers. The ombudsman is meant to be independent with investigatory powers but, crucially, without the power to impose a remedy – only to recommend one. The remit of the original parliamentary ombudsman has been extended: e.g. to the health service and local government. (The filter only applies to departments other than the NHS.) Most, if not all other public sector ombuds have been established by statute, either Westminster or devolved. The role of Financial Services Ombuds (2000) in providing oversight of financial services has produced a hybrid ombud with powers to grant financial compensation, but this is very much a special case because it is arguably part of a regulatory framework.

Although an anomaly in the common law system of England and Wales, there are many examples of an ombuds-like jurisdiction both in pre-modern Europe and other parts of the world. In classical Rome, the Roman Tribune had the authority to veto acts that infringed on the rights of the plebians. A prototype of ombudsmen is found in China during the Qin dynasty (221 BC) and in Korea (Amhaeng-eosa) during the Joseon dynasty, where an official directly appointed by the ruler was mandated to investigate government officials while travelling incognito. In Islamic law, the Al-Mazalim courts derive from the authority of the sovereign to redress injustice and operate as a parallel system to the Quda courts, which administer ordinary justice (Long 1973). The Turkish Diwan-al-Mazalim goes back to the second Caliph Umar (634–644).

The Ombuds in the public sector has statutory powers to adopt an investigative approach to complaints and imports an element of civil law into the investigation of maladministration in the UK. The process is more informal than court adjudication and does not require lawyers. The Financial Ombudsman Service resolves nearly 300,000 complaints each year, and the housing ombuds close some 15,000 cases. While the ombuds process is itself a type of ADR, an ombudsman may frequently encourage parties to try mediation to resolve a dispute amicably rather than by their determination.

Decisions are based on written evidence, and ombuds will only investigate after a complainant has taken steps to resolve the dispute by internal complaint procedures. An ombuds first needs to be satisfied that a complaint falls within their jurisdiction and that the service has been given an opportunity to remedy any maladministration. While most in-depth investigations involve written submissions, there may also be an opportunity for face-to-face meetings and interviews.

Ombuds processes form part of the oversight of significant public services under the Parliamentary Commissioners Act 1967, and their recommendations cannot be easily ignored. The Health Services Ombudsman covers all aspects of NHS. The Local Government Ombudsman (1974) oversees the work of local authorities. The Legal Services Ombudsman, under the Courts and Legal Services Act (1990), investigates complaints against solicitors, barristers, and patent attorneys. Public Service Ombuds have powers similar to those of a High Court judge and can compel witnesses and parties to give evidence and draw legal inferences from evidence given. One of the strengths of the ombuds system is that findings become a matter of public record. This contributes to public accountability and institutional learning and improvement. The Legal Services Ombudsman provides accountability for its decisions by making annual reports to Parliament and the Lord Chancellor/Ministry of Justice.

Remedies that an ombuds can provide include recommending compensation, an apology, and rectification of defects. The Financial Services Ombudsman can order compensation in their own right. In the case of the Pensions Ombudsman Scheme, decisions are binding on both parties. Decisions of the Financial Services Ombudsman and Legal Ombudsman are binding once a complainant has accepted the decision. Decisions will generally be binding on the public body or members of the industry concerned but do not preclude a complainant bringing a claim to a court. Public service ombuds have powers similar to those of a High Court judge. Decisions of ombuds in relation to the public sector will be subject to judicial review on the basis of irrationality, illegality, proportionality, and procedural impropriety. In *R (Crawford) v Legal Ombudsman* (2014) and *Hafiz & Haque Solicitors, R (On the Application Of) v Legal Ombudsman* (2014), the High Court quashed decisions of the Legal Ombudsman on the grounds of irrationality.

The term 'ombuds' is used for both public and private sector examples, but there is a fundamental distinction. While public sector ombuds exist under a statutory framework, private sector examples support industry standards under private law agreements. This impacts the limits of powers and methods of enforcement. While the jurisdiction of a private ombuds scheme is contractual, decisions of public ombuds will be subject to judicial review.

Public Service Ombudsmen

Parliamentary and Health Service Ombudsman (1967)
Local Government Ombudsman (1974)
Prisons and Probation Ombudsman (1994 extended to Probation 2001)
Housing Ombudsman (1996)
Northern Ireland Police (2000)
Scottish Public Service Ombudsman (2002)
Public Service Ombudsman for Wales (2005)
Legal Services Ombudsman (2010)

Private Sector Ombudsmen

Insurance (1981)
Banking (1986)
Building Societies (1986)
Investment (1989)
Pensions (1991)
Financial Services (2000)
Estate Agents (1990),
Property (1990)
Pensions (1991)
Financial Services (2000)
Telecommunications (2003)

Expert Determination

Expert determination is a private form of ADR in which parties submit their dispute to the determination of a technical expert, typically using the words 'who shall act as expert and not as arbitrator.'

Unlike arbitration, there is no statutory safety net for expert determination along the lines of the Arbitration Act 1996. It is governed purely by what the parties have agreed to in their contract. As an essentially private process, it is not bound by the rules of natural justice or the ECHR obligations of Article 6. Unlike arbitration, there are no statutory provisions regarding expert determination. Parties who refer a matter to an expert for decision can obtain a relatively quick, inexpensive, and binding decision 'on a matter that calls for informed judgment' (per Moore-Bick L.J. in *Premier Telecom Communications Group Ltd v Webb* (2014)).

As a contractual process, expert determination does not engage judicial review principles of natural justice. In *Bernhard Schulte v Nile Holdings* (2004), Cook J held, 'There is no requirement for the rules of natural justice or due process to be followed in an expert determination in order for that determination to be valid and binding between the parties.'

Expert determination may take place by agreement or according to an expert determination clause in a business contract. Disputants agree that an expert (or panel of experts) will be appointed to determine specific issues that are referred to them. There will be two contracts: one that governs the ADR clause and the second, between the parties and the expert, setting out the ambit of the expert's role. Experts may be from a variety of backgrounds, including accountants, surveyors, engineers, agronomists, architects, nutritionists, and lawyers. The process is most suitable for disputes in which the issues are of a highly technical or specialist nature.

Determinations made by experts may be binding on the parties or binding for a limited period. Parties agree on whether or not written reasons should be given for a decision. Limited grounds for challenging the expert's decision include:

1. Lack of jurisdiction;
2. Material departure from instructions (for example, breach of procedure);
3. The expert not being properly appointed;
4. Improper delegation of decision-making by the expert;
5. Actual bias on the part of the expert; and
6. Collusion or fraud, as in the decision of Denning LJ in *Campbell v Edwards* (1976).

The court may interpret the terms of a particular contract as permitting challenge where:

1. An obvious mistake is made by the expert. Per *Owen Pell Ltd v Bindi (London) Ltd* (2008), a mistake made in good faith by an expert will not invalidate the determination provided that the expert has answered the case put to them.
2. An error of law on an issue within the jurisdiction of the expert.
3. An error in interpreting words in the contract if within the expert's exclusive jurisdiction to decide what those words mean.
4. A lack of independence of the expert.
5. Apparent bias on the part of the expert.

Any clause for providing expert determination needs to be precisely drafted. In *Barclays Bank Plc v Nylon Capital LLP* (2011), the Court of Appeal considered whether there should be a stay of court proceedings pending expert determination under an agreement between the parties. It ruled that the expert in the case did not have jurisdiction to decide the dispute, so there should be no stay of the proceedings.

The advantages of expert determination can include:

- Finality.
- Effectiveness.
- Cost – which is less thSan arbitration.
- Speed.
- Confidentiality.
- Parties set the parameters of the determination while ceding the decision to an independent third party.
- Preservation of relationships.

Expert determination is commonly used in the following types of disputes:

- Valuation of shares in private companies.
- Valuations of partners' interests in business disputes.
- Construction and engineering disputes.

- IT and communication technology projects.
- Insurance disputes.
- Pension rights transfers.
- Price adjustments on takeovers.
- Rent reviews.

Mediation Arbitration Hybrids

Various hybrid forms attempt to combine mediation and arbitration.

In Med-Arb, the prevalent variant in the USA, a mediator becomes an arbitrator if they are unable to effect a settlement. In Japan, Hong-Kong, and Singapore, where a more evaluative form of mediation is practiced, this form of Med-Arb is frequently used in commercial disputes and is the prevalent form of dispute resolution in the China International Economic and Trade Arbitration Commission (CIETAC).

In Arb-Med, an arbitrator who is also an experienced mediator may raise the prospect of mediation during the preliminary arbitration conference. Alternatively, the arbitration takes place, but the award is sealed and maintained by the arbitrator. The parties then mediate in the knowledge that if they are unsuccessful in reaching an agreement, the arbitral award will be published, and any attempt at reaching a compromise cannot have an influence on the award.

In Arb-Med-Arb, a dispute is first referred to arbitration before mediation is attempted. If parties are able to settle their dispute through mediation, their mediated settlement may be recorded as a consent award. The consent award is generally accepted as an arbitral award is enforceable in over 170 countries under the New York Convention. If parties are unable to settle their dispute through mediation, they may continue with the arbitration proceedings.

In others models, when mediation is unsuccessful, it is followed by arbitration conducted by another person. Alternatively, a mediator may offer an 'outcome settlement,' and if this is not accepted by both parties, the case proceeds to arbitration.

These processes are particularly prevalent in commercial hearings in China, where 'med-arb' is an entrenched preference for resolving disputes' (Palmer and Roberts 2020). The dual role of mediator-arbitrator is consonant with a legal culture predicated on settlement in the interests of a 'harmonious society.' The ideal outcome is that of an agreement reached in mediation, and this is made more likely by the threat of an imposed settlement when the function of arbitration is to make a mediated outcome more likely. Yong'an and Ming (2023) define four separate categories in a Chinese context:

1. Pure mediation followed by arbitration pure mediation. The parties initiate mediation to resolve their dispute and then proceed to arbitration after mediation fails or is successful.

2. Med-Arb-Diff-Recommendation. The mediator submits a proposal for an award to the arbitrator prior to the commencement of the arbitration proceedings, based, *inter alia*, on the facts of the case known during the mediation proceedings.
3. Med-Arb-Opt Out. A pure mediation is followed by arbitration, with the parties having the right to reject the conversion of the previous mediator into an arbitrator.
4. Mediation and last-offer arbitration. This is a hybrid process like the original Med-Arb process; their difference is in the arbitration phase. If the parties do not reach a voluntary settlement through mediation, each party submits a last offer to the mediator-arbitrator, who must choose between one of two final offers. This process limits the discretion of the arbitrator to decide what they believe to be the most appropriate solution since the award must be limited to one of the offers.

These are all hybrid processes in the sense that they are neither fully facilitative nor fully adjudicative. There are a number of dangers in combining processes in this way. Mixing processes may compromise the integrity of both mediation and arbitration. While mediation is consensual and non-judicial, arbitration is confrontational and adversarial. Whereas mediation involves optimal settlement between parties, arbitral authority is derived from a contractual relationship. Private meetings are indispensable to mediation but anathema to arbitration. There is a tension between the confidentiality required in mediation and the fairness required of an arbitrator. A mediator turned arbitrator will find it difficult to hear evidence with an open mind; they will either be obliged to exclude information heard in confidence during the mediation stage (a nearly impossible task as this has not been accepted by the other party), or, if evidence is taken into account without the consent of the other party, the fairness of the arbitral process is compromised. Med-Arb encourages parties to inflate claims in the mediation stage to strengthen their case at subsequent arbitration. While this kind of mediation with 'sharp teeth' may be a common practice in civil law jurisdictions, in Med-Arb, judges and arbitrators are used to taking on the role of mediator to encourage settlement between the parties during the proceedings, so it is less common in a common law context.

Consumer Adjudication

Consumer adjudication offers a form of redress for individuals bringing complaints against companies for participating schemes. While similar to arbitration, the process is not subject to the Arbitration Act 1996.

These schemes invite the consumer and subscribing company to submit evidence weighed up by an independent adjudicator. Schemes are generally free to the consumer or available at a modest cost. In many of these schemes, hearings are conducted entirely on the papers, and contact between the parties and dispute resolution services is limited to conversations with an administrator. When an adjudicator has issued a written decision, including their reasoning, a consumer has the option to accept it, in which case it becomes binding on the trader or, alternatively, reject it and pursue other remedies, including going to court. From the perspective of the consumer, an individual may be able to find practical redress more readily than in court adjudication. A remedy in the CISAS scheme, for instance, might be for a telecommunication provider to send an engineer to reconnect an individual to fast-fibre broadband or to reposition a receiver. A funeral services adjudication might include a written apology in a particular form and the provision of a memorial. Companies benefit from feedback that allows them to identify problems and patterns of complaint across the industry, which may lead to improved customer satisfaction and internal complaint handling and reduce potential future complaints.

In 2022, CEDR had 24,000 cases registered, resulting in over 7,000 decisions, which would have required an estimated 706 judicial days to process in the court system, at a cost of nearly two million GBP. This work relates to 18 industries, including schemes for funeral services, gambling and lotteries, private health care, OFSTED inspections, jewelry, garages, flights, holidays, surveyors, solicitors, water, and sewage.

Construction Industry Adjudication

The Housing Grants, Construction and Regeneration Act 1996 provides for a specific right to refer construction disputes to adjudication. The scheme is intended to avoid the cost and delay of going to court and to prevent the stalling of construction contracts. The decision by an independent third party, generally from a construction industry background, is binding on an interim basis until determined by the court or arbitration or resolved by agreement. The underlying principle informing construction adjudication is 'pay now, argue later' (*RJT Construction Engineers Ltd v DM Engineering Northern Ireland Ltd* (2002)). All construction contracts must include written terms that enable a party to give notice of their intention to refer a matter to adjudication, provide a timetable for the appointment of an adjudicator, require the adjudicator to reach a decision within 28 days, permit the adjudicator to extend the period by 14 days with the permission of the party referring the dispute, impose a duty to act impartially, and enable the adjudicator to ascertain facts and the law and to correct clerical errors. Where a construction contract does not include such a clause, the terms of the Scheme for Construction Contracts under Section 108 of the act are implied. An adjudicator may be named in the construction contract or be selected from a nominating body such as AICA, RIBA, RICS, CEDR, or TeCSA.

Adjudication is widely used regarding payments, construction delays, construction defects, breach of contract, and professional negligence. Fees are typically between £250 and £350 per hour. Parties are jointly and severally liable for the fees, which the adjudicator may apportion between the parties.

There is a duty on the adjudicator to decide matters impartially and to avoid incurring unnecessary expense. Reasons are only required if one of the parties requests them, and there is no obligation to have an oral hearing. There is no right of appeal, and decisions can be enforced in the High Court, generally in the Technology and Construction Court.

Rent a Judge

In some states in the USA, including California and Texas, parties can employ a third-party referee appointed by the court. Unlike an arbitrator, however, the 'rent a judge' is an official element of the state court system, and decisions can be appealed in the state courts (Palmer and Roberts 2020). Many of the appointments are made through Judicial Arbitration and Mediation Services (JAMS). Referees are generally retired judges or senior lawyers, appointed with the consent of both parties. Both parties present evidence to the referee, and decisions are appealable on the grounds of factual evidence and applicable law. This process in the UK would require primary legislation and fall outside the generally accepted interpretations of the rule of law. It would both privilege rich litigants and detract from the public accountability of the judiciary.

Ministry of Justice Call for Evidence on Dispute Resolution (2021)

MOJ's summary of responses to its Call for Evidence on Dispute Resolution (2022) identified a number of themes.

The emotional state of the parties, understanding of the process, financial considerations, lack of awareness, and safeguarding issues are all factors influencing the engagement of participants. Respondents highlighted the complexity of the dispute resolution landscape as a significant barrier for vulnerable parties.

Most responses supporting mandatory ADR came from consumers, the public services sector, and insurers while unsupportive respondents came mainly from the legal profession, academia, and the advice sector.

Many respondents expressed concern over the lack of regulation and support for more training and continuing professional development. Alternatives to statutory regulation proposed included the Ministry of Justice setting qualifying conditions for dispute resolution providers, which could be monitored and enforced by independent bodies.

Respondents stated that the cost effectiveness of dispute resolution in comparison with litigation was contingent on several factors. In low-value claims conducted by litigants in person, court costs are frequently lower than using dispute resolution. When dispute resolution is unsuccessful in resolving or narrowing the dispute and recourse to court is required, the overall costs of achieving resolution may be increased. In arbitration, respondents recognised that the costs of these processes were usually high, but they could deliver savings through their capacity to shorten timescales for decisions.

Current costs ranges from hourly rates of around £100 for non-lawyer mediators to several thousand pounds for experienced lawyers in arbitration cases. There are some examples of pro bono mediation in family or not-for-profit mediation services. NHS Resolution, for instance, pays the costs of dispute resolution for litigants in person and mediator fees and other expenses if liability has been admitted in full.

A number of respondents indicated that minority groups may not be benefitting from dispute resolution services and referred to lack of diversity in dispute resolution providers, particularly in terms of race and ethnicity.

An ombudsman scheme identified cultural barriers as including a deference to authority alongside a fear that complaining could have negative repercussions affecting future care or access to services. Academic respondents identified black and minority ethnic groups as having low levels of trust in authority and take-up of dispute resolution.

Case types considered not suitable for dispute resolution included test cases; disputes around discrimination and whistleblowing; cases that give rise to regulatory issues and those for which dispute resolution would be contrary to the public interest: for example, where a confidential settlement could conceal serious and repetitive wrongdoing.

Respondents discussed dispute resolution as part of a whole approach to justice. Many saw the need for dispute resolution as an integrated pathway to justice which should also include early legal advice; support from professionals from other sectors such as benefits, mental health, and employment; dispute resolution as a pathway to litigation.

Respondents identified a gap in the housing and property sector: private landlords are not required to join any redress scheme, and they are not covered by any dispute resolution provision or ombudsman.

Conclusion

In the taxonomy offered in this chapter, the primary distinction is between adjudicative and non-adjudicative forms. Each has its own benefits and challenges. Non-adjudicative forms are generally more conducive to maintenance of relationships while adjudicative forms have the benefit of certainty and finality. Arbitration, while resembling adjudication in court, has the benefits of privacy, finality, and speed.

The distinction, however, breaks down in relation to Med-Arb, which contains elements of both. Non-binding forms of evaluation are similar to mediation in enabling parties to form a more realistic view of their prospects of success and therefore return to a form of negotiation and settle. While, in theory, as in Sander and Goldberg's (1994) *Fitting the Forum to the Fuss*, parties have the right to choose the system that is most suited to them, in practice, the choice of dispute resolution procedure is likely to be determined by institutional parties. An individual in dispute with a telecommunication company over a contract for services may have little practical choice but to accept the independent scheme which the company subscribes to – at least, as an initial avenue if they do not want to incur costs and penalties. One of the advantages of ADR is that its categories are not closed systems, and courts and disputants will continue to develop and devise new ways of resolving intractable disputes. At the same time there has been a process of formalisation and judicialisation of dispute resolution systems.

Questions

What type of dispute resolution process might be used in each of the following circumstances? Give reasons for your choice and explain the merits and limitations of the process involved.

1. **A dispute between a builder and her sub-contractor over the value of the work performed where there is no dispute as to the existence of a contract but widely differing opinions of the value of the work performed.**

2. **A dispute between separating spouses over the value of a divorce settlement where spouses are also business partners with shares in a family firm.**
3. **A claim for unfair dismissal where the employer is adamant that he will not reinstate the employee, and the employee needs a reference from the employer.**
4. **A personal injury claim taking place at work where issues include liability; quantum, possibly contributory negligence; and whether the employer had provided a safe system of work.**
5. **A dispute between a homeowner and their insurer of 20 years as to whether the owner has been unfairly denied a no-claims bonus after speaking to the insurer about a possible claim for flooding which was not pursued.**

Further Reading

Menkel-Meadow, C. (2020) 'Hybrid and Mixed Dispute Resolution Processes: Integrity of Process Pluralism'. In F. Moscati, M. Palmer & R. Roberts (Eds.), *Comparative Dispute Resolution: A Research Handbook*. Edward Elgar Publishing.

Palmer, M. & Roberts, S. (2020) *Dispute Processes, ADR and the PrimaryS0 Forms of Decision-Making* (3rd ed). Cambridge University Press.

Sander, F. E. A. & Goldberg, S. (1994) 'Fitting the Forum to the Fuss: A User Friendly Guide to Selecting an ADR Procedure', *Negotiation Journal* 10 (1), 49–68.

12 Mediation Ethics

For the purposes of this chapter, 'ethics' is used to describe morality as applied to the professional role of mediator. Any profession needs a shared set of values and enforceable standards of behaviour as a part of its boundary definition. Mediation in the UK (although not to the same extent in Ireland, Italy, or the USA) remains a rather disparate set of practices that operate outside the scope of professional regulation. The need for professional guidelines is as much about protecting the reputation of a professional body as about providing a guarantee of security for those using it. The scope of professional ethics depends on the shared understanding of the role involved. This, in turn, may vary according to the style of mediation adopted. In both the UK and abroad, legal ethics have developed in the context of strong professional self-regulation over centuries, whereas the current state of regulation regarding mediation in the UK is almost non-existent. While many lawyer-mediators may be bound by the regulation of the Law Society or Bar Council, ethics are poorly equipped to deal with non-adversarial contexts. Mediation ethics will need to be developed and judged according to the purpose and justification of ADR which, in significant ways, diverges from that of adjudication. If the legitimacy of ADR depends on the values of democratic and empowering participation, informed consent, and quality of solutions (Menkel-Meadow 1997), this will need to be manifested in its ethical regulation.

In the case of third-party facilitated negotiation, there is no single body with the authority to regulate those holding themselves out as mediators. Insofar as guidance offered by the Bar Council and Law Society is helpful, it often relates to a duty owed to safeguard the best interests of the individual client rather than the integrity of a process of negotiation in which disputants compromise their interests in the shadow of the law. Over the last ten years, there has been a significant increase in non-lawyer mediators in civil mediation. In a context where anyone can legally hold themselves out to be a mediator, the adoption of a code of conduct still remains a voluntary decision.

Ethical norms derive from a multiplicity of sources. They may comprise binding legal norms; guidance offered via professional bodies with explicit or implicit sanctions for breach, norms flowing from responsibility that are attributed to a professional role where deviation incurs the risk of professional and reputational damage, contractually accepted commitments, and commitments to fairness

DOI: 10.4324/9781003112617-12

and equity that are internally binding in conscience. Mediation is, in essence, third-party facilitated negotiation. Parties remain free to settle or withdraw from the process at any time. While some commentators (Shapira 2016) have questioned whether mediator impartiality/neutrality is an intrinsic part of this process in terms of the factual-descriptive definition of mediation, for the purposes of this chapter, I consider professional integrity, confidentiality, impartiality, fairness of process, and party autonomy all core ethical imperatives. Without these ethical values and others flowing from them, including competence, disclosure of conflicts of interest, diligence, honesty, and respect (Shapira 2021), mediation, however effective, would be defective in the sense that a mediator would be falling short of professional expectations.

Solicitors

The Law Society delegated its regulatory powers to the Solicitors Regulation Authority in 2007. Solicitors currently provide legal service under the Solicitors Regulation Authority Code of Conduct. Its most recent 21st version (October 2019) contains six mandatory principles (SRA Principles), supplemented by mandatory outcomes (SRA outcomes) and indicative behaviours (SRA indicative behaviours) that all solicitors should comply with:

SRAP 1: To uphold the constitutional principle of the rule of law and the proper administration of justice;
SRAP 2: To uphold public trust and confidence in the solicitor's profession and in legal services provided by authorised persons;
SRAP 3: o act with independence;
SRAP 4: To act with honesty;
SRAP 5: To act with integrity; and
SRAP 6: To act in a way that encourages equality, diversity, and inclusion.

These essentially give support to an expanded definition of these ethical imperatives, which derive from the implications of professional integrity.

A solicitor may offer services as a mediator, neutral evaluator, adjudicator, or expert determiner but, in doing so, must avoid any conflict of interest with other aspects of their practice. In acting as a mediator or ADR practitioner, a solicitor has a duty to ensure that any dispute resolution activities comply with these duties of independence, honesty and integrity, equality, and upholding the rule of law. A solicitor acting as a mediator is also bound to ensure that they are not subject to any conflict of interest (Chapter 3 SRA Code of Conduct).

If a solicitor is advising a client about options for dispute resolution, they would be potentially negligent not to advise on ADR options. Dyson LJ set out in *Halsey v Milton Keynes NHS Trust* (2004) that 'all members of the legal profession who conduct litigation should now routinely consider with their clients whether their disputes are suitable for ADR.' The Law Society has established specialist panels of mediators.

Bar Council

While US lawyer-mediators are required to comply with the American Bar Association (2005) Model Standards of Conduct for Mediators, there is no direct equivalent for the English Bar. The Bar Standards Board (BSB) has not published specific ethical standards for barristers practicing as mediators, but its Handbook (2024) considers that the standards applicable would apply whatever the function of a barrister is and contains ten core duties (BSB core duties), which cover all aspects of practice; a set of mandatory rules (BSB rules) and outcomes to be achieved (BSB outcomes). Barristers are required to act with independence and impartiality in whatever role they assume. A barrister who breaches one of these core duties is subject to sanctions for bringing the profession into disrepute.

The Bar Code of Conduct (2023) Version 7 sets out ten core duties for Barristers. CD2, CD3, CD4, CD5, CD6, CD7, CD8, and CD10 are all potentially engaged in mediation.

These are all uncontestable general ethical principles but have not been developed by the Bar Council in a distinctive way that applies to the specifics of the professional practice of mediation. For example, the best interests of the client (CD2) may legitimately be viewed differently by the barrister in a court proceeding and a mediator providing mediation services to two or more clients with divergent interests. 'Competent service' (CD7) and acting with integrity (CD3) may require different courses of action depending on the role performed (e.g. a mediator might be obliged to withdraw from the mediation in certain events: for example, upon learning information about hidden assets in a private meeting that he is prevented from sharing, yet failure to do so would undermine the integrity of the mediation).

CD1. You must observe your duty to the court in the administration of justice.
CD2. You must act in the best interests of each client.
CD3. You must act with honesty and with integrity.

This would include ensuring that mediation and other forms of ADR are not used for an improper purpose such as delay or inappropriate discovery of business information in the absence of a genuine willingness to settle.

CD4. You must maintain your independence.
CD5. You must not behave in a way which is likely to diminish the trust and confidence which the public places in you or in the profession.
CD6. You must keep the affairs of each client confidential.
CD7. You must provide a competent standard of work and service to each client.
CD8. You must not discriminate unlawfully against any person.
CD9. You must be open and cooperative with your regulators.
CD10. You must take reasonable steps to manage your practice, or carry out your role within your practice, competently and in such a way as to achieve compliance with your legal and regulatory obligations.

Many chambers now offer ADR services, including mediation. A specialist barrister may provide an expert opinion as part of an early neutral evaluation where the law is unclear.

ADR and the Practice of Law

Some commentators consider mediation wholly distinct from legal practice while others in the USA (Menkel-Meadow 1997) argue that some forms of mediation involve, in part, 'the practice of law.' This will become increasingly important in the context of the closer relationship between mediation and adjudication that may arise with mandatory mediation.

Non-lawyer mediators could be prohibited from drafting mediated settlement agreement in jurisdictions which reserve the drafting of legal agreements to lawyers alone, and even lawyer-mediators would be unwise to do so out of the risk of violating impartiality. While lawyer-mediators may find it difficult to define the boundary between offering legal information (acceptable) and legal advice (unacceptable), non-lawyer mediators offering either information or advice risk straying into the unauthorised practice of law.

One of the most important duties of a mediator (whether or not it falls within the practice of law) is to explain clearly the nature of the role they are offering to play, as this is what will shape their ethical responsibilities. This should be made clear prior to parties signing the agreement to mediate, which should be accompanied by any code of conduct which binds the mediator. Mediators should draw attention, explicitly, to a party's right to withdraw from the process at any time. This is an intrinsic aspect of safeguarding party autonomy.

The extent to which evaluation is acceptable in mediation depends on culture and jurisdiction.

Providing legal information as such is not practicing law. Some forms of 'soft evaluation' (reality checking) can be done by both lawyers and non-lawyers on the basis of their knowledge and experience. Supporting parties in writing their settlement agreements will not necessarily amount to practicing law. Shapira (2021) affirms the importance of practitioners distinguishing between legal practice and mediation practice as a matter of integrity. While providing legal information and questioning legal premises are acceptable, there may come a point at which explaining the normative framework surrounding a dispute crosses the boundary into the provision of legal advice. Current proposals for automatic reference of small claims to mediation may need to confront this issue in deciding which mediators can be accredited in the court process.

Civil Mediation Council

The Civil Mediation Council (CMC) is the leading body representing the professional interests of mediators in the UK. It was established in 2003 under the chairmanship of Lord Justice Sir Brian Neill to promote civil and commercial mediation as alternatives to litigation. It aims to provide a single unified voice for civil and commercial mediation in the United Kingdom. The CMC has adopted the EU Model Code of Conduct for Mediators and expects its mediators to adopt this code or a code of equivalent rigour but does not specify what this should be. The CMC offers a Members' Complaints Resolution Service which enables their clients to resolve conflicts that are not resolved through mediation providers' internal complaints process. This provides for resolution via a fixed-fee, time-limited mediation.

EU Code of Conduct

EU Code of Conduct (ECOC) (2018) includes competence, independence, fairness of process, impartiality, and confidentiality within its scope.

For the purpose of the code, mediation is defined as:

> any structured process, however named or referred to, whereby two or more parties to a dispute attempt by themselves, on a voluntary basis, to reach an agreement on the settlement of their dispute with the assistance of a third person – hereinafter 'the mediator.'
>
> Mediators shall be competent and knowledgeable in the process of mediation. Relevant factors include proper training and continuous updating of their education and practice in mediation skills, having regard to any relevant standards or accreditation schemes.
>
> (1.1)

> Mediator must verify that they have the appropriate background and competence to conduct mediation in a given case before accepting an appointment. Upon request, they must disclose information concerning their background and experience to the parties.
>
> (1.2).

A mediator must be open and honest about their fees:

> Where not already provided, mediators must always supply the parties with complete information as to the mode of remuneration which they intend to apply. They must not agree to act in a mediation before the principles of remuneration have been agreed by all parties concerned.
>
> (1.3)

Under ECOC, ADR 'Mediators may promote their practice provided that they do so in a 'professional, truthful and dignified way' (1.4).

> A mediator has a continuing obligation of independence and neutrality and must disclose any conflicts of interest. 'In such cases the mediator may only agree to act to act if he is certain of being able to carry out the mediation with full independence in order to ensure complete impartiality and the parties explicitly consent.
>
> (2.1)

'A mediator may only agree to act or continue to act if he is certain of being able to carry out the mediation with full independence in order to ensure complete impartiality and the parties explicitly consent.' Illustrative circumstances include:

- any personal or business relationship with one or more of the parties;
- any financial or other interest, direct or indirect, in the outcome of the mediation,
- the mediator, or a member of his firm, having acted in any capacity other than mediator for one or more of the parties.

(2.1)

Impartiality requires that the mediator 'must at all times act and endeavour to be seen to act, with impartiality towards the parties and be committed to serve all parties equally with respect to the process of mediation' (2.2).

Under the ECOC, a mediator is responsible for the fairness of the process and for ensuring the parties have understood the characteristics of mediation and the role of the mediator as an aspect of 'party autonomy.' There is a specific reference both to the rule of law and power imbalances.

> The mediator shall conduct the proceedings in an appropriate manner, taking into account the circumstances of the case, including possible power imbalances and the rule of law.
>
> Fairness of procedure includes a commitment to 'taking into account the circumstances of the case including possible imbalances of power and any wishes the parties may express, the rule of law and the need for a prompt settlement of the dispute.
>
> (3.1)

> Fairness of process may also require the exercise of legal judgment: 'The mediator must inform the parties, and may terminate the mediation, if:
>
> - a settlement is being reached that for the mediator appears unenforceable or illegal.
>
> (3.2)

The Code of Conduct also makes specific reference to the right of parties to 'withdraw from the mediation at any time without giving any justification' (3.3).

The ECOC also covers confidentiality, both of the whole process and of private (UK) or caucus (USA) meetings.

> The mediator must keep confidential all information, arising out of or in connection with the mediation, including the fact that the mediation is to take place or has taken place, unless compelled by law or public policy grounds. Any information disclosed in confidence to mediators by one of the parties shall not be disclosed to the other parties without permission, unless compelled by law.
>
> (4)

Lawyers Acting as Mediators in the USA

The American Arbitration Association, the American Bar Association's Section of Dispute Resolution, and the Association for Conflict Resolution prepared a Model Standards of Conduct for Mediators in 1995 and revised it in 2005.

In the USA, the CPR-Georgetown Commission on Ethics and Standards in ADR has developed a proposed model rule addressing the significant ethical and professional responsibility issues faced by lawyers who act as third-party neutrals. The commission comprises a group of private and public lawyers, academics from Georgetown, Ohio State School of Law, and Pennsylvania. The model rule includes the requirement of diligence and competence, the need for confidentiality, the requirement of impartiality, the avoidance of conflict of interest, clarity regarding arrangements for fees, and fairness and integrity of process.

In the USA, at least 27 states now have statutory or judicially sanctioned standards of conduct, including formal disciplinary boards for court-appointed mediators (Kallipetis 2015).

The USA Uniform Mediation Act standardising the mediation process and establishing privilege for mediators and mediation participants has been adopted by 13 states, including Georgia, Hawaii, Idaho, Sout Dakota, Utah, Vermont, Iowa, New Jersey, Ohio, Washington, Illinois, and Nebraska, as well as the District of Colombia.

The ABA Model Rules of Professional Conduct (2024) require mediators to distinguish their role clearly from that of representing clients as counsel. Rule 2.4 regarding third-party neutrals provides:

> (a) A lawyer serves as a third-party neutral when the lawyer assists two or more persons who are not clients of the lawyer to reach a resolution of a dispute or other matter that has arisen between them. Service as a third-party neutral may include service as an arbitrator, a mediator or in such other capacity as will enable the lawyer to assist the parties to resolve the matter.
>
> (b) A lawyer serving as a third-party neutral shall inform unrepresented parties that the lawyer is not representing them. When the lawyer knows or reasonably should know that a party does not understand the lawyer's role in the matter, the lawyer shall explain the difference between the lawyer's role as a third-party neutral and a lawyer's role as one who represents a client.

Summary of Core Ethical Dimensions of Mediation

The nature of mediation as third-party facilitated negotiation raises several distinct issues, arising from the nature of the role, that are common to the various frameworks discussed. Professional integrity, confidentiality, impartiality, party autonomy, and fairness of process all raise significant challenges. The limits of confidentiality will only be addressed briefly here as they are covered more fully in Chapter 9 in the context of mediation privilege. Dilemmas arise when these principles conflict with each other.

Core Ethical Dimensions

- Professional integrity.
- Confidentiality.
- Impartiality.
- Party autonomy.
- Fairness of process.

Professional Integrity

Professional integrity includes commitment to the role and profession of mediator, including core competence and guaranteeing the integrity of the mediation process. A mediator has the responsibility to explain the nature of their role and its difference from that of a judge or lawyer. For lawyer-mediators, this will involve ensuring that their role will not conflict with any role as a lawyer. Professional integrity and competence are core requirements in any code of practice while what exactly they require is contested. Professional competence implies that a mediator should have adequate knowledge, skills, and experience in the area that they are holding themselves out as providing. Mediators should have adequate training and take part in continuing professional development. Mediators and mediation providers should ensure that parties have adequate information about a proposed mediator and the mediation process to ensure that they can make an informed choice. Mediators need to communicate clearly to their clients the nature of the service, the role they are providing, and how this differs from adjudication. While in family mediation, mediators need to be a member of a body affiliated with the Family Mediation Council (FMC) to take part in legally aided processes, in civil mediation, membership in the CMC is voluntary.

Professional integrity includes exercise of discretion on the basis of good reasons and responsibility for process. On the basis of such integrity, a mediator should refuse to accept a case for mediation when there is a clear conflict of interest and terminate a mediation to prevent an illegal outcome (Shapira 2021).

Confidentiality

This issue is dealt with more completely in Chapter 9 on mediation privilege. There are several overlapping strands to privacy in mediation:

1. Materials disclosed to a legal representative will be covered by legal professional privilege. This includes material disclosed when a mediator is present.
2. Communications made during a mediation with the aim of compromising a claim will be covered by without-prejudice privilege.
3. The mediation contract will almost certainly include confidentiality as an express term.

4. A mediator has a professional duty to maintain confidentiality.
5. Some commentators have argued for a specific mediation privilege.

The starting point for confidentiality is that information arising in the mediation is confidential to those taking part in the mediation, and material shared with disputants in a private meeting is subject to an additional layer of confidentiality and should not be shared with other disputants or beyond the mediation. Problems arise when a mediator feels a conflict between a ground rule of confidentiality and a moral or legal duty to disclose. There are certain clear exceptions to the duty of confidentiality. In civil mediations, money laundering regulations, including the Proceedings of Crime Act 2002, provide a clear exception, and in family mediations, there is an overriding obligation to breach confidentiality when failing to do so might risk significant harm to a child's welfare. Blake (2016) lists three specific exceptions to an express confidentiality clause:

- Where parties agree it is important that a public rather than a private meeting takes place during the mediation to air issues that affect a number of interested parties (e.g. where a meeting takes place in a planning or environmental dispute);
- Where the parties want a provision of their settlement agreement to be made public (e.g. in regulatory matters or where the provision of a public apology is part of an agreement); and
- Where the parties agree that confidential information given during a private mediation can be revealed to an opposing party.

In private (caucus) meetings, more complex issues arise. Mediators may either adopt an approach of saying everything in private meetings is confidential, except where otherwise explicitly stated, or adopt an approach of what the Harvard Project on Negotiation has referred to as 'noisy translation,' in which the mediator asks parties to be explicit about what disputants do not want shared and apply their discretion as regards sharing other details. Problems here may arise when there is a disjuncture between what is said in private and public meetings or when a mediator has been shown material that contradicts what has been communicated directly between the parties. Here, a duty of confidentiality conflicts with a duty of fairness, integrity, and party autonomy; by remaining silent, a mediator may become party to a deception. It might also undermine the other parties' autonomy or self-determination (making an uninformed decision, undermining the integrity of process).

While the dilemma can be resolved by persuading the misleading party to share the undisclosed material or to correct an erroneous assertion, if a disputant refuses to do this, the mediator may have no alternative but to withdraw from the mediation as the only way of maintaining their professional integrity.

Problems with confidentiality arise when the process breaks down, and a party may wish to adduce evidence from the mediation: for instance, on the terms of a proposal or agreement or when a party in the dispute attempts to call a party to the mediation as a witness.

A further ethical dilemma may arise if a mediator becomes aware that there is a significant overlap between the bottom lines of both parties and is asked informally to offer guidance or advice. Here, there may be a conflict between neutrality and fairness – how far should a mediator go in redressing power imbalances (or perceived power imbalances) between the parties?

Impartiality

The more proactive a style adopted by a mediator, the more important impartiality becomes. Impartiality and neutrality are sometimes used interchangeably. Whereas neutrality implies freedom from conflict of interest, impartiality is sometimes used as a more positive value to imply the equal treatment of all parties, here during the process of mediation. The EU Code includes a duty to 'serve all parties equally' under impartiality (2.2). The ABA Model Standards define impartiality as 'freedom from favoritism, bias or prejudice.' Kallipetis (Richbell 2015) summarises the difference between interpretations of the role:

> [S]ome commentators argue that neutrality means that mediators should prevent their own values from biasing the outcome. Other argue that neutrality requires a structuring of process that will ensure meaningful participation, informed decision-making and a reasonable balance of power between the parties to promote fairness of process.

While some commentators, such as Boulle and Nesic (2001), consider impartiality a core requirement in mediation, in the sense that its absence would fundamentally undermine the nature of the process, and 'it is inconceivable that parties could waive the impartiality requirement without fundamentally altering the nature of the mediation process.' Shapira (2016) considers that 'a biased mediation process is flawed but does not lose its identity as mediation.' Although research into unconscious bias suggests that pure impartiality is impossible, it nevertheless remains an important ideal to be guided by. In some community mediations, mediators may be assertive in ensuring that parties act in a way that respects the core principles of equality and non-discrimination and withdraw from a mediation if it is impossible to counter discriminatory behaviour. Legal codes of conduct tend to emphasise the duty to an individual client and fail to capture the importance of impartiality when the role of a mediator involves a duty to several clients with seemingly opposing interests or helping them expand the size of the pie or assets available for allocation between them.

While mediators do not impose solutions, their range of interventions influences the negotiating process in subtle and varied ways. In seeking to be impartial and equidistant from the parties, mediators have a responsibility to interrogate their own values and to become aware of their own psychological preference, including unconscious or hidden biases. Kallipetis in Richbell (2015) suggests the formulation of a mediator's role of impartiality as 'the mediator is impartial as to the outcome of the mediation but cannot be neutral as regards the facts of the dispute,' but a mediator would be compelled to terminate a mediation if it would lead to an illegal outcome.

As a function of independence, a mediator is required to ensure that they ae not involved in a conflict of interest with any of the parties. A mediator should not act if there is a conflict of interest with a party: for instance, if they have any financial stake in a dispute or they have acted for one of the disputants on a related matter. Where there is a perceived conflict of interest – e.g. a mediator has acted for a party on an unrelated matter or has had social contact with them – the mediator may be able to remedy this by disclosure and the informed consent of both parties. If in doubt, a mediator should always disclose any conflict. Some conflicts of interest may only become evident at the mediation: for instance, if a mediator has an indirect interest in a planning decision or has acted for one of the lay clients on a different matter. Here, the mediator should withdraw in the absence of written consent.

Fairness of Process

Fairness is often one of the most elusive qualities in a mediation. Mediators should ensure that all parties are enabled to fully participate in the process and that parties remain responsible for deciding when and whether to settle. Conventional wisdom is that while a judge is responsible for the substance of a judgment, a mediator is responsible for fairness of the process. The distinction is sometimes a complex one. While a mediator can ensure that an equal share of their time is allocated to both parties in private sessions, how far can they go in redressing power imbalances? Time spent with a party may be more about helping them recalibrate their interests in light of new information to the benefit of a party who is not in the room. Mediators will often explain that they will spend time wherever it is needed to help settlement and that strict equality of time may not help the process.

Some commercial mediators consider they have no responsibility for the fairness of a mediation's outcome. Others think they have a responsibility not to let a party enter into an 'unconscionable bargain' on the grounds of their professional integrity. There is a spectrum between these points. To what extent does fairness of process require a mediator to illuminate potential difficulties in a settlement agreement or to ensure that parties are entering into an agreement with full knowledge and informed consent? The ECOC refers specifically to a mediator's responsibility to take into account 'power imbalances and the rule of law' (3.1). How does this apply when one party is professionally advised, and one litigant in person is negotiating 'in the shadow of the law'? ECOC makes reference to withdrawing when a settlement would compromise legal values by being illegal or unenforceable (3.2), but conventional wisdom, the value of professional integrity, and the requirement to separate professional roles as recognised in ABA suggest that while a mediator can give legal information, they cannot give legal advice. The balance is a fine one, and simply advising a disputant to take professional advice may be more about formal than substantive ethical compliance. A mediator may seek to redress power imbalances by drawing a party's attention to a legal provision of which they are unaware, but in doing so, they might be seen as undermining impartiality. Even harder would be to address the question of interpretation, which may be pivotal to assessing litigation risk. Problems may arise with fairness if a duty to consider power imbalances conflicts with the value of neutrality. While a mediator may develop techniques for redressing inequalities of power, the arguments of Hazel Genn (2009) and the US critics of informalism (Auerbach 1983; Fiss 1984; Nader 1979; Abel 1982) provide a cogent analysis of the limitations of mediation in this regard.

Party Autonomy (Self-Determination)

The nature of facilitated negotiation requires party autonomy and voluntary participation.

Shapira (2016) considers participation party autonomy as comprising three elements: (1) capacity/competency (to grasp information and to understand), (2) voluntariness (to make free and uncoerced choices/decisions), and (3) informed consent (basing the decision on relevant and necessary information). In its common law form, disputants must be free to walk away from the process. A mediator can coax, question, inform, and recommend but cannot compel. Voluntariness is an intrinsic aspect of affirming party autonomy, particularly in family mediations, in which, because of the dearth of legal aid, disputants may feel they have no choice but to mediate. With disputants who may be depressed or suffer from other mental health conditions, an important aspect of affirming party autonomy is ensuring not just that disputants agree to mediate but also that there is informed consent. Informed consent becomes especially difficult in the case of unrepresented litigants who are unaware or have a defective understanding of their legal rights.

While some mediators consider that a degree of mandation into mediation may be compatible with its nature as voluntary facilitatSed negotiation (Ahmed 2012) or that a 'limited restriction of party self-determination with respect to entry to the process and participation is not regarded as a denial of mediation's nature and identity,' others consider that there is a 'continuum of mandatoriness' and that 'coercion into mediation' cannot be wholly distinguished from 'coercion within mediation (Quek 2010; Bartlet 2019).

Process Dilemmas

Conflict Between Fairness, Party Autonomy, and Impartiality

One of the ethical dilemmas in mediation is the extent to which a mediator is responsible for seeking to redress power imbalances. Moore (2014) describes the dilemma as follows:

> The independent mediator, because of his or her commitment to neutrality and impartiality, is generally ethically barred from direct advocacy on behalf of the weaker party, yet is also ethically obligated in to assist the parties in reaching a relatively fair, acceptable and durable agreement.

Adopting a formal neutrality – for instance, in a case in which only one party is legally represented – could compromise the value of fairness in that the unrepresented party would not be able to participate fully and make informed decisions, whereas to seek to redress imbalances could compromise impartiality in the sense of favouring one party over another.

Others consider that there is little a mediator can do to redress serious power imbalances and that mediation is therefore unsuitable for these kinds of dispute. Pre-existing power imbalances are an inevitable aspect of any dispute, and it is hard to decide at precisely what point they become so serious as to make mediation oppressive or unethical. A serial litigant in person may have access to significant legal resources and be in a better position than a poorly represented party. Imbalances of power can be particularly complex in family mediation in relation to long-term abusive relationships in which patterns of behaviour may become both unconscious and entrenched.

Some of the ways that mediators may seek to redress imbalances include ensuring that relevant and proper information is brought into the process to redress balance in access to data; assisting parties in considering data; offering legal information on an even-handed basis but never advising; ensuring both parties are respectfully heard and listened to; setting ground rules to prevent abusive conduct; and, if necessary, consulting outside experts.

In community and family mediation, disputants are often asked to make an express commitment to respect and non-discriminatory behaviour. When, as is often the case, parties are not accompanied by their lawyers and rely solely on the mediator for the protection of their dignity, a respectful atmosphere during the mediation becomes particularly important. In family mediation, the FMC Code of Practice provides

> [T]he Mediator must seek to prevent manipulative, threatening, or intimidating behaviour by any Participant, and must conduct the process is such a way as to redress, as far as possible, any imbalances of power between the participants. If such behaviour or any other imbalance seems likely to render the Mediation unfair or ineffective, the Mediator must take appropriate steps to seek to prevent this, including terminating the Mediation if necessary.
> (6.3.2)

Conflict Between Fairness, Autonomy, and Confidentiality

There is an inherent tension between confidentiality and fairness of process. Any disclosure in mediation is generally legally privileged (*Aird v Prime Meridian* (2006), although in *Farm Assist Limited v Secretary of State for the Environment and Rural Affairs (No2)* (2009), Ramsay J dismissed the assertion of mediation privilege). There are, however, exceptions to this principle. If the mediation is being used as a cloak for illegality there is 'no privilege in iniquity.'

If information given in confidence in private meetings leads mediators to consider that the mediation process is being used for an improper purpose or a party is behaving in unconscionable ways, the mediator has little way of ensuring compliance. Problems may arise when mediators are told information in confidence by a party who then negotiates in a way incompatible with that disclosure.

The ignorant party cannot exercise autonomy if the information is required for exercising informed consent decision-making. The mediator cannot reveal the confidence, but to become complicit in a deception would both undermine their integrity and lead to manifest unfairness. While they may urge the party to disclose the information to the other party, they cannot compel them to do so. The clash of values dilemma arises because the mediator must respect the wishes of the party who objects to the disclosure. If, after appropriate warning, a party continues to act in a way that contradicts the information, the only option open to a mediator may be to withdraw from the case. This, however, will do little to resolve the case, and the disadvantaged party may either be left with no option but to pursue adjudication or to find another, less morally scrupulous mediator, with whom the problems will be replicated.

Conflict Between Party Autonomy, Impartiality, and Integrity

If a mediator considers a proposed agreement manifestly unfair, they have a responsibility to ensure that a vulnerable party is aware of the full implications of a decision they are entering into and to encourage a process of reality testing. Whereas in civil mediation, a party's legal representative would normally be the guarantor of their autonomy, in community or family mediation and in some small civil claims, the capacity of an unrepresented party for fully informed consent may be impaired. In many areas of practice, a mediator may need to withdraw from a process both out of a concern for fairness and to protect their personal integrity and that of the profession, rather than becoming an agent of injustice. This potential tension is one of the reasons that screening for domestic violence is so important in family mediation. Controlling or coercive behaviour and subtle forms of manipulation may become part of the primary dynamics of violent relationships. The fact that mediation may offer a physically safe environment does not guarantee informed consent to the process or the outcome of mediation. Severe depression or mental illness that impairs a party's understanding of critical information may limit their capacity for fully informed consent. In family or community contexts, patterns of coercive behaviour may undermine full party autonomy.

Redressing Power Imbalances

Mediators differ over the extent to which it is possible and/or desirable to redress power imbalances. Civil mediators often see the presence of solicitors as holding the responsibility for their clients' interests. There may be acute problems, however, when only one party is legally represented, and some mediators will not act in this context. The EU code directs the mediator to 'take into account' imbalances of power. Winslade and Monk (2000) suggest mediators assist parties who are silenced in ways that do not alienate those who are more powerful. For Bush et al. (2004), empowerment and recognition are at the heart of the process of mediation. Mediation may be more about unmasking power inequalities on the basis of respect than about redressing them. In family mediation, the FMC Code of Practice (2018) (5.4.1) requires mediators to be alert to power imbalances, Parkinson

(2020) considers that remaining strictly impartial at all times would limit interventions to assist individuals. Shapira considers (2016) mediators cannot correct imbalances of power and cannot balance powers but can 'empower,' although this falls short of balancing (equalising) the powers of the parties. He describes an intervention that 'seeks to provide a minimum safety-net ensuring that all parties have the basic conditions for exercising self-determination within the mediation.'

Some of the ways that mediators might seek to redress power imbalances without compromising the mediation process include agreeing on rules and processes with both parties, trying to ensure that relevant and proper information is brought into the process to redress balance in access to data, assisting parties in considering data, advising parties who are not legally represented to take independent legal advice or include legal representatives in the process, providing unrepresented parties with legal information on an even-handed basis but never advising, ensuring all parties are respectfully heard and listened to, enforcing ground rules regarding equality and preventing abusive conduct, and helping parties articulate positions and proposals. In family law, a mediator has the responsibility to advise both parties if a proposed settlement would fall outside the spectrum of awards a judge might make.

Brown and Marriot (Shipman et al. 2019) suggest that mediation may be inappropriate if parties are unable to participate because of mental or other incapacity, if a party is unable to participate because of fear or intimidation, and when power imbalances are so great as to prevent an equitable outcome. They suggest that mediators proceed with caution if there is past evidence of abuse, intimidation, or threat but both parties nevertheless wish to proceed, if there is uncertainty over any of the preceding circumstances; if it appears that a party does not intend to negotiate in good faith, and if it appears from the *Halsey* principles that mediation is not appropriate. If strong antagonism exists between the parties, a process should not be proposed that requires joint meetings unless both parties feel ready for this. While the participation of skilled and effective legal representatives may resolve some of these tensions, there is little point of mediation unless, at least to some extent, both parties are willing to participate in a process of facilitated negotiation and come to it with a genuine openness to compromise.

Conclusions

Institutionally, mediation is still in its infancy. Many litigants coming to mediation as an aspect of civil litigation, especially lay clients, are unclear as to what to expect. The ethical regulations of mediation in the UK have not yet caught up with the development of ADR as an aspect of civil process. This will become more pressing if there is automatic reference to mediation. When the state's judicial arm requires participation in ADR as an inherent part of its civil procedure, it takes on a moral responsibility for guaranteeing its fairness. The morality of mediators acting in good faith cannot be a substitute for adequate accountability for their provision of professional services.

Automatic referral to mediation takes place not just in the shadow of the law but, more directly, in the shadow of the court. The more mediators adopt an evaluative style of predicting adjudicative outcomes, including likely costs orders, the more acute the need for a binding set of enforceable norms becomes. If courts refer parties to an exclusive panel of mediators, they will need to ensure that those mediators conform to a clear and comprehensive set of ethical standards that do nothing to impair the parties' access to justice. Failure to do so could potentially be a breach of Article 6 ECHR.

While the growing popularity of mediation makes it important to ensure that mediators conform to a professional standard and maintain the integrity of the process, there is a risk that too much regulation may compromise its advantages. The very informality of mediation is one of its unique attractions.

Questions

1. **To what extent does a mediator have a responsibility for fairness in a mediation?**
2. **What are power imbalances in a mediation and to what extent can (and should) a mediators seek to redress them?**
3. **What are the boundaries of mediator impartiality?**
4. **When might a conflict of interest arise for a mediator, and how should they seek to address it?**
5. **In what circumstances should a mediator withdraw from a case?**

Exercises

How Might a Mediator Deal With the Following Scenarios?

Scenario One

Sifa is an assured shorthold tenant of a first-floor flat in Pimlico. Her landlord, David, lives in the floor above here. When Sifa returns from a holiday, she discovers that the ceiling of her flat has collapsed, causing serious damage to her Kashmir rug, and she is unable to use her kitchen for a week. In prior conversations between the parties, David has agreed to repair the ceiling but refuses to pay compensation for damage to Sifa's possessions. When Sifa withholds a month's rental as what she considers fair compensation for the damage, David threatens to terminate the lease. Both parties have agreed to mediation under the auspices of the Pimlico Mediation Service. In the mediation, David offers to allow Sifa to live in the flat for another two months and to waive the final month's rental but not to return her deposit. Sifa reluctantly agrees to this without taking legal advice. The mediator is aware that Sifa has an assured shorthold tenancy and that David is required to give Sifa two months' notice to quit.

Scenario Two

Catherine and Adam agree that their relationship of ten years has irretrievably broken down and have applied to the court for a divorce. They have agreed on arrangements for their children on the basis of shared parental responsibility but have not resolved the financial matters of their separation. Both parties have given financial disclosure via their solicitors, and Adam has offered to give Catherine 50% of the equity in a family home that is currently owned in their joint names. This would be an order that a court would probably make if neither party had significant other assets. The mediators in the case are aware that, although Adam has disclosed the value of his IT business, which, on the basis of last year's tax returns, has little value, he may have seriously misrepresented its value by not disclosing the full extent of debts that are owing to it and the prospect of new business.

Scenario Three

Janice is claiming ownership of a parcel of land against Sigma Property by reason of long-term adverse possession. In discussion with both parties, you become aware that neither Janice nor Sigma is aware of a significant precedent that would benefit Janice. What is your responsibility as a mediator? Would it make any difference if the precedent favoured the commercial party?

Further Reading

Kallipetis, M. (2015) 'Chapter 9 Mediation Ethics'. In D. Richbell (Ed.), *How to Master Commercial Mediation*. Bloomsbury Professional.

Menkel-Meadow, C. (2007) 'The Lawyer as a Consensus: Ethics for a New Practice', *Tennessee Law Review* 70, 63–119.

Shapira, O., ed (2022) *MeSdiation Ethics: A Practitioner's Guide*. American Bar Association.

Susskind, L. (1981) 'Environmental Mediation and the Accountability Problem', *Vermont Law Review* 6, 1–47.

13 Arbitration

Arbitration provides a system of privatised justice and is the most common adjudicatory form of ADR. Its hallmark is the autonomy and consent of parties as regards jurisdiction, rules of procedure, evidence, and confidentiality. Although both mediation and arbitration require the presence of an impartial third party, their roles are completely distinct. While in mediation, the resolution of the dispute remains the responsibility of the parties, in arbitration, they relinquish this decision and choose the person who will make it. As Simmel points out, this gives them a unique authority as it presupposes a 'greater subjective confidence in the objectivity of judgment than does any other form of decision making.' Even in court adjudication, it is only the action of the complainant that results from confidence (Simmel 1950).

History

Arbitration predates the existence of courts' providing adjudication in a system of sovereign states. There are references to arbitration in the Old Assyrian Empire, in the Old Testament, and in pre-Islamic Arabia. Arbitration agreements in commercial contracts date back to 1224 in England. In the Middle Ages, merchant disputes in England were frequently arbitrated by guilds rather than by litigation in the Royal Courts. In its simplest form, arbitration might involve a third-party expert being asked to make a judgment on the quality of cotton or coffee.

In England, the philosopher John Locke was asked by the newly founded Board of Trade to draft the Arbitration Act of 1698, the first statute on arbitration to be enacted in England. The act authorised the common law courts to imprison individuals for contempt of court if they did not comply with an arbitral award. The only defence was misbehaviour by the arbitrators.

In the 18th century, Lord Chief Justice Mansfield encouraged court-approved arbitration, and cases registered at the King's Bench increased dramatically during his tenure. During the 19th century, commerce and the law of contract developed to meet the needs of a changing economy. The City of London Chamber of International Arbitration, later the London Court of International Arbitration (LCIA), was established in 1892.

DOI: 10.4324/9781003112617-13

Disputes regarding British support for the Confederacy during the American Civil War were resolved under the Jay Treaty of 1795 between the USA and Great Britain. The Alabama Claims case (1872) is sometimes seen as the first example of modern international arbitration in which the tribunal awarded the USA $15.5 million in gold for seizing ships during the American Civil War. An 1895 dispute between the United States and Britain over the boundary between Venezuela and British Guiana was peacefully resolved through arbitration. During the Hague Peace Conference of 1899, the major world powers, including Britain, France, Russia, and the USA, agreed to a system of voluntary arbitration and the creation of a permanent Court of Arbitration.

Process

As a private form of adjudication, arbitration mirrors the due process requirements of the civil justice system. It is widely used in commercial, employment, and consumer disputes. It can take place in state-to-state and individual-to-state contexts and is now the default option for international investment and trade disputes. While lightly supervised by the courts, there are very limited rights of appeal.

Arbitrators with specific subject-matter expertise are often employed, which, for many disputants, makes the arbitral award more acceptable. Parties can choose both the procedural and the substantive body of rules and law to be applied. This may be the law of a foreign jurisdiction, trade rules, or the principles of religious law.

In arbitration, the disputants contract to accept the decision of an arbitrator or arbitral tribunal, which will make a binding determination of the issue brought before them. An arbitration might be presided over by a single arbitrator or a panel, invariably with an odd number of members (generally three), with one appointed by each party and the chair agreed between them or appointment made according to the arbitral institution. Arbitrators can choose to use an adversarial or an inquisitorial (civil law) process. As with other forms of ADR, there is a tension over the respective claims of business efficacy and legal clarity. Some businesses prefer a decision being made on the basis of trade custom and practice, rather than a reasoned decision based on formal law.

Religious communities may want to have disputes resolved by consent by respected community leaders. Muslim arbitration tribunals in the UK in London, Bradford, Manchester, and Nuneaton apply Sharia law to decide commercial and private law family disputes with the consent of both parties. The arbitral jurisdiction is contractual and, in the UK, subject to statutory regulation. Arbitration (*tahkim*) is exhorted by the Qur'anic verse 4.35: '[I]f they desire reconciliation, Allah will restore harmony between them.' Islam encourages members of the community to seek mediation (*wasta*) before going to arbitration. In family disputes, this might be conducted by an imam from the community mosque or Sharia council and, in commercial disputes, by a lawyer under Muslim arbitration tribunal exercising jurisdiction under Section 1 of Arbitration Act 1996.

Essential Features of Arbitration

- Consensual process in which disputants ask a third-party neutral to make a decision.
- Impartial arbitrator or panel.
- Contractual jurisdiction.
- Party autonomy – parties choose the arbitrator(s) and process.
- Location agreed to by the parties.
- Process generally private and confidential.
- Finality subject to light legal regulation with limited rights of appeal.

Arbitrability

Not all disputes are suited to arbitration. Arbitration is suitable for the determination of private rights and generally not appropriate where the rights of those not party to the arbitration are affected. Criminal cases require justice to be open and subject to the control and appeal of the courts and cannot be arbitrated. Cases regarding the grant of patents and public law cases which may affect the rights of third parties would not be arbitrable for the same reason.

In *Riverrock Securities Limited v International Bank of St Petersburg* (2020), the High Court adopted a pro-arbitration approach and held that the avoidance claims brought in bankruptcy proceedings fell within the scope of the LCIA arbitration agreement between the parties and were arbitrable under English law. Further, the dispute between the parties concerned contractual rights, and an arbitral tribunal was capable of granting the relief sought.

In *NDK v HUO* (2022), the English Commercial Court dismissed NDK's Section 67 challenge to an LCIA award, finding that a proposed shareholder was covered by the arbitration clause in the shareholders' agreement.

The Court affirmed the principle that arbitration clauses governed by English law will be interpreted with a presumption that the parties, as rational businessmen, intend it to apply to all disputes arising from the relationship between them.

Statutory Framework for Arbitration in the UK

In many jurisdictions, arbitration is regulated by statute. In the UK, the Arbitration Act 1996 covers domestic and international arbitration and has helped to make London one of the preferred seats of arbitration, perhaps partly because of its Section 69 provision for an appeal on a point of law as a default right. Other jurisdictions have differing domestic statutory regimes. In the USA, the Federal Arbitration Act 1925 provides for contract-based binding arbitration. In India, the Arbitration and Conciliation Act 1996 sought to make arbitration the preferred form of commercial dispute resolution.

The Arbitration Act 1996 distinguishes between mandatory provisions, which apply regardless of the decision of the parties, and non-mandatory or default provisions, which can be derogated from and will be applied if the parties haven't specified a procedure.

Arbitration Act 1996

The guiding principles of arbitration in the UK are set out in the Arbitration Act 1996.

Section 1 provides:

> a) the object of arbitration is to obtain the fair resolution of disputes by an impartial tribunal without unnecessary delay or expense;
>
> (b) the parties should be free to agree how their disputes are resolved, subject only to such safeguards as are necessary in the public interest;
>
> (c) in matters governed by this Part the court should not intervene except as provided by this Part.

The Arbitration Bill (2024) responds to recommendations of the Law Commission to amend some of these provisions in the following ways:

- Codifying an arbitrator's duty to disclose potential conflicts of interest.
- Strengthening arbitrator immunity to ensure that arbitrators can continue to act in a way which is robustly impartial.
- Introducing the capacity for arbitrators to dispose summarily of issues that have no real prospect of success.
- Strengthening court orders to ensure that arbitral proceedings and the orders of arbitrators are fully effective.
- Clarifying the applicable law governing international arbitration agreements.

Mandatory Provisions of Arbitration Act 1996

Sections 9 to 11 (stay of legaSl proceedings);
Section 12 (power of court to extend agreed time limits);
Section 13 (application of Limitation Acts);
Section 24 (power of court to remove arbitrator);
Section 26(1) (effect of death of arbitrator);
Section 28 (liability of parties for fees and expenses of arbitrators);
Section 29 (immunity of arbitrator);
Section 31 (objection to substantive jurisdiction of tribunal);
Section 32 (determination of preliminary point of jurisdiction);
Section 33 (general duty of tribunal);

Section 37(2) (items to be treated as expenses of arbitrators);
Section 40 (general duty of parties);
Section 43 (securing the attendance of witnesses);
Section 56 (power to withhold award in case of non-payment);
Section 60 (effectiveness of agreement for payment of costs in any event);
Section 66 (enforcement of award);
Sections 67 and 68 (challenging the award: substantive jurisdiction and serious irregularity);
Sections 70 and 71 (supplementary provisions; effect of order of court), so far as relating to those sections;
Section 72 (saving for rights of person who takes no part in proceedings);
Section 73 (loss of right to object);
Section 74 (immunity of arbitral institutions, etc.);
Section 75 (charge to secure payment of solicitors' costs).

Confidentiality

Except where otherwise agreed, arbitration proceedings are private and confidential. Confidentiality is a creature of the common law and considered to be an implied term of the arbitration contract. The 1996 Act does not specifically address confidentiality. In *Emmott v Michael Wilson and Partners* (2008), Collins LJ described confidentiality as a 'rule of substantive law masquerading as an implied term' and summarised the following exceptions:

1. Consent of all parties including by trade custom;
2. By leave of the Court or where there is a contrary Court order;
3. Documents in the public domain;
4. Where it is reasonably necessary to protect the legitimate interests of an arbitrating party;
5. In the interests of justice, including in foreign proceedings, to avoid a subsequent tribunal being misled; and
6. Where it is in the Public Interest.

The court in each instance weighs the public interest in open justice against the desirability of maintaining confidentiality. In *Hayat v Raddison Hotels* (2023), the judge held that an expectation of privacy did not outweigh the public interest in making the judgment accessible, so the judgment should not be anonymised.

In *Department of Economic Policy and Development of the City of Moscow v Bankers Trust Company* (2004), the Court of Appeal held unanimously that challenges to an aspect of arbitration proceedings should generally be heard in private. In *Halliburton v Chubb* (2020), the Supreme Court considered that, due to the private nature of arbitration, when an arbitrator is appointed in relation to multiple overlapping references, the non-common party cannot discover what evidence or submissions have been made or the arbitrator's response.

In *CDE v NOP* (2021), where court proceedings overlapped with the subject matter of an LCIA arbitration, the court upheld an application that a case management conference should be held in private. While the starting point is that arbitration claims under CPR 62.10 are held in private, the default position for court proceedings, even if they refer to arbitrations, is that they are heard in public. Confidentiality does not necessarily extend to arbitration claims.

Publication of Judgments

In *Moscow v Bankers Trust* (2004), Mance LJ affirmed the significance of public scrutiny of decisions regarding the administration of justice, holding in the Court of Appeal that a judgment regarding matters in arbitration should be made public, stating that 'even though the hearing may have been in private, the court should, when preparing and giving judgment, bear in mind that any judgment should be given in public, where this can be done without disclosing significant confidential information.' He emphasised the desirability of public scrutiny as a means by which confidence in the courts can be maintained and the administration of justice made transparent, stating 'Arbitration is an important feature of international, commercial and financial life, and there is legitimate interest in its operation and practice.'

In *Manchester City v. F A Premier League* (2021), the court ordered publication of its judgment on a dispute between a football club and the Premier League, holding 'It is desirable for any judgment to be made public in order to ensure public scrutiny and the transparent administration of justice,' and 'the confidential nature of the arbitration has to be weighed against the public interest in ensuring appropriate standards of fairness in the conduct of arbitrations.'

Agreement to Arbitrate

While any form of dispute (subject to the rules on arbitrability) may be referred to arbitration, most arbitrations in the UK arise from a clause in a contract which provides for prospective disputes to be determined by arbitration. Where this is the case, the arbitration clause will be separable from the underlying contract. An arbitration agreement may still be valid and enforceable even if the main agreement in which it is contained is found to be invalid and unenforceable.

Examples of general arbitration clauses:

Chartered Institute of Arbitrators

Any dispute, controversy, or claim arising out of or in connection with this contract, or the breach, termination or validity thereof, shall be submitted to the Chartered Institute of Arbitrators (CIArb) and settled by final and binding arbitration in accordance with the CIArb Arbitration Rules. Judgment on any award issued under this provision may be entered by any court of competent jurisdiction.

London Court of International Arbitration

Any dispute arising out of or in connection with this contract, including any question regarding its existence, validity or termination, shall be referred to and finally resolved by arbitration under the LCIA Rules, which Rules are deemed to be incorporated by reference into this clause.

Examples of a post-dispute submission clause:

Chartered Institute of Arbitrators

We, the undersigned parties, hereby agree that the dispute concerning [insert a brief and accurate description of the dispute] shall be submitted to the Chartered Institute of Arbitrators (CIArb) and settled by final and binding arbitration in accordance with the CIArb Arbitration Rules. Judgment on any award issued under this provision may be entered by any court of competent jurisdiction.

London Court of International Arbitration

A dispute having arisen between the parties concerning [], the parties hereby agree that the dispute shall be referred to and finally resolved by arbitration under the LCIA Rules.

Arbitration is governed by the following law:

1. The law applicable to the substantive dispute
2. The law that governs the procedure of the arbitration, which will generally be the law of the seat.

Enka v Chubb (2020) confirms that the law applicable to the arbitration agreement will be: (1) the law expressly or impliedly chosen by the parties or (2) in the absence of such choice, the system of law 'most closely connected' to the arbitration agreement. Although the law applicable to the arbitration agreement will generally be that of the seat, it is not uncommon for an arbitration to be seated in England and Wales but for the arbitration agreement to be governed by a foreign law.

To resolve any ambiguity, Clause 1 of the Arbitration Bill (2024) creates a statutory rule that the law governing an arbitration agreement is the law expressly chosen by the parties to an agreement or, by default, the law of the chosen seat. This occurs regardless of where the arbitration is seated. When an arbitration is seated in England or Wales, then, by default, the agreement to arbitrate would be governed by the law of England and Wales. An exception can be made if the parties expressly agree a different law to govern the arbitration agreement.

Process

Section 33 of AA 1996 sets out the duties of the tribunal. These include the duty to act fairly and impartially between the parties, to give each party a reasonable opportunity to put their case and to respond to the case against it, and to adopt suitable procedures, avoiding unnecessary delay and expense.

Process may vary from a relatively simple procedure in consumer arbitrations to complex procedures (and costs) analogous to commercial litigation in investment disputes.

The arbitral tribunal can decide all procedural and evidential matters referred to it. Parties can decide whether the arbitral tribunal will dispense with oral hearings of evidence. Procedure may include:

- Where hearings should take place and whether there will be an oral hearing.
- The language of the proceedings.
- What documents should be disclosed and produced, at what time, and in what form.
- What expert evidence may be required and whether joint or independent experts should be appointed.
- Time limits for directions.

In commercial arbitrations, there will generally be a preliminary meeting, increasingly held virtually by video conference or telephone, to discuss jurisdiction, procedure, and consequent directions. Parties will prepare and exchange bundles of evidence and statements of their case, and the tribunal will, at an early stage, set out a timetable for the arbitration, including deadlines for submissions of evidence. In higher-value cases, there will generally be an oral hearing. The procedure is similar to a court of law, although less formal.

One of the attractions of arbitration in some areas, such as construction disputes, is the practice of compromise as opposed to a winner-take-all approach. Some commentators suggest that the lack of legal supervision may undermine the integrity of the process.

Arbitral Award

The arbitral award is equivalent to a court judgment. A final award deals with all the issues submitted to the tribunal while partial awards deal with discrete issues.

To be valid, an award must:

1. Be signed by all the arbitrators
2. Contain reasons for the award (unless it is an agreed award)
3. State the seat of the arbitration or where the award was made and the date

Supervision of the Courts

As with other forms of ADR, arbitration both represents an alternative to the courts and depends on them for its effectiveness. Courts are guided by two contending principles. The courts have a responsibility to uphold the rule of law and ensure that the private process of arbitration doesn't displace or undermine them. At the same time, if arbitration has been freely chosen, the courts will respect the principle of party autonomy and the right of disputants to choose their own means of dispute resolution. Under the doctrine of 'competence-competence', arbitrators are almost universally recognised as having the autonomy to determine their own jurisdiction in the first instance.

Arbitration remains subject to the supervision of the court throughout, and awards may only be appealed on limited grounds.

Prior to arbitration, parties can apply to the court to obtain a stay of proceedings or anti-suit injunction for breaches of the arbitration agreement. When the parties cannot agree on the arbitral tribunal or there is no default method for appointing arbitrators, the court can appoint them. The court can also extend time limits for commencing arbitral proceedings.

During an arbitration, the court may exercise statutory powers for the purposes of supporting the arbitration. These include:

- Injunctions to restrain court or arbitral proceedings.
- Deciding disputes about the jurisdiction of arbitrators.
- Procedural steps that an arbitral tribunal cannot order or cannot enforce: for example, issuing a witness summons.
- Maintaining the status quo by, for example, the grant of urgent interim injunctions.
- Extending time limits for making the award.
- Determining preliminary points of law under Section 45 AA 1996.
- Removing arbitrators and appointing replacements under Section 24 AA 1996.
- Determining the recoverable costs of the arbitration under Section 63 (4) AA 1996.

Post arbitration, the courts can hear challenges to the award. They can be asked to enforce awards and make orders relating to the professional fees of arbitrators. As a matter of public policy, arbitration awards are generally enforced by the courts.

Correction of Defective Decisions

Section 57 of AA 1996 provides a limited right for a party to request the correction of errors or the removal of ambiguities in an award or request an additional award in respect of a claim that has not been addressed. Grounds on which a decision can be challenged are very limited, as Sir Michael Kerr commented: 'Remember when parties agree arbitration they buy the right to get the wrong answer' (Mr Justice Eder 2014).

Challenge to Substantive Jurisdiction

Challenges to the tribunal's jurisdiction (Arbitration Act, Section 67) may include issues of whether there is a valid arbitration agreement, whether the tribunal is properly constituted, or whether matters have been submitted to arbitration in accordance with the arbitration agreement.

Serious Irregularity

The Arbitration Act 1996 (Section 68) provides for challenge on the grounds of serious irregularity. Serious irregularity can include:

- Failure to give each party the opportunity to fairly put its case or answer the case against them.
- The tribunal exceeding its powers.
- Failure to conduct the proceedings in accordance with the agreed procedure or law.
- Failure by the tribunal to deal with all the issues that were put to it.
- An arbitral institution or person acting beyond their jurisdiction.
- Uncertainty or ambiguity as to the effect of the award.
- The award being obtained by fraud or the way in which it was procured being contrary to public policy.
- Failure to comply with the requirements as to the form of the award.

Appeal on Point of Law

Findings of fact cannot be appealed. Parties may, in addition, agree to exclude a right of appeal on a point of law (Section 69).

Permission to appeal will be granted where:

- Determination of the question would substantially affect the rights of one or more of the parties.
- The question of law is one which the tribunal was asked to determine.
- The decision of the tribunal on the question of law is obviously wrong, or the question is one of general public importance, and the tribunal's decision is open to serious doubt.
- Despite the agreement of the parties to resolve the matter by arbitration, it is just and proper in all the circumstances for the court to determine the question.

Enforcement

Arbitration awards can be enforced by bringing a civil claim on the award in the High Court or using a summary procedure under the Arbitration Act 1996. Cross-border or foreign awards can generally be enforced under the New York Convention 1958 if the necessary conditions are met.

Section 66 of the Arbitration Act 1996 deals with enforcement of arbitration awards, whether made domestically or abroad.

> (1) An award made by the tribunal pursuant to an arbitration agreement may, by leave of the court, be enforced in the same manner as a judgment or order of the court to the same effect.
>
> (2) Where leave is so given, judgment may be entered in terms of the award.

(3) Leave to enforce an award shall not be given where, or to the extent that, the person against whom it is sought to be enforced shows that the tribunal lacked substantive jurisdiction to make the award.

The right to raise such an objection may have been lost (see Section 73).

(4) Nothing in this section affects the recognition or enforcement of an award under any other enactment or rule of law, in particular under Part II of the [1950 c. 27.] Arbitration Act 1950 (enforcement of awards under Geneva Convention) or the provisions of Part III of this Act relating to the recognition and enforcement of awards under the New York Convention or by an action on the award.

Section 103 provides for circumstances in which enforcement of the award may also be refused. This includes awards in respect of matters not eligible for settlement by arbitration or those contrary to public policy. In the case of *Payward Inc and Ors v Chechetkin* (2023), the Commercial Court refused to enforce a California arbitration award in favour of a crypto-asset exchange on public policy grounds, within the meaning of section 103(3) of the 1996 Act. The judge noted that the professed priorities of the JAMS arbitration system were to 'save time and money' and promote 'efficiency, speed, and results,' which he considered may well have meant that the arbitrator had favoured the short and simple route to disposing of the claim over one that would require the investigation of foreign laws.

International Arbitration

Arbitration has increasingly become the preferred forum for deciding international business disputes.

The New York Convention 1958 provides for the mutual recognition and enforcement of arbitration agreements and awards in the 172 state parties.

The United Nations Commission on International Trade Law (UNCITRAL) Model Law 1985 (revised 2006) sets out a model regarding international commercial arbitration for national governments to adopt as part of their domestic legislation. According to Model Law Article 1(3), an arbitration is international if:

(a) the parties to an arbitration agreement have, at the time of the conclusion of that agreement, their places of business in different States; or

(b) one of the following places is situated outside the State in which the parties have their places of business: (i) the place of arbitration if determined in, or pursuant to, the arbitration agreement; (ii) any place where a substantial part of the obligations of the commercial relationship is to be performed or the place with which the subject-matter of the dispute is most closely connected; or

(c) the parties have expressly agreed that the subject matter of the arbitration agreement relates to more than one country.

UNCITRAL separately provides arbitration rules (initially 1976 and revised 2010) which may be incorporated as part of a contract or govern the conduct of an arbitration intended to resolve a dispute or disputes between themselves.

In the USA, the Federal Arbitration Act 1925 has led to the enforcement of pre-dispute agreements. In India, the Indian Arbitration and Conciliation Act 1996 reproduced the UNCITRAL Model Law in national legislation. In the UK, arbitration is regulated by the Arbitration Act 1996, although this is not identical to the UNCITRAL Model Law. Decisions of the arbitrator and the arbitral award are binding and enforced by the Courts, subject only to very limited rights of challenge. Unless otherwise agreed by the parties, the arbitration award is treated as having been made in the seat of arbitration, which will be the supervisory jurisdiction for the purposes of enforcement.

The International Chamber of Commerce (ICC) has played an influential role in the development of international commercial arbitration. The ICC was founded in Paris in 1919 to promote global trade, and its dispute resolution services decided 28,000 cases in the period to 2023. The ICC does not draw on the rules or regulations of any individual nation-state and has developed its own arbitral rules and international culture of arbitration. There is a tension between French and English approaches to law. In French law, according to the Cour de Cassation *Putrabali* decision (2007), an international arbitral award is 'not anchored in any national legal order' but 'a decision of international justice, whose validity must be ascertained with regard to the rules applicable in the country where its recognition and enforcement are sought.' French courts hold that the setting aside of an international arbitral award by the courts of the seat of the arbitration is irrelevant and does not prevent its recognition and enforcement in France. In English law, decisions of the court of the seat are decisions which the parties must be taken to have accepted when that seat was chosen and should be treated as final and binding. According to the French approach, it is arguable that the ICC is developing its own *Lex Mercatoria*, representing a secondary source of non-national law in relation to international business actors as a source of settling disputes in international commerce.

International Investment Arbitration

International investment arbitration enables a private entity to bring a claim against a foreign state for breach of investment treaties. Less-developed countries have disproportionately been the targets of these actions. Those in support of investment treaties including mandatory arbitration agreements argue that they encourage growth by protecting investment. Typically, bilateral investment treaties offer investors no expropriation without compensation, fair and equitable, and due process.

Critics of investment arbitration argue that powerful multinational companies can coerce states into changing public policy. Ontario has abandoned environmental initiatives because of the threat of investment arbitration; the tobacco company Philip Morris changed its corporate nationality to bring a case against Australia for changes to a labelling law it believed would depress the tobacco market; and states have been sued for changes to social policy that have impacted profitability. Public information on overall and specific arbitration cases is limited by confidentiality clauses and the fact that there is no need to involve the courts unless there is a dispute.

The governments of Venezuela, Bolivia, and Ecuador have stated that their bilateral investment treaties and foreign investors' claims have impeded social and political change and left the ICSID Convention (the multilateral framework for investment arbitration). The current system of international investment arbitration permits the private determination of disputes that impact profoundly important issues of public policy, such as environmental protection, public health and safety, and market competition (Argen 2015).

Arbitration in Family Law

Arbitration is increasingly used in family law regarding financial matters. The Institute of Family Law Arbitrators was set up in 2011 as a collaboration between Resolution, the Family Law Bar Association, the Chartered Institute of Arbitrators, and the Centre for Child and Family Law Reform. It initiated the Family Law Arbitration Financial Scheme in 2012. The scheme offers arbitration in cases involving property and finance. In early cases, appeal was based on the jurisdiction of the Arbitration Act 1996 and limited to very narrow circumstances. In *S v S* (2014), President of the Family Court, Sir James Munby gave guidance on the proper approach of family courts in incorporating arbitral awards as consent orders, saying that judges would not disturb an award 'unless something leaps off the page to indicate that something has gone so seriously wrong in the arbitral process as fundamentally to vitiate the arbitral award.' In *DB v DJ* (2016), a case in which one party refused to accept an arbitral award, the court declared the scope for challenging an award to be exclusively governed by the Arbitration Act 1996. The most recent case of *Haley v Haley* (2020) in the Court of Appeal has widened the scope of appeal from an arbitral award in family cases, deciding that the proper test is the appeals test under MCA 1973. In *A v A (Arbitration Guidance)* (2021), Mostyn J ruled that any challenge to the substance of an arbitral award should be dealt with in the same way, applying the same principles, as an appeal from a district judge to a circuit judge. In *G v G* (2022), the court decided that grounds for appeal were not limited to those set out in the Arbitration Act 1996; the court has a duty to assess the fairness of any remedies based on an arbitral award; the legal test for challenging arbitration determinations is whether the decision is wrong; and the principles in applying to challenge decisions in family cases apply to both financial disputes and disputes regarding children.

Court-Annexed Arbitration

Court-annexed arbitration has not been used in the UK, although a County Court may order that small claims be heard by a district judge as a binding arbitration with the force of a court order. As with consumer adjudications, these are not subject to the Arbitration Act 1996.

Court-annexed compulsory arbitration has been used in the USA since the 1970s: in Pennsylvania, for instance, since 1978, for claims not in excess of $75,000 (1989). Arbitrators are appointed on pro bono basis – three per trial.

Judgment becomes final within 30 days unless one or both parties file demand for trial *de novo*. Arbitration fees are deposited with the court and returned only if the party receives a final judgment more favourable than arbitral award. Over 10 years, 388 cases (2% of 17,006) placed in an arbitration programme in the Eastern District of Pennsylvania required traditional courtroom trial.

High-Low Arbitration

This is a way of managing risk and more prevalent in USA, where it is used in personal injury claims. It is often used when liability is not at issue, and the parties agree that an award may not be higher or lower than certain boundary figures. The figures are communicated to the arbitrator in advance, and if an award is made outside these boundaries, the claimant will only receive the lower figure or the defendant only pay the upper figure.

In final-offer arbitration, sometimes used in labour disputes, an arbitrator is required to choose between the final offer of one party or the other.

Amiable Composition

Under UNCITRAL Model Law (28.3), with the consent of the parties, arbitrators can dispense with strict legal rules and decide a case by amiable composition. The principle of '*Ex aequo et bon*' (acting according to the right and good) permits an arbitral tribunal to act on the basis of an equitable jurisdiction. It requires the express consent of the parties and is in practice rarely used.

Advantages of Arbitration

- As with mediation, arbitration proceedings are private and confidential.
- The procedure is flexible and can be less formal than court hearings, leading to benefits of speed and economy. In some jurisdictions, there may be several years' delay in getting cases listed for court hearing, and commercial arbitration enables much swifter resolution.
- Parties, in theory, have the liberty to choose a tribunal with a particular industry expertise.
- For parties who want to cut down on the potential time and costs of appeal, awards are binding, and there are more limited appeal rights than with court-based adjudication.
- When arbitration takes place on written submission, the hearing may be significantly cheaper than court adjudication.
- In cross-border disputes, arbitration can relieve parties of some of the costs of litigating in the opposing party's jurisdiction.

Disadvantages of Arbitration

- With arbitrations resulting from a compulsory arbitration clause, the right to choose an arbitral tribunal may be illusory or non-existent.

- Compulsory arbitration clauses are often contained in the small print of employment or consumer contracts and may effectively oust the jurisdiction of the courts.
- If an arbitrator or arbitral tribunal depends on a corporation or sector for repeat business, they may develop a structural bias against the consumer or employee, and there may be an incentive to rule against them or set a high evidential threshold for success.
- In commercial arbitrations, lead arbitrators may suggest industry norms that suppress the level of compensation.
- Limited rights of appeal may make it harder to correct defective decisions.
- Arbitrators lack the capacity to enforce interlocutory measures against a party. This may make it easier to obstruct procedural justice.

Commentary

The more often parties use arbitration and the closer they are to the process in terms of choosing arbitrators and the drafting the arbitration agreement, the more advantageous the process will be for them. The myth of a cheap, effective, and informal means of access to justice is often subverted in practice. In complex commercial investment cases, the cost of arbitration may be no less than court adjudication. In disputes in which a party desires vindication, confidentiality may be a disadvantage rather than a benefit. In a particular business context in which the bulk of cases are decided at arbitral tribunals, there may be an erosion of clear precedent, leading to the erosion of the bargaining endowments of the weaker parties.

In her seminal article 'Commercial Arbitration?' Mentschikoff (1961), considering the way the structure and the process of commercial arbitration are determined according to the different institutional contexts in which it arises, distinguished between three institutional contexts:

1. When two parties in a business relationship 'agree to settle any disputes that may arise under the contract by resort to arbitration before named arbitrators or persons to be named at the time of the dispute.' In this category, all arrangements, including the procedures for arbitration, rest entirely with the parties concerned.
2. When arbitration arises within the context of a particular trade association, 'The group establishes its own arbitration machinery for the settlement of disputes among its members, either on a voluntary or compulsory basis.'
3. When administrative groups 'provide rules, facilities, and arbitrators for any persons desiring to settle disputes by arbitration.'

While 80% arbitrators in Mentschikoff's experiment thought they ought to reach their decisions in the context of the principles of substantive rules of law, 'almost 90 per cent believed that they were free to ignore these rules whenever they thought that more just decisions would be reached by so doing.'

Gross (2020) has offered a typology of arbitration, suggesting that for arbitration to enhance parties' access to justice, the process needs to:

1. Cost less and take less time than litigating the same claim in court;
2. Result in a published, explained award;

3. Preserve the parties right to assert any claim, remedy, or procedure that would be available in court; and
4. Permit the parties to be represented.

Sternlight (1996) argues that arbitration can be deployed as a corporate tool that systematically disadvantages less-powerful parties. Nolan-Haley (2020), Resnik (2014), and Colvin (2014) criticise arbitration for delegating to private and unaccountable parties the power to deprive less-powerful parties of their rights. Palmer and Roberts (2020) identify 'an inherent tendency for arbitration to lapse into a very second-rate version of court adjudication,' in which arbitrators tend 'not to adjudicate properly but rather to try to compromise, – in particular, in order to maintain good relations with an otherwise "losing party."'

Ware (2021) concludes that the vision of 'merchants arbitrating their disputes before fellow merchants – largely free of the substantive law, adjudication procedures, and enforcement tools provided by government – may initially sound like something lost in the mists of time since the medieval Law Merchant, (but) Mentschikoff showed it to be thriving in the mid-twentieth-century United States.'

Arbitration has become increasingly prevalent in employment, consumer law, and the gig economy on both sides of the Atlantic, where compulsory arbitration can become a fetter on access to justice. In an examination of 19,000 California mandatory arbitration clauses approved by the National Arbitration Forum, the non-profit public interest group Public Citizen found that the companies prevailed over citizens in 94% of disputes (Program on Negotiation 2016).

Uber's use of mandatory arbitration clauses provides an extreme example of how an arbitration clause can deprive those required to sign it of any remedy against a powerful multinational enterprise. Here, drivers were required to accept *pro forma* service agreements before driving.

The terms contained a clause stating that the agreement was exclusively governed by the laws of the Netherlands, and any dispute must first be dealt with by mediation before proceeding to arbitration. The process required upfront payment of US$14,500. At the time of the hearing of the case in Canada, not one of five million drivers had invoked the clause.

While in the USA, the Supreme Court has generally taken a broad view of the Federal Arbitration Act 1925 and enforced compulsory arbitration clauses, the Canadian Supreme Court in *Heller v Uber* (2020) showed a refreshing willingness to develop the doctrine of unconscionability for the majority (or public policy for the dissent) to prevent a multinational company from enforcing an unfair and one-sided arbitration clause.

In considering the advantages of arbitration, context is everything. Businesses require mandatory arbitration in *pro forma* contracts because they face lower transaction costs and will have to pay out less. A company can use arbitration to limit discovery against itself, choose arbitrators, and consolidate its advantage by depriving the consumer of a significant opportunity to appeal.

Conclusion

As with other forms of ADR, arbitration has become increasingly formalised. It risks losing some of its benefits even as it comes to challenges state courts as the preferred form of resolving international investments disputes. At best, arbitration offers resolution that is pragmatic, confidential, quick, and informal. It affirms values of autonomy, empowerment, and consent in a process which provides access to a richer type of justice than that offered by the courts. To parties with equal bargaining power, arbitration may deliver on this promise. However, when the arbitration clause is embedded in the contract out of which the dispute arises, arbitration becomes a compulsory and non-consensual process in which 'repeat players' gain a distinct advantage. The degree of consent and equality of power of single-shot disputants who have not drafted the arbitration clause may be illusory. The *ad hoc* nature of arbitration and its finality and privacy all make it hard to ensure consistency or transparency of process.

At worst, arbitration is an effectively mandatory process sacrificing transparency and accountability while mimicking the court resolution to which it purports to be an alternative. It can shield businesses from legal accountability for their actions and offers second-class justice without the safeguard of appeal for less-powerful litigants.

Questions

1. **In what ways is arbitration like and in what ways is it different from other forms of ADR?**
2. **What do you consider the values underpinning arbitration?**
3. **What are the advantages and disadvantages of arbitration as opposed to mediation in the following contexts:**

   a) **Family law**
   b) **Consumer disputes**
   c) **Business-to-business disputes**
   d) **Cross-border business disputes**

Further Reading

Blackaby, N. et al. (2022) *Redfern and Hunter on International Arbitration: Student Version*. Oxford University Press.

Boorman, F. (2022) 'Developments in the History of Arbitration: A Past for the Present?', *Amicus Curiae*, Series 2, 4 (1).

Bull, C., ed. (2023) *Arbitration's Age of Enlightenment*. ICCA Congress Series No. 21, Kluwer.

Roebuck, D. (2001) *Ancient Greek Arbitration*. Oxford University Press.

14 Mediation in Comparative Context

Earlier chapters have considered how the form and style of mediation may vary according to legal and social context. This chapter will extend the enquiry to pre-modern forms of dispute resolution before comparing the contemporary practice of mediation in Ghana, India, and China. These case studies have been chosen to exemplify mediation practice in three different jurisdictions that are more collective and hierarchical than in the UK or the US and illustrate these cultural values in divergent political and economic contexts.

In examining these contexts, we will consider the extent to which core principles of mediation, such as party autonomy, voluntariness, and confidentiality, may be contingent on the cultural contexts and political systems within which they operate. All three contexts illustrate a history or tradition of mediation as an indigenous practice, and all three have, to an extent, adopted mandatory forms of mediation.

Pre-modern forms of dispute resolution are a near-universal phenomenon. Capelletti (1978) recognised the relevance of anthropological perspectives to facilitating access to justice and learning the importance of 'settling disputes through negotiation, mediation, conciliation and arbitration rather than through adjudication according to the adversary system.' Palmer and Roberts (2020) highlight the perennially recurring role and diversity of form of the mediator in anthropological research in pre-industrial society. Fiadjoe (2013) understands non-coercive means of resolving disputes as essential for 'building long-term relationships' and traces the origins of ADR to traditional societies which, without the power of enforcement of the modern state, had no coercive means of resolving disputes.

In Anglo-Saxon England, forms of mediation and reconciliation, based on the Germanic value of *comitatus* (community loyalty), precede the development of the court system. Anglo-Saxon assemblies preferred the dispute to be mediated to a settlement rather than adjudicated. Roebuck (2007) cites examples of a land dispute in the eighth century and the role taken by the Church in mediating: for instance, in Bede's narrative of Theodore of Tarsus, the Archbishop of Canterbury mediated a settlement between Northumbrians and Mercians (679). In medieval England, boundaries between government, law, and religious authority remained porous. Until the reign of Henry II (1154), royal justice was dispensed wherever the king travelled. From the reign of Richard I (1189), knights, as feudal tenants, were appointed by Hubert Walter (Archbishop of Canterbury and the king's chief justiciar) to preserve the peace

DOI: 10.4324/9781003112617-14

in unruly areas. While the Royal Courts dealt with disputes between the aristocracy over land (all ultimately held under feudal tenure from Crown), the boroughs developed their own 'courts' and informal institutions (Piepowder courts – *pieds poudre*) for hearing disputes relating to trade and commerce between merchants and artisans. Mediaeval guilds prioritised trade customs over the laws of the state in settling their own disputes without resort to court adjudication.

A study of the emergence of the common law and the Royal Courts of Justice

> reveals a world in which many litigants, preferring local knowledge and expertise of local dispute institutions, relied on these institutions rather than the Royal Courts to handle their grievances and even when invoking the system of royal justice to pursue their grievance, the parties were inclined to settle when they perceived settlement to be in their best interests.
>
> (Palmer and Roberts 2020)

In mediaeval England, a distinction rooted in the one between the New and Old Testaments was drawn between the principles of charity or love (*Caritas*) (New) and law (*Lex*) (Old). Civil cases were settled out of court on so called Love Days, according to the principle *Pactum legem vincit et amor iudicum*. (Agreement prevails over law and love over judgment) (Clanchy 1983), during which hearings were adjourned to enable settlement. In 14th-century England, there are records of actions before the Court of Common Pleas met with the statement being recorded as settled *per mediacionem facta* (made through mediation).

Koch in Klaus-Friedrich, ed. (1979), draws on ethnographic accounts of disputes in Fiji, the Friendly Isles, Iran, early Utah, Zincacantan, and Chiapas in Mexico to illustrate the polymorphous shape of disputes and the role played by dispute processes in legitimating the social order in which they occur. In the Pacific, Middle Eastern, Maya Indian, and Mormon communities, 'their enmeshment in a village-wide network of multiple, reciprocal and cross-cutting relationships promotes the use of mediation over adjudication.' Barton (1919) describes the role of Kalinga and Ifugao *Monkalun,* or 'go-between,' in the Philippines, whose role encompasses judge, prosecutor, and defending counsel and who has a duty to exert diplomatic efforts and persuade the parties to achieve a peaceful settlement but, crucially, no authority to enforce it.

Religious authorities have often proffered forms of dispute resolution to their communities based on shared values. Ismaili Conciliation Boards offer this in Shi'a Islam. *Beth Din* rabbinical courts offer a similar role in Jewish communities. Dissenting religious communities, such as Quakers and Mennonites, have a settled distrust of state-backed adjudication and a strong preference to resolve disputes within their own communities on a consensus model, almost as an article of faith.

In nomadic Tibet, the function of a mediator was often fulfilled by a Buddhist lama. A mediator or mediators would perform numerous roles in peace-making between individuals and communities. The role of mediator was socially prestigious. Mediators were *Bar Mi* (between men), centered between two sets of claims; *Bar aDum Ba* (between reconcilers), who listened to both sides and deployed powers of 'argument, persuasion, cajolery and appeal to self-interest to bring both sides to the point of agreement'; and *gZu Ba* (straightforward witness ones), who collected and evaluated evidence and pronounced findings which 'drew the function of mediation closer to the more authoritarian function of arbitration' (Ekvall 1964). Lamas brought to the process the transcendent ethics of Buddhism and the deepest beliefs of the Tibetan world view:

> When of great sanctity, they brought . . . . reflections of clairvoyant wisdom, and by divination they could refer knotty problems to the will of the gods. Mediation uniformly had greater prospect of success when the red and yellow robed ones initiated it, or headed the delegation of the 'between ones.' All mediators, laymen and clergy alike, should be KHa NGo Can (mouth-face possessors).

The term stresses two basic qualifications of acceptable and successful mediators: 'mouth,' the power of speech, belonging to those who exacted attention and respect when they spoke and were true orators and eloquent in a speech conscious culture and 'face,' which was an indefinable combination of status, worth, reputation, and relationship, which made it possible for a mediator to say, 'Regard my face and . . .' as a consciously and carefully chosen form of final appeal (Ekvall 1964). Pirie (2013) describes a continuation of forms of mediation in the 21st century, where 'the process of mediation is tentative and contingent' and dependent on persuasion; threat and cajolery in a process 'characterized by appeals to pride and honour, rather than reference to laws and legalistic adjudication.'

Aris in Hutt (ed) (1994) discusses traditional methods of settling antagonisms in rural Bhutan, contrasting the use of mediation with formal litigation. High-status intermediaries (*bar-mi*) liaise between lay or clerical independent figures (*kha-mchu* or *rtsod-gzhi*) and the parties to the dispute. More formally, cases can be put to the village headman to negotiate a compromise outside the court system. The aim of the process is to forge 'settlement' or 'accord' (*grigs-kha*, *cham-kha*, *bsdums-grigs*). A contract is drawn up including a pledge (*ba*) to be forfeited if a statement is proved false, or the contract is broken. Such private contracts carry equal authority to those imposed by a court. Formal litigation is costly and has stigma attached to it. The process of ligation is seen as the 'total failure of the community itself to effect a settlement.'

In Lebanon, Jordan, and Palestine, patronage-based *wasta* and community-based *sulh* (mediation) and *musalaha* (reconciliation) processes steer disputing parties to a middle point.[1] The mediatory role is traditionally performed by the head of the family but may be contracted to others; the principle *wasta* (mediatory) task involves intercession for economic benefit (Cunningham and Saravrah 1994). In the Gulf region, the *Majlis* (place of sitting in Arabic, but also the meeting itself) is traditionally a tent set aside for legislative social gathering, but incorporated as a room for social gatherings in many houses is one of the cornerstones of Emirati civilization and a significant means of conflict resolution and fact of social life. Friends, neighbours, and families gather in a *Majlis* at sunset to resolve community disputes.

African traditional justice has a variety of forms of dispute resolution. Evans Pritchard (1940) identifies the role of mediator in the Nuer leopard-skin chief in disputes such as cattle theft or blood feuds. The power of the leopard-skin chief is religious rather than political in nature but may become a focus for community cohesion in arranging compensation and closure rituals (Gulliver 1971). Avruch (1998) examines collective decision-making among the Southern Tanzanian Ndendeuli, for whom mediation is a source of social prestige, and mediators, equidistant in kinship from both parties, convene meetings between disputants and supporters.

In Ethiopia, customary leaders and elders are elected by the *Kebele* (the lowest administrative unit of 500 or more families). While some work as judges, many more work as customary mediators, handling cases regarding land use, grazing rights, or property at a village level. Elders attempt to reconcile disputants by urging them to negotiate and make compromises. Their main concern is to achieve reconciliation through a restorative process and prevent escalation of the dispute. Customary mediators use rituals as part of the reconciliation process. The popularity of traditional mediation is based on the fact that it is accessible, quick, and free, but faced with an adamant defendant, it may be powerless to effect any compensation and appeal to the *Woreda* (district) court, which may be unable or unwilling to offer a remedy. Many customary elders still accept harmful traditional practices such as female genital mutilation and forced marriage. To protect land that belongs to the clan, women have little claim on collectively owned land (Baker 2013).

Some forms of traditional justice have been adapted to meet contemporary conflict and disputes. *Mato Oput* (the drinking of bitter root) in Acholi decision-making has played a role in the reintegration of child soldiers after abduction by the Lord's Resistance Army. In this ritual, former adversaries share a drink made of bitter herbs as a metaphor for the enmity between them and place their foreheads against each other in a ritual of community reconciliation (Bartlet 2009; Murithi 2006). In Rwanda, *gacaca* courts were developed out of a pre-existing system of community courts as a form of popular justice. The term *gacaca* can be translated as 'short grass,' referring to the public space where neighborhood elders (*abagabo*) meet to solve local problems. Adaptation is not simple, and there is a tension between reconciliation and the danger of impunity for serious crimes.

Gacaca developed as a form of transitional justice in dealing with the aftermath of the genocide in which as many as 800,000 people were murdered by an estimated similar number of perpetrators. *Gacaca* could not hear cases of war crimes, which means that reprisals carried out by the Rwandan Patriotic Front (RPF), the Tutsi-led rebel force that ended the genocide, were outside their jurisdiction. *Gacaca* courts illustrate the danger of alternative forms of justice being co-opted to political ends, in his case by furthering the narrative of the Hutus as the authors of the genocide while leaving the crime of Tutsi led army unaddressed.

The boundaries between customary arbitration and mediation are porous, in that while those resolving disputes take what, in Western terms, might be seen as an adjudicatory decision, the process of resolving a dispute is participatory and voluntary and the binding force of a decision depends not solely on the status of the elder or chief concerned but on the consent of the parties to the outcome proposed. The role of mediator in many African contexts is conceptually distinct from the Western model. In West African communities, they are expected 'to be fair-minded, unbiased elders, knowledgeable in the customs and traditions of their particular community.' Not only is there no requirement for them to be independent of the disputants, 'but they would inevitably be connected to those in dispute by ties of kinship, clan, and tribal identity' (Onyema in Moscati 2020). The role of a mediator could require clarifying information, promoting clear communication, interpreting standpoints, summarising discussions, emphasising relevant norms or rules, envisaging the situation if agreement is not reached, or repeating the agreement if already attained (Brock-Utne 2001).

Writers on mediation often credit indigenous practices as the sources of contemporary Western mediation practice. In New Zealand, mediation mirrors the traditional Māori decision-making process. The principle of *Kotahitanga* in Māori political practice seeks to reach unity through consensus in a way that recognises individuals and include all their concerns (Ritchie 1986). Forms of mediation are applied in the family courts (Family Proceedings Act 1980; Children, Young Persons and Their Families Act 1989), in industrial relations (Labour Relations Act 1987), and in international relations. The Treaty of Waitangi Act 1975 (1988 amendments to the Second Schedule) confer on the Waitangi tribunal the power to refer claims to mediation.

Ghana

Non-adversarial consensual dispute resolution has deep roots in Ghana. Chiefs, heads of families, elders and queen mothers continue to play significant roles in the resolution of disputes by consensus. These authority figures manage and resolve conflicts through processes that could be identified as negotiation, mediation, arbitration, or other forms of adjudication. Customary arbitration remains the dominant form of dispute resolution.

Customary dispute resolution operates within a communitarian framework with regional variation. It remains an integral part of people's lives in many communities. African customary dispute resolution is a consensual undertaking. The process is voluntary, and any decision must be agreed by the disputants. Although chiefs and elders have authority to make decisions, the consent of the parties involved in the conflict and that of the community validates the decision-making process. Consent to customary arbitration is given by the parties by giving a token to the arbitrators. Reconciliation is an important goal of these processes, and in a criminal context, the offender may be required to make restitution, offer an apology, or make other forms of atonement to appease the 'gods of the land' in the hope of forgiveness (Grande 1999).

In Ghana, there is a blurring of the distinction between mediation and arbitration. In customary arbitration, the elders or tribal leaders seek resolution by consent according to rules of natural justice founded on local mores and norms in adjudicating a claim. 'Customary arbitration,' as referred to in the ADR Act (2010) (Act 798), is used to describe both customary mediation and arbitration. While mediation is a significant part of customary dispute resolution, it differs in style from the US/UK model (discussed in Chapter 6). Values of community and tradition are more significant than the shibboleths of confidentiality and voluntariness. Customary dispute resolution focuses on restoring harmony to the community, building consensus, and reconciling competing interests.

Ahorsu and Ame (2011) describe a process in which confidentiality and neutrality are qualified values:

> Under the traditional flavor 'model,' the principles of confidentiality and neutrality are qualified, especially where power asymmetry among the parties are evident. The essence is to create an opportunity for a new relationship among parties to transform their 'structural violence.' On confidentiality, if the matter affects the whole community, as in some land disputes, the deliberations are held openly. The open hearings ensure greater trust and amplify the confidence of the community in the process; yet, only chosen representatives of parties are allowed to speak to questions that are directed at them. An offending party may be required to apologise to the community or to a specific individual before any settlement is finalised.
>
> (Nolan-Haley 2015)

As the first sub-Saharan country to gain independence from Britain, Ghana has had 60 years of independent legal development. In a dual-law system, customary law is incorporated into the common law by the 1992 Constitution.

> The common law of Ghana shall comprise the rules of law generally known as the common law, the rules generally known as the doctrines of equity and the rules of customary law including those determined by the Superior Court of Judicature.

Mediation is promoted by the judicial system under the aegis of the judicial services of Ghana, co-ordinated by a secretariat headed by a justice of the Court of Appeal and subject to a comprehensive statutory framework. The Courts Act 1993 (Act 459) provided for the promotion of reconciliation of civil and criminal disputes. In 1996, the Ghana Arbitration Centre was established to resolve commercial issues. The ADR Task Force was created to make recommendations for implementing ADR in the judicial system in 2001. The Labour Act 2003 (Act 651) provided for labor disputes to be settled through ADR. In 2005, the Lord Chief Justice created a five-year Strategic Plan for ADR Program. The Alternative Dispute Resolution Act 2010 (Act 798) consolidated previous legislation and integrated customary arbitration and court-connected mediation into a single legal framework subject to the jurisdiction of the courts. The judicial services of Ghana collaborated with the United Nations Development Program (UNDP) to develop a court-connected ADR manual, setting out a uniform style of court-connected mediation that largely follows a Western model.

The commercial division of the High Court provides for mandatory pre-trial settlement conferences in which the pre-trial judge acts as a mediator. In court-connected mediation, a judge refers a case for mediation at a case management conference, and trials are stayed for 30 days to allow for amicable settlement, but there are no sanctions for not participating. Mediation under the court-connected service is free to the participants. Mediation is highly settlement focused, and mediators are only paid for mediations that reach a settlement.

Customary mediation still plays a significant role in Ghana and is offered by churches, mosques, in a tribal setting, and across the country. It is incorporated into the civil justice system by the ADR Act 2010, and, where formalised through the process of customary arbitration, its outcome may be registered at the nearest district, circuit or High Court as an enforceable agreement subject to the jurisdiction of the courts (Section 110 of the ADR Act 2010). Decisions are only appealable on narrow grounds. Ghana National Association of ADR Practitioners (GNAAP) has a statutory mandate of providing education, training and refresher training, and research and ensuring professional development and maintenance of high standards of ADR practice in the Republic of Ghana in line with best international practices and procedure.

Court-connected alternative dispute resolution, as practiced across Ghana, represents a more Western form of mediation and is mandatory in commercial contexts. The pre-existing familiarity with forms of customary mediation, the social imperative to participate in these processes, and the active promotion by the state have all made the adoption of effectively mandatory mediation more acceptable, although state intervention may, at times, lead to negative reactions.

Contemporary styles of mediation in Ghana depend on context. Customary mediation may be either private or, where there is more of a community interest, a public process. Mediation of land disputes takes place in a community setting and would hear evidence from members of the community. After listening to all sides of a dispute, mediators may meet with the disputants privately and seek to 'persuade' them of the truth of the dispute. In disputes of a family nature, boundaries of confidentiality are more scrupulously respected. Court-connected mediation follows a Western style more closely (as discussed in Chapter 6), except where this involves the use of a customary arbitration process, such as when the matter has been referred to a community chief or community leader for customary arbitration. When court-connected mediation involves the services of trained mediators, the Western-style approach is used. Nolan-Haley (2015) describes 'tensions between the principles of neutrality and, self-determination and communitarianism, and confidentiality and public participation.' These tensions reflect the challenges and complexity of seeking to superimpose Western standards, as prescribed by the UNDP, onto pre-existing forms of mediation and illustrate the need to respect local traditions of justice and incorporate consensual decision-making into modern African dispute resolution if civil justice reform is to have popular consent.

Table 14.1 Judicial Service of Ghana – National ADR Secretariat (Breakdown of Annual Performance 2007–2020)

Year	*Month*	*Cases Mediated*	*Cases Settled*	*Percentage*
2007	January to December	853	466	53
2008	January to December	1,723	807	47
2009	January to December	5,358	3,871	72
2010	January to December	3,754	1,633	43
2011	January to December	4,392	2,025	46
2012	January to December	5,924	2,722	46
2013	January to December	6,668	2,806	42
2014	January to December	4,416	1,999	45
2015	January to December	1,464	635	43
2016	January to December	1,372	605	44
2017	January to December	3,486	1,571	49
2018	January to December	4,112	2,075	50
2019	January to December	6,384	3,041	49
2020	January to December	5,455	2,312	42
Total		55,361	26,568	48

India

Mediation as a method of resolving disputes is deeply rooted in Indian legal history. The mediation training manual of India, produced by the Mediation and Conciliation Committee of the Supreme Court presents the values of wisdom, reason, and prudence from Vedic tradition as informing the originating philosophy of mediation:

> The early Aryans . . . invoked the unwritten law of divine wisdom, reason and prudence, which according to them governed heaven and earth. This was one of the first originating philosophies of mediation – Wisdom, Reason and Prudence, which originating philosophy is even now practiced in western countries.
>
> (*Mediation Manual of India*, 2017)

The manual suggests that the modern theory of arbitrage has its roots in ancient customary law. Historically, law in India was viewed as *dharma* or a moral code rather than as a system of laws. The purpose of *dharma* as spiritual discipline is to enable each member of society to fulfill their human potential. Krishna is referred to as mediating between Kauravas and Pandavas in the Mahabharata.

Disputes between different communities were conducted by non-adversarial indigenous methods, as exemplified in the *Kula* tribunal developed by the scholar Yagnavalkya in Vedic times, which dealt with disputes between families, communities, tribes, or races; the *Shreni*, a corporation of artisans dealing with internal disputes; and the *Puga*, an association of traders in any branch of commerce. Buddhism advocated mediation as the wisest means of dispute resolution, and the manual cites the Buddha as saying:

> Meditation brings wisdom; lack of mediation leaves ignorance. Know well what leads you forward and what holds you back; choose that which leads to wisdom.

Ancient Indian jurist Patanjali, living between the second and fourth centuries BCE, was regarded as the avatar of demi-god Adi Sesha. He is reported to have said:

> Progress comes swiftly in mediation for those who try hardest, instead of deciding who was right and who was wrong.

In pre-colonial India, most disputes were settled in village meetings or *Panchayat*. These assemblies of five (*ayat*) respected elders (*panch*) became revered as a decision-making body with some of the attributes of mediation and some of court judgment. In addition to local government, *Panchayats* play a role in resolving conflict at a communal level in rural villages.

Ghandi envisaged the *Panchayat raj* (rule) as the foundation of self-sufficient rural governance. *Gram Sarehas* and *Panchayat raj* offer contemporary examples of community-based non-legal dispute resolution.

During the colonial era, arbitration became the favoured form of ADR, recognised in 1879 and referred to in Civil Procedure Code of 1908.

The Industrial Disputes Act 1947 recognised ADR in providing for the appointment of 'conciliators,' chosen in accordance with Section 4 of the act to mediate and advance the resolution of industrial disputes. Mediation was extended to family matters in 1976 through an amendment to the Code of Civil Procedure 1908. It placed a duty on courts dealing with family disputes 'to assist the parties in arriving at a settlement.'

Lok Adalat (People's Court) as a form of popular justice can be traced to village- and community-based mediation. Initially a tribally based form of dispute resolution, *Lok Adalat* was introduced in its modern form in Gujarat in 1982 and in Chennai (1986) and given statutory recognition under the Legal Services Authorities Act 1987. *Lok Adalats* are formed on district, state, and national levels and provide settlement conferences in cases being heard in a *Panchayat* or a formal court of law. The composition of each *Lok Adalat* varies, but there are often senior members of the bar or retired judges (Xavier 2006).

The *Lok Adalat* is free to litigants and presided over by members, who have the role of statutory conciliators only but no judicial role. Members often adopt a highly evaluative style but can only persuade the parties to come to a settlement. The decision of a *Lok Adalat* is deemed final, and any award or decree issued is enforceable on competing parties. The mechanism can provide for interim and final relief.

In family law proceedings in India, parties are required to meet with social workers at the first hearing after the case has been petitioned. (Section 9 Family Courts Act 1984). Reference is made to voluntary no-cost mediation, with lawyers at a later stage. Mediators here are court appointed and legally qualified.

The judiciary has sponsored modern facilitative mediation since the 1990s. In 1996, Chief Justice Ahmadi led a national team to examine case management and dispute resolution as part of a joint project with the United States. This group proposed procedural reforms, including legislative changes to authorise the use of mediation. Chief Justice Ahmadi called a meeting of all the High Courts of Indian states in 2002 to persuade them of the importance of mediation and the need to implement Section 89 of the Civil Procedure Code (Code of Civil Procedure Amendment Act 1999), which provides for referral of cases pending in the courts to mediation. The Commercial Courts Act 2015 provides for mandatory pre-institutional mediation in certain classes of commercial suits.

Mediators in court-appointed mediations are invariably legally qualified. While theoretically voluntary, disputants who do not wish to mediate can feel that while referral to mediation is voluntary, it is a request that is difficult to refuse.

The Mediation Act 2023 provides a regulatory framework for the promotion and facilitation of mediation at a national level. It aims to provide for the enforcement of mediated settlement agreements, establish a mediator registration body, encourage community mediation, and promote the acceptance of online mediation.

It was initially proposed that the act would provide for mandatory pre-litigation mediation, but to date, this has not been introduced.

Section 5 (1) provides for voluntary pre-litigation mediation:

Subject to other provisions of this Act, whether any mediation agreement exists or not, the parties before filing any suit or proceedings of civil or commercial nature in any court, may voluntarily and with mutual consent take steps to settle the disputes by pre-litigation mediation in accordance with the provisions of this Act.

Section 7 (2) provides for refence to a court-appointed mediator:

> (1) Notwithstanding the non settlement of dispute under sub-section (1) of section 5, the court or tribunal may, at any stage of proceeding, refer the parties to undertake mediation.
>
> (2) If the court or tribunal refers the parties to undertake mediation, it may pass suitable interim order to protect the interest of any party if deemed appropriate.
>
> (3) The parties shall not be under obligation to come to a settlement in the mediation pursuant to a reference under sub-section (1).

The Commercial Courts Act 2015 provided for mandatory pre-institutional mediation in certain classes of commercial suit. Since 2019, mediation has been ordered in most civil disputes and criminal cases where there is a maximum sentence of less than seven years imprisonment. It also may also take place in writ petitions filed before the Supreme Court.

Ethnographic research by Basu (2012) in the Family Courts of Kolkata confirms the prevalence of authoritarianism in the court and mediation sector and challenges the idea that alternate dispute resolution 'provides more satisfactory outcomes for marginalized subjects, as well as the assumption that new ways of speaking and listening can be transformative.' These comments suggest the pervasiveness of authoritarianism in the civil justice system in India and that mediation may not offer a way out of oppressive trials or gender norms.

The anecdotal experience of a practising mediator suggests that 'as in the litigation sector women and young mediators are unrepresented.' Another lawyer commented:

> In India many mediators who may be judges or senior lawyers, expect their guidance to be taken rather as if their relationship to the disputants, and their

> lawyers, were that of a strict parent to recalcitrant children. Far from being neutral in the conventional CEDR sense they would see themselves as guardians of norms and values of the legal community of which they are a part.

Another mediator commented, '[M]any mediators are senior lawyers and sometimes retired judges,' and the

> cultural obligation to 'listen to your elders' has seeped into the mediation setting. . . . This is done within professional boundaries most of the time, but I have seen some mediators get more personal and involved in their advice and suggestions; it has at times felt a bit directory.

While mediators in court-annexed mediation theoretically follow the UK/US Western model, the collectivist culture and tradition of *Panchayat*, still largely male and patriarchal, probably makes disputants more amenable to pressure to mediate and, subsequently, to settle.

China

Mediation in China can be traced back to the period of Emperors Yao and Shun (Fu and Palmer 2017) (2250–2100 BC) and has been the dominant form of dispute resolution from the Western Zhou dynasty (1046 to 771 BC). Confucius (551 to 478 BC) discouraged litigiousness. Confucian thinking prioritised the values of harmony and duty and put an emphasis on the virtue of 'yielding' and not standing on rights, emphasising moral leadership, self-sacrifice, and education, reinforcing an innate conservatism which encouraged the maintenance of existing relationships. In dynastic China, mediation in guilds, clans, and families became the ordinary mechanism of dispute resolution at a local level. Popular Chinese proverbs included 'It is better to be vexed to death than to bring a lawsuit' and 'Win a lawsuit; lose your money!' One of the analects of Confucius records: 'In hearing litigation I am not different from any other man. But if you insist on a difference it is perhaps, that I try to get the parties not to resort to litigation in the first place' (Analects of Confucius XII.13).

These values co-existed with a distinct philosophy of 'legalism,' in which a strong, centralised state provided for adjudication according to comprehensive legal codes in a hierarchy of courts. For the governing class, legalism was a conscious strategy to extend political control by exaggerating the risk of litigation and re-enforcing the fear of and aversion to litigation among citizens.

In this context, 'The function of law is not to provide a legal channel for people to satisfy with selfish desire' but to 'try its best to constrain the selfish desire of people to reach finally the purpose of making people have no disputes' (Zhiping 1991). Judge Wang Zuhui, in the Qing Dynasty, opined:

> It is good to be diligent to hear and judge. However, where it is unnecessary to distinguish black and white excessively for amity, it is better to mediate through relatives and friends. Therefore, we hear and judge according to law,

> while mediate with emotions. Law must distinguish the clear and the muddy, while emotion allows somewhat mistakes in distinguishing the right or wrong.
>
> (Yong'an and Cong 2023)

China today is a vast and diverse country immersed in a tradition of Confucianism and shaped by the ideology, campaigns, and strategy of the Communist Party. Since 1978, economic expansion, domestically and nationally; urbanization; and industrialisation have further changed the nature of its society to one in which increasingly educated individuals now engage with strangers through electronic terminals and face to face. Mediation has become a pragmatic way of dealing with challenges that might otherwise overwhelm a formal litigation system.

The conventional definition of mediation in China is

> a legal institution and dispute resolution mode of facilitating the parties to a dispute to conclude, on the basis of independent will, an agreement for eliminating the dispute by means of convincing, persuading and educating under the moderation of a third party.
>
> (Liao 2019)

Article 2 of the People's Mediation Law of China provides:

> [P]eople's mediation referred to herein deals with the activities of the people's mediation committee to facilitate, in the mode of convincing and persuading, the parties to reach voluntarily a mediation agreement and settle the folk dispute on the basis of equal consultation.

While emphasising the importance of voluntariness, China's form of mediation includes 'convincing,' 'educating,' and 'persuading' as aspects of a proactive mediation style that seeks to maintain the dominance of the party state. The mediator is not only a 'facilitator' but can propose solutions and overcome the 'pauperization of consensus' by putting pressure on the parties to come to an agreement. According to Liao and Cong (2023) 'If it is really necessary to find a word in English corresponding to Chinese mediation, then "reconciliation" may be more appropriate.'

Contemporary Chinese mediation, *tiaojie*, adopts a highly evaluative style which may involve moral and political judgments as well as the assessment of legal context. The political function of mediation as a source of implementing communist ideology has been grafted onto a traditional search for compromise in a network of social relationships. The revised Chinese Civil Procedure Law (2023) creates a framework for court-annexed mediation. While mediation is not mandatory, litigants may face strong expectations that they will settle. Mediation continues to be shaped by the parallel values of Confucianism and the contemporary role of the Communist Party as a normative force at every level of society. Mediation is seen both as a form of public education (following the opening of China, post 1978) and as containing or resolving social conflict. Since 2002, China has promoted mediation as part of its campaign for a harmonious society (*hexie shehui*). Article 122 of the Civil Procedure Law, as amended in 2012, provides: '[A]s for the civil disputes brought by the parties to the people's court and applicable for mediation, mediate first, except where the parties refuse mediation.'

Mediation in contemporary China takes place in a diversity of socio-civil-legal contexts. While people's mediation is statutorily regulated by the People's Mediation Law and industry mediation by the Labour Dispute Mediation and Arbitration Law (2008), other types of mediation have emerged and developed through judicial practice and international commercial mediation, in part influenced by the United Nations Convention on International Settlement Agreements Arising from Mediation signed in 2019 (Singapore Mediation Convention).

I have followed Liao and Cong's (2023) categorisation of 'people's mediation,' 'administrative mediation,' 'industry mediation,' 'commercial mediation,' and 'mediation and arbitration.' In addition, China is now also sponsoring an ever-expanding range of online mediation (Liao and Cong 2023). Gu (2021), following Fu and Palmer (2017), considers six types of mediation dependent on context: (1) people's mediation (*renmin tiaojie* 人民调解), (2) administrative mediation (*xingzheng tiaojie* 行政调解); (3) judicial mediation (*sifa tiaojie* 司法调解); (4) mediation combined with arbitration or Med-Arb (*tiaojie yu zhongcai xiangjiehe* or *tiaozhong* 调解与仲裁相结合或者调仲); (5) international commercial mediation (*guoji shangshi tiaojie* 国际商事调解); and (6) private mediation (*siren tiaojie* 私人调解).

People's mediation takes place in Peoples Mediation Committees (PMCs) before non-lawyer grassroots mediators. In the early years of the People's Republic of China (PRC) Ma Xiwu, as chief justice of a provincial-level people's High Court set up processes of informal justice and established people's mediation committees from 1949 as a way of incorporating popular participation in informal justice. If mediation failed, cases could be heard in front of the masses.

Mediation involved a strong didactic element in spreading both the understanding and the acceptance of party policy and promoting harmony (Palmer and Roberts 2020).

Article 111 of the Constitution of the PRC provides that 'resident committees' and 'village committees' are 'mass organisations of self-management at the grassroots level.' It stipulates that

> the resident and villagers' committees establish committees for people's mediation, public security, public health and other matters in order to manage public affairs and social services in their areas, mediate civil disputes, help maintain public order and convey resident opinions and demands and make suggestions to the people's government.

Article 5 of the Regulations for the Organisation of People's Mediation Committees sets out their aim: 'The mission of the People's Mediation Committee is to mediate civil disputes, and through such mediation, publicise laws, regulations, rules and policies and educate citizens to abide by laws and respect universally accepted morals.'

Table 14.2 People's Mediation Statistics (2008–2018)

Year	*Total Number of PMCs*	*Total Number of Civil Disputes Mediated by PMCs*
2008	827,412	4,981,370
2009	824,000	5,797,300
2010	818,130	8,418,393
2011	811,000	8,935,341
2012	817,121	9,265,855
2013	820,025	9,439,429
2014	802,957	9,404,544
2015	798,417	9,331,047
2016	784,000	9,019,000
2017	759,000	8,741,000
2018	752,000	9,532,000

Source: Table 5.1, p. 129, *Dispute Resolution in China: Litigation, Arbitration, Mediation, and Their Interaction*. First edition by Gu (2021). Reproduced by permission of Taylor & Francis Group.

PMCs exist in in villages, residential blocks, and factory work units. People's mediation is conducted by volunteers and is free at point of use. Some people's mediation is now provided by government-purchased social mediation. Since 2003, individual mediation studios have been set up, named after chief mediators. In Shanghai, the most influential examples are the Li Qin People's Mediation Studio and the Yang Boshou People's Mediation Studio. People's mediation may also be offered by NGOs.

The outcome of a people's mediation is not automatically enforceable but is considered to have the force of a contract. According to statistics of the Chinese Ministry of Justice (2023), there were 693,000 people's mediation committees nationwide, with 3.2 million people's mediators (including 412,000 full-time mediators). In 2022, people's mediation committees nationwide mediated 14.94 million cases of various types.

Prior to the People's Mediation Law 2010, people's mediation was conducted in public, but participants can now request that their mediation be conducted privately or publicly. Mediators are no longer required to 'educate' their disputants and are encouraged to 'persuade and guide' (*shuofu* and *shudao*) (Art 2) instead of 'mobilising' (*dongyuan*) disputants to mediate. Police and judges should 'inform the disputants about the option of mediation' (Fu and Palmer 2017).

Administrative mediation is conducted by government institutions. Despite an explicit ban on mediation in administrative cases, the People's Supreme Court has recognised the pressure from below by recognising mediated agreements as negotiated settlements (*hejie*) (Palmer 2020).

Administrative Procedure Law, Art 60 (2015) provides that although people's courts hearing administrative cases shall not apply to mediation, in cases of administrative compensation or where the exercise of discretion is provided for by laws or regulations, mediation may be used. Mediation must abide by the principles of voluntariness and lawfulness and not harm the national interest, societal public interest, or other lawful rights and interests.

Where a citizen, legal person, or organisation applies for administrative reconsideration of a specific action taken by an administrative organ, a written agreement can be submitted to the administrative reconsideration department, and if the settlement agreement 'does not prejudice the public interests and the legal rights and interests of others, the administrative reconsideration department shall consent to the settlement agreement' (Implementing Regulations of Administrative Reconsideration Law of the People's Republic of China, Art 40).

While such agreements cannot become orders of the court, the state entity, as defendant, can request the claimant to notarise the written settlement so the state agency can bring closure to the case and prevent the claimant from resurrecting another claim based on the same grievance (Palmer 2014). Ministries have supplemented the general guidance of the People's Mediation Law (2010) with advice on processes in specific industrial sectors such as hydroelectric, maritime, land, and labour disputes.

Court mediation is performed by judges prior to a trial in civil proceedings. In the pre-trial phase, judges are encouraged to liaise with local community organisations and industrial enterprises to get the disputants to agree to mediate their differences. Judicial mediation can take place pre-filing, post-filing, immediately prior, or during the trial. It is common practice for judges in charge of filing cases, who are different from the judges hearing the cases, to appoint relevant mediation organisations or individuals to conduct mediation. If the parties reject the mediation or if no settlement results, the case proceeds to trial with the same judge adjudicating the case. If agreement is reached, the court makes a 'settlement statement,' which can be enforced in the same way as a judgment. Gu (2021) identifies four stages in the development of judicial mediation. In the first stage (before 1991), mediation was the major method of dispute resolution for various disputes in the Chinese courts. In the second stage (1991 to mid-late 2000s), mediation was still preferred, but with civil litigation strengthened under the Chinese court reform of formal justice and dispute resolution and the wishes of the parties being important. In the third stage (late 2000s to early 2010s), mediation was prioritised under the Chinese mediation campaign and became politicised to maintain social stability. This involved a change of judicial self-image from 'professional, elite, authoritative decision makers' to 'stability-maintaining citizens' (Fu and Palmer 2017). Parties often entered judicial mediation due to judicial pressure. Judges were constrained by performance targets to settle cases through mediation and assessed by mediation rates both professionally and politically. In the fourth stage (early-mid 2010s to present), judges have adopted a more nuanced approach toward the use of judicial mediation.

Research, including that sponsored by Chinese courts themselves, has shown that the impact of enhanced emphasis on judicial mediation 'has not necessarily increased political stability and social harmony.'

The Supreme People's Court issued the *Opinions on Further Deepening the Reform of ADR Mechanisms within the Judiciary in* 2016. This proposed the separation of mediation and litigation, and since then, a more rational approach has been taken to promoting mediation in judicial practice. Chinese courts now generally refer cases to

Table 14.3 Caseload of Chinese Courts (2013–2018)

Year	*Caseload of SPC*	*Caseload of Chinese Lower-Level Courts Combined*
2013	11,016	14,217,000
2014	11,210	15,651,000
2015	15,985	19,511,000
2016	22,742	23,030,000
2017	21,430	16,558,000
2018	34,794	28,000,000

Source: Table 2.1, p. 24, *Dispute Resolution in China: Litigation, Arbitration, Mediation, and Their Interaction*. First edition by Gu (2021). Reproduced by permission of Taylor & Francis Group.

Table 14.4 Judicial Mediation in China's First-Instance Civil Litigation (2009–2018)

Year	*Total Number of First-Instance Civil Litigation Cases Concluded by All Chinese Courts*	*Total Number of First-Instance Civil Litigation Cases Concluded by Judicial Mediation*	*Percentage of Judicial Mediation in All Concluded Civil Litigation*
2009	5,797,160	2,099,024	36.21%
2010	6,112,695	2,371,683	38.80%
2011	6,558,621	2,665,178	40.64%
2012	7,206,331	3,004,979	41.70%
2013	7,510,584	2,847,990	37.92%
2014	8,010,342	2,672,956	33.37%
2015	9,575,152	2,754,843	28.77%
2016	10,763,889	2,787,475	25.90%
2017	11,651,363	2,885,318	24.76%
2018	12,434,826	3,133,015	25.20%

Source: Table 6.1, p. 160, *Dispute Resolution in China: Litigation, Arbitration, Mediation, and Their Interaction*. First edition by Gu (2021). Reproduced by permission of Taylor & Francis Group.

an out-of-court mediator, but the same judge may hear a case and mediate up until the point of judgment. In 2023, there were 12.04 million successful cases of pre-litigation mediation in courts nationwide, accounting for 40.3% of the total number of civil and administrative cases brought to court (statistics from the Supreme People's Court).

For Gu (2021), the development of judicial mediation or 'mediatory justice' reflects a 'juggling path between adjudicatory and mediatory justice in China, as well as the tension between professional and popular justice.' In mediation initiated by judges, parties may yield to the judge's authority or are reluctant to reveal information that may be used to be against them in subsequent litigation proceedings.

Industry Mediation

China has encouraged industry mediation, conducted by associations in a particular industry, since 2015 by reference to the People's Mediation Law. Industry and professional mediation organisations are sponsored by administrative authorities with the participation of industry representatives and experts. One example is the People's Mediation Committee for Intellectual Property Disputes in Hunan Province established by the Hunan Intellectual Property Association in 2016. Other sectoral mediation organisations include medical services, property services, consumer protection, road traffic accidents, and insurance.

Commercial mediation has been conducted by arbitral administrative bodies, including private entities, since 1987, in areas such as investment, finance, securities and futures, insurance, e-commerce, intellectual property rights, and international trade. Commercial mediation has experienced growth since the Belt and Road Initiative (2013) and now plays a significant role in China. More recently, the adoption of the United Nations Convention on International Settlement Agreements Resulting from Mediation (Singapore Convention) has accelerated the application of commercial dispute resolution in China as part of a process of globalisation. Organisations include the China Council for the Promotion of International Trade/China Chamber of International Commercial Mediation Centre, the Beijing Arbitration Commission Mediation Centre (2011), the Shanghai Commercial Mediation Centre (2011), and the Guangdong, Hong Kong, and Macau Commercial Mediation Alliance (2013).

Lawyer Mediation

Although technically not a separate form of mediation, since 2017, China had encouraged lawyers to offer mediation in courts, legal service centres, law firms, and bar associations. China's Ministry of Justice requires lawyers to adopt a low-price model, which, in some contexts, must be no more than 50% of court costs in similar circumstances.

Mediation in Arbitration

China's arbitration law provides for mediation in arbitration: i.e., an arbitrator will mediate the dispute after the arbitration proceedings have been initiated. Some arbitral institutions, such as the China International Economic and Trade Arbitration

Table 14.5 Med-Arb Adoption in China (2014–2018)

Year	*2014*	*2015*	*2016*	*2017*	*2018*	*Average*
Total number of arbitration cases	113,660	136,924	208,545	239,360	539,542	**247,606**
Number of arbitration mediations (i.e., by consent award)	74,200	56,659	121,527	69,450	140,281	**92,441**
Percentage of arbitration cases concluded by successful mediation (i.e. percentage of consent award)	65%	41%	58%	29%	26%	**47.07%**

Source: Table 8.1, p. 219, *Dispute Resolution in China: Litigation, Arbitration, Mediation, and Their Interaction*. First edition by Gu (2021). Reproduced by permission of Taylor & Francis Group.

Commission and the Beijing Arbitration Commission, have innovated and developed forms of combining arbitration and mediation on the basis of the arbitration law.

In the period 2014 to 2018 almost half (47.07%) of arbitration cases are concluded by successful mediation. As these figures do not include cases where mediation was futile, it appears that med-arb is applied in the majority of arbitration cases.

Online mediation has been widely adopted by Chinese courts and industry-supported platforms such as the China (Hangzhou) Intellectual Property-International Commercial Mediation Cloud Platform and self-contained e-commerce platforms such as the Taobao ODR Center. The Supreme Court established a national online dispute resolution platform in 2017. In its first year, over 1,000 courts and 12,000 mediation organisations had joined this platform. Through this online mechanism, parties can apply for mediation, select a mediator, attend via video, and sign an agreement through their cell phone, tablet, or computer. Online mediation can be (1) government led, (2) court led, or (3) civil organisation led (Liao and Cong 2023). Zhejiang province has set up a comprehensive online dispute resolution platform providing a variety of services, including consultation, evaluation, mediation, and arbitration. The first internet court was established in Hangzhou in collaboration with China Telecom (2017) to handle internet-related cases, including disputes over purchases, and to cater to the increasing number of online disputes. Statistics from the Zhejiang ODR platform indicate that the number of new user visits between January and June 2020 was 1,072,249, and the number of newly registered users was 181,985.

The growth of growth of online dispute resolution (including online mediation) and the adoption of ODR technologies in Chinese courts have been spectacular. According to the annual work report of the Supreme People's Court published in March 2023, a total of 38.32 million disputes were mediated online in 2022, with an average of 75 cases per minute successfully resolved online before litigation.

Mediation in China is more than an adjunct to civil procedure and a form of dispute resolution; it expresses deep cultural values and has its place in popular culture. In a recent development, 'grand mediation' may be applied to highly individualised environmental, labour and socio-economic disputes. Grassroots government officials identify large-scale disputes and attempt to resolve them before they escalate into protest (Fu and Palmer 2017). Television mediation, in which publicly aired disputes are resolved, has become a popular form of entertainment. Generally concerning family disputes between socially disadvantaged citizens, mediations are broadcast live to an audience of millions. According to the Department of Justice, these mediations have are a 92.6 % success rate (Fu and Palmer 2017) and are binding in the same way as other people's mediations.

The diversity of mediation in China illustrates the way contemporary mediation has been shaped, both by historical antecedents and the normative force of the Communist Party. Domestically, many local disputants regard a willingness to settle and move on as a virtue on a par with seeking justice in adjudicated outcomes. While people's mediation is driven by the government and the party's priority of maintaining social stability, international commercial mediation is shaped by China's adherence to the Singapore Convention and the desire to maintain the confidence of international investors. In Chinese legal philosophy, there appears to be an entrenched view that while 'facilitative mediation' is the culturally appropriate style of mediation outside the PRC, a 'more robustly evaluative approach' (Fu and Palmer 2017) is appropriate to the domestic context in PRC. Pragmatism is the cornerstone of the mediation system in China and is evident in both the highly assertive nature of mediator interventions and the range of dispute resolution forms that may be deployed.

Conclusion

This chapter has been able to do no more than scratch the surface of the legal anthropology of dispute resolution in the Global South. The modern ADR movement has sometimes been depicted as a return to the 'idyllic past' of consensual dispute resolution (Grande 1999). This ignores the different structure of modern and traditional legal processes. Whereas in the modern state, courts are seen as the sole guarantor of legal rights, in acephalous societies, the individual exists in a group which is the guarantor of a mutual pattern of rights and duties. It is natural, therefore, that the community should play a significant role in the resolution of disputes. It is clear, however, that the more collective a society and the stronger its ties of reciprocity, the greater the potential for non-adversarial means of dispute resolution. The wealth of evidence of non-adversarial dispute resolution procedures attests to a near-universal need for processes that resolve disputes in ways that re-engage parties with each other rather than referring them to an adjudicator for their decision and, in so doing, also create and affirm community cohesion.

These studies confirm the comment of Golbert (2009) that 'cross-cultural and international mediation that is truly responsive to context and to culture must do more than explain and translate important cultural differences; it must attempt to incorporate dimensions of cultural differences into the mediation model.' Price (2018) has suggested that ADR 'offers a bridge between traditional and modern dispute resolution, creating a mutually supportive, collaborative relationship.'

While in the individualistic cultures of the UK and the USA, facilitative forms of mediation are premised on an interest-based style of mediation, this is only one potential form. In more collective cultures, a wider range of parties (friends, neighbours, community members) will be drawn into a dispute. An insider third-party mediator may play a significant role as a representative and interpreter of social norms, whether traditional or derived from political practice. As Wehr and Lederach (1991) have argued, in more collective societies, an effective model of mediation may involve the 'insider partial' mediator 'whose acceptability to the conflictants is rooted not in distance from the conflict or objectivity regarding the issues but rather in connectedness and trusted relationship with the conflict parties.'

While individualistic culture puts an emphasis on the struggle for individual rights, in more collectivist cultures, such as Ghana, India, and the PRC, there is a preference both to avoid conflicts in the first place and to take active measures to resolve conflicts when they occur. This provides favorable conditions for a culture of negotiation, mediation, and reconciliation.

Although clearly, there are significant cultural and political differences between these distinct cultural and political contexts, more collective cultures both provide an incentive for mediation and shape the form that it takes. Ghana, India, and China have all adopted forms of de facto mandatory mediation that go beyond contemporary practice in the UK. As Nolan-Haley (2015) has observed, 'mediation programs, as implemented in Africa under the banner of access to justice have at times conflicted with local customs and traditions,' resulting in a clash of values. Models which seek to transpose Western, interest-based mediation as a uniform model without regard to local traditions are likely to encounter resistance. It is too early to judge the impact of the Mediation Act (2023) in India. In China, the confluence of Confucian values and the normative force of the Communist Party make mediation the dominant form of dispute resolution but in a highly evaluative form that would not always meet Western definitions. In Ghana, pre-existing familiarity with mediation has made court-annexed mediation more acceptable but created tensions between the favoured US/UK model and expectations built on traditional dispute resolution.

Questions

Exercise

Research and prepare a 500-word summary of how mediation in a non-European context differs from and is similar to the USA/UK model. Discuss similarities and differences with your tutorial partners and consider possible reasons for these variations.

Question

What do you think mediators in the US and the UK might learn from other jurisdictions that could be applied to their practice?

Further Reading

Capelletti, M. (1978) *Access to Justice, IV Anthropological Perspectives. Giuffre.*

Golbert, R. (2009) 'An Anthropologist's Approach to Mediation', *Cardozo Journal of Conflict Resolution* 11, 81.

Moscati, F., Palmer, M. & Roberts, R., eds (2020) *Comparative Dispute Resolution a Research Handbook.* Elgar.

Note

1 *Wasta* means 'the middle' and is associated with *yatawassat* – 'to steer conflicting parties to a middle point' – in Eastern Arabic. *Wasta* refers both to the act and actor of mediation.

15 Online Dispute Resolution

This short chapter offers a brief introduction to online dispute resolution (ODR). It will introduce some of the issues that it raises for the development of ADR and its relationship with the courts. While ADR has its origin in an alternative to the court system of adjudication, ODR has developed in a context in which courts have not previously operated. 'Online dispute resolution' is used to describe any dispute resolution process conducted online and describes a range of distinct phenomena:

1. Forms of ADR that have been around since the mid-1990s for resolving disputes which have arisen as a result of and to cater for the internet and virtual reality. The vast majority of these processes take place online.
2. Forms of ADR involving information and communication technology (ICT) and artificial intelligence (AI) that are increasingly being deployed to develop ADR processes that may be used to deal with disputes arising both in cyberspace and in a real-world context.
3. Forms of dispute resolution taking place online, which may be used to describe both ADR processes and state-sponsored adjudication accessed by an online portal.

Katch and Rabinovich-Einy (2017) describe three shifts in the evolution of the ODR landscape: the first from a physical to a virtual setting; the second from human-based to automated processes; and the third from 'processes that value confidentiality in resolving disputes to processes that focus on collecting, using, and reusing data to prevent disputes.' According to the analysis of Katch and Rabinovich-Einy (2017) and Quek (2019), technology has the potential to become a 'fourth party' in a dispute, distinct from the 'third party' of the courts, with the potential to prevent as well as resolve online disputes.

First-Generation Online Dispute Resolution

Amazon, eBay, the expansion of e-commerce, and the gig economy have given rise to huge numbers and new forms of disputes. ODR initially dealt with these disputes by mimicking ADR procedures. Amazon and eBay created their own online dispute resolution systems, including technology-assisted negotiation taking place in a virtual forum followed by low-cost online virtual mediation for resolving disputes

DOI: 10.4324/9781003112617-15

arising from their platforms. These systems have been adapted and developed in systems such as Modria, used by CEDR.

One of the earliest experiments was eBay's contract with SquareTrade (1999) to provide dispute resolution services for e-commerce consumer transactions. By 2003 SquareTrade was handling several million disputes per year (eBay currently handles over 60 million disputes a year) (Rabinovich-Einy and Katsh 2017). In this process, a buyer or a seller files a complaint by filling out a web-based standard claim form that identifies the type of dispute and provides a list of common solutions. Most disputes fall into one of ten discrete categories, facilitating the creation of generic forms that parties can use to explain grievances and seek solutions. Software tools limit the free text space, encourage the proposition of agreements, set deadlines, and shape the tone and content of exchanges. When initial agreement cannot be reached, parties are offered an interactive web interface to shape communications into a courteous and constructive negotiation. If this is unsuccessful, they can request the services of an experienced mediator who uses email to communicate with disputing parties in much the same way as in a face-to-face setting. The greater cost of mediation was born by eBay as an encouragement of confidence in its sales platform. SquareTrade technology intervenes in the negotiation by enabling parties to formulate and reformulate the problem and the solution in ways that facilitate a potential solution.

Second-Generation ODR

MODRIA (the modular online dispute resolution implementation assistant) is currently one of the most sophisticated platforms for dispute resolution used by both government agencies and dispute resolution services. It developed out of the first generation of systems such as that provided by SquareTrade. Modria offers 'preconfigured resolution flows, an online "resolution room" for each issue, and a unique user experience.' The system claims to resolve 60% to 90% of e-commerce disputes without customer service intervention.

Modria technology has resolved hundreds of thousands of disputes for clients, including the American Arbitration Association (traffic accident cases), the Dutch Legal Aid Board (Rechtwijzer), the state of Ohio (tax appeals), various county governments throughout the United States (property assessment disputes), CEDR, and e-commerce and payments companies. From the point of view of the trader, Modria enables the company to gather and analyse detailed information about the types of dispute arising, including the number of disputes filed by case type; the number of disputes resolved by outcome, such as those mutually agreed on by buyer and seller or resolved after escalation; settlement rates; and awards.

Second-generation ODR has developed artificial intelligence (AI) to help parties identify their concerns and interests and suggest resolution and draft agreements. Cybersettle software developed out of work settling insurance claims and offers a blind-bidding system that creates a ZOPA for settlement. The system can generate suggestions that fall within certain negotiating ranges. Parties may exchange visible proposals or contribute their own suggestions to the mix. These suggestions remain anonymous, thus avoiding the loss of face of accepting a suggestion made by another party. Confidential offers will only be disclosed when both offers match certain standards (usually ranging from between 30% and 5% of each other) or a given amount of money. The settlement will usually be set at a midpoint of the two offers. If the bids come near each other in any particular round, then the system splits the difference between them and declares settlement.

The United Nations Commission on International Trade Law (UNCITRAL) has provided the UNCITRAL Technical Notes on Online Dispute Resolution, which can be used by ODR providers as a base model to draft their own rules, specifically tailored to their specifications.

Third-Generation ODR

State courts and legal services are increasingly devising online portals to access the court systems. Some of these relate to filing cases for adjudication, so they are not, strictly speaking, ADR. Others blur the distinction between adjudication and ADR.

The Civil Justice Council's Advisory Group on ODR (2015) has recommended that HMCTS establish a new, internet-based court service, to be known as HM Online Court. The report recommended a three-tier service:

1. Providing online evaluation, helping users with a grievance classify and categorise their problem, to be aware of their rights and obligations, and to understand the options and remedies available to them.
2. Online facilitation, bringing a dispute to a speedy, fair conclusion with the support of online facilitators. Communicating via the internet, facilitators would review papers and statements and help parties through mediation and negotiation. Additionally, there would be some automated negotiation via systems to help parties resolve their differences without human intervention.
3. Online judges – full-time and part-time members of the judiciary – deciding appropriate cases or parts of cases online, largely on the basis of papers submitted to them electronically as part of a structured process of online pleading. This process would be supported, where necessary, by telephone-conferencing facilities.

Online dispute resolution subsequently became a central part of Briggs LJ's 2016 proposals for reform as part of his review of the structure of the civil courts. He recommended the introduction of an online court (OC) for 'resolving the lack of adequate access to justice for ordinary individuals and small businesses.' His recommendations included:

- The OC should eventually 'be compulsory for claims within its jurisdiction (subject to the courts' power to transfer cases to a higher court on grounds of complexity or public importance).' (Recommendation 5 and paragraph 6.16, BFR.)
- In the conciliation phase (stage 2), a Case Officer should recommend the best option for each case, which might include ODR, face-to-face and telephone

mediation or judicial early neutral evaluation. (Recommendation 12 and paragraphs 6.112–3 and 7.22–3, BFR.)
- HMCTS and the voluntary agencies should work on improving the provision of public legal education. (Recommendation 25 and paragraphs 6.115–119, BFR.)

In England and Wales, Pre-Action Protocol for Low-Value Personal Injury Claims in Road Traffic Accidents adopted a portal (2010) for dealing with personal injury claims online. The process has been accelerated by COVID. The probate portal provides an online service for members of the public and probate professionals to apply for probate (2020). The family public law portal provides an online service which allows local authorities to complete and submit applications for care and supervision orders. Lawyers can respond to and access information on family public law applications (2021). There is an access to damages claims portal, offering online services for lawyers to issue and respond to a claim for damages on behalf of their clients (2022).

Other Jurisdictions

European Union

EU Reg 524/2013 (Online Resolution for Consumer Disputes) created a web-based platform in 2016 for out-of-court resolution of contractual disputes. The ODR platform provides a website that acts as a hub to transmit disputes to ADR providers nominated by member states. All online merchants and marketplaces that operate within the EU must provide an accessible link to the ODR platform. Some EU countries have already built national ODR platforms to complement the EU platform.

As a result of Brexit UK (EU Exit), the Online Dispute Resolution Regulation was revoked by the Consumer Protection (Amendment etc.) (EU Exit) Regulations 2018, meaning that, from 1 January 2021, businesses and consumers in the UK are no longer able to use the ODR platform, although they are still able to access EU ADR entities through other means.

British Colombia passed Civil Resolution Act 2012, and its tribunal was launched in 2016. The act deals with small claims with maximum value of Can$25,000 and motor vehicle injury disputes up to $50,000 and also related to condominium disputes via a four-phase process:

Stage 1 Assisted self-help plaintiff needs to access CRT's Solution Explorer Software before filing a claim, which gives the party education about context.

Stage 2 Claimant fills in request for dispute resolution by responding to preset questions in set fields.

Stage 3 Settlement encouragement – information on negotiating effectively on the assisted-negotiation platform for interparty communication.

Stage 4 Adjudication – tribunal member decides the case on the basis of electronically submitted evidence. If oral hearing is necessary, it takes place by phone or video conferencing.

China

The first internet court was established in Hangzhou (2017) to handle internet-related cases and cater to the increasing number of online disputes, cases against ISPs, and product liability for products bought online. The process begins with a claimant filing a claim online. Within 15 days, a mediator contacts the parties to offer mediation via text, telephone, or video conference. Party autonomy is a foundational principle of online mediation. Article 4 of the Rules for Online Mediation in People's Courts (2022) specifies that 'to adopt online mediation, a people's court shall obtain the consent of the parties concerned and comprehensively consider the specific circumstances of the case, technical conditions and other factors.' Only if a mediation does not take place or is unsuccessful does the defendant respond to the claimant, after which a judicial hearing is held via video conference and open to the public via video stream.

China has adopted a court system which relies on computer technologies to enable big data use, blockchain formation and advisory, and determinative forms of artificial legal intelligence. Online mediation can be (1) government led, (2) court led, or (3) civil organisation led (Liao and Cong 2023). The Supreme Court Online Resolution platform was launched in 2011. In its first year of operation, over 1,000 courts and 12,000 mediation organisations joined the platform. Parties can apply for mediation through an online mechanism, select a mediator, attend via video, and sign an agreement through their cell phone, tablet, or computer. According to the Annual Work Report of the Supreme People's Court (March 2023), 38.32 million disputes were mediated online in 2022, with an average of 75 cases per minute successfully resolved online before litigation.

Quasi-Judicial Forms of Dispute Resolution

Many disputes are now resolved without reference to a court. The Financial Ombudsman Service resolved 438,802 complaints in 2015–2016. The Traffic Penalty Tribunal assessed 12,734 penalty charges in the same period, of which 76% were assessed on the papers only with e-decision. Of these, 16% required telephone hearings, and 8% involved face-to-face proceedings.

Private Online Adjudication

Consumer disputes are increasingly diverted to online dispute resolution at an early stage. Internal processes (e.g. requests for flight refunds) are themselves increasingly digital. CEDR handles disputes in relation to the following sectors: accountancy, cars, finance, flights, funerals, gambling, health care, holidays, post, communication and internet service providers, removals, funerals, surveyors, solicitors, and water and sewage. Customers are obliged to raise complaints internally prior to CEDR investigation. These processes are generally free to the customer but at a charge to the business.

Communication with both consumer and provider is via an online platform (Modria). If the customer is not content with the result of the adjudication, they can then pursue legal avenues. Recent BBC coverage regarding flight refunds has highlighted a gap in the law between a customer's right to compensation for cancelled flights and the reality of being offered vouchers. Th British Airways website displayed two buttons: one labelled 'change booking' and the other 'cancel booking.' The cancel booking button then took customers to a webpage that offered vouchers rather than a refund.

Benefits of ODR

- ODR can enhance access to justice.
- Parties don't need to meet face to face.
- It can reduce linguistic barriers through translation software.
- It can enhance consistency through automation.
- It reduces costs.
- Asynchronous communication increases the speed of resolution.
- It offers business insights for the merchant through analysis of data.
- It provides lawyerless resolution for consumers for disputes that aren't legally complex.

Challenges of ODR

- ODR tends to prioritise efficiency at the expense of individual fairness.
- Procedural justice depends on the design of each ODR system.
- ODR may have serious implications for open justice.
- Lack of direct contact between parties can erode trust and empathy on which ADR depends.
- Classification of violations of legal liability cannot be resolved through electronic mediation.
- Ease of access to ODR may encourage litigiousness.

Discussion

Proponents of ADR maintain not just that it can resolve disputes but that it has the potential to manage and prevent disputes in the future. The use of blockchain technology with its decentralised structure and sophisticated approach to data security could drastically reduce the potential for factual disputes. CEDR's use of Modria for consumer adjudications illustrates the potential for businesses in the technology sector to identify problems and patterns of complaints and improve internal handling to enhance customer satisfaction and limit future disputes. In China, the ODR platform has been used to enable musicians to safeguard their copyrights by self-service e-discovery against infringements.

In the Sir Brian Neill lecture to the Society of Computers and Law, Voss (MR) (2022) offered a vision in which digital records and crypto-assets 'could make factual disputes almost entirely a thing of the past' in most civil claims. Litigation, arbitration, and associated mediations create and rely on the same data in their pleadings, witness statements, expert reports, skeleton arguments, and opening and closing written submissions. In his McNair lecture (2023), he outlined a vision for an 'online funnel' with artificial intelligence taking minor judicial decisions and effectively providing a fusion of systems dealing with ADR (proper) and adjudication. His proposal includes a system in which:

> pre-action portals will be provided by a mixture of public and private entities. If resolution is not achieved within the portals, the data constituting the claim will be transmitted by API (application programming interface) directly into the digital court system that is already well on its way to completion.

Technology should be applied to ensure 'every case has a single data set that can be used at every stage of the dispute resolution process, whether judicial, mediation or other forms of [A]DR.'

There is relatively little research into public attitudes to ODR. A National Center for State Courts (NCSC) poll found US citizens are not as enthusiastic as some may suspect. Only 44% of those surveyed who earn $75,000 or more were likely to want online resolution of tenancy disputes.

Blankley (2020) considers ODR may help protect victims during family law processes, referencing evidence that online processes may provide different results to in-person hearings. Bail for Immigration Detainees in UK found online applications for immigration received less favourable outcomes than face-to-face hearings. The Bail Observation Project (2013), in a study of 211 immigration bail hearings, found that 50% of cases heard via video link were refused bail, compared to 22% of those heard in person (Hynes 2019). Rabinovich-Einy and Katsh (2017) consider that private ODR systems operate sporadically, with little monitoring regarding procedural fairness or disclosure of the nature of the dispute prevention activities being performed.

Prince (2019) draws attention to the need for open and procedural justice in the design of the online court and calls for further empirical data. Schmitz (2020) adopts a precautionary approach, highlighting the risks of online processes undermining due process by becoming click-through processes without the presence of facilitators. Her study references a National Centre for State Courts survey in which 'poorer, older and less educated people generally seem less willing to engage with ODR' and concludes that it can enhance access to justice, 'but only if properly deployed, improved and monitored.'

Conclusion

Forms of ADR that were developed to cater for the web have now become incorporated into mainstream adjudication. At the same time, technology has changed the way we relate to each other in both private and public adjudication processes. Information technology is having a profound impact on the administration of justice and blurring boundaries, both between public and private and ADR and court adjudication. In the case of proposals such as Voss's online funnel, it may also elide the distinction between ADR and court adjudication.

Precisely because it is so powerful and potentially disruptive, the use of AI in ODR raises legitimate concerns. Some of the most persuasive advocates of ADR are profoundly sceptical of its claims for its prioritisation of efficiency at the expense of individual justice (Menkel-Meadow 2016). While ODR deals effectively with large volumes of disputes, it presupposes a level of technical literacy that may impair or impede access to justice for a significant proportion of disputants (Rabinovich-Einy 2017). While in some contexts, technology and ODR may enhance access to justice, in others, they may raise barriers or create new types of dispute for which there are limited means of redress.

ODR may be swift, economic, and effective in low-cost claims if the parties don't know each other, but these advantages are less apparent when the continuation of a relationship, whether business or personal, is a significant aspect of a dispute. Although, for some litigants, the anonymity of ODR may be helpful in preventing emotional exposure, in others, it may erode the unique characteristic of mediation as a process anchored in human experience with the potential to transform or restore broken relationships by re-orienting parties towards each other and what is most significant for them, rather than settling disputes on the basis of some social or industrial norm.

Questions

1. **What are the challenges that ODR raises for the administration of justice?**
2. **What impact has ODR had on alternative dispute resolution?**
3. **What are the potential advantages and disadvantages of ODR from the perspectives of disputants and judges?**
4. **What are some of the particular ethical issues raised by ODR?**

Further Reading

Anderson, D. Q. (2019) 'The Convergence of ADR and ODR Within the Courts: The Impact on Access to Justice', *Civil Justice Quarterly* 38, 126–143.

Mania, K. (2015) 'Online Dispute Resolution: The Future of Justice', *International Comparative Jurisprudence* 1, 76–86.

Prince, S. (2019) '"Fine Words Butter No Parsnips": Can the Principle of Open Justice Survive the Introduction of an Online Court', *Civil Justice Quarterly* 38 (1), 111–125.

Rabinovich-Einy, O. & Katsh, E. (2017) 'A New Relationship Between Public and Private Dispute Resolution: Lessons from online Dispute Resolution', *Ohio State Journal of Dispute Resolution* 32 (4), 695–724.

16 Conclusions

'Everything must change so that everything can stay the same' (Giuseppe de Lampedusa, *The Leopard*). Mediation is almost as ubiquitous as conflict. The resurgence of mediation and ADR has come about both as a result of the withdrawal of the state from its traditional function of dispute resolution and as a movement to create forms of justice that do not solely depend on adversarial means. Its processes will vary with the function that it fulfills.

The Promise of Mediation

Mediation, in its non-coercive forms, can offer a transformative response to conflict and access to a type of justice that is not available in the courts. With a skilled and conscientious mediator and parties of broadly equal bargaining power, mediation enables disputants in difficult and potentially hostile disputes to prioritise what in their experience is most important and negotiate a solution to a dispute. Mediation can be the key to unlocking a deeper understanding of justice that is not about the imposition of authoritarian norms but about crafting an agreement that reflects what is right between people. At best, skillful mediators, through empathy and intuitive listening, enable those in a dispute to imagine a better future and encourage them through fruitful dialogue and negotiation to transcend the destructive patterns and cycles of their conflict.

Mediation is pragmatic and democratic; at best it represents a form of decision-making that goes 'beyond majority rule' (Sheeran 1991) to ensure the interests of all those involved in a dispute are heard. Mediation has the potential to influence the processes, whether political or legal, that it complements or replaces. One example of this is increasingly frequent settlement conferences between counsel in personal injury cases in which, although there may not be a mediator present, both parties may have had mediation training and use mediatory skills of reality testing and managing expectations in facilitating settlement. Another would be the sea change within the civil justice system in England and Wales, which now understands the role of a judge is not just to determine a case according to law but to promote a settlement.

Mediation is always and everywhere as much about psychology as law. It is an art that is learnt through practice and not a science. Despite variations, the different

DOI: 10.4324/9781003112617-16

forms of mediation examined here show striking similarities. Though the social contexts differ, the psychological elements of fear, anger resentment, and suspicion that impede resolution are similar in conflicts at all levels. The role of the mediator is to 'encourage adversaries to stand back from the obsessive fears, suspicions and hatreds' to understand each other and their dispute more rationally and 'consider however skeptically, the possibility of restoring the relationship' (Curle 1990). In performing this role, the mediator is listener, interpreter, catalyst, facilitator, enabler, and guide to help protagonists change their perceptions of each other and collaborate with them in finding creative solutions to intractable conflict.

Mediation can offer a distinct but potentially congruent process with adjudication according to the rule of law. Both are anchored in the value of equality: equality before the law in the case of adjudication and equal participation, dignity, respect, and rationality in the case of mediation. Both mediation and adjudication take place in the context of the ties that bind, which form the complex web of relationships of culture and society of which we are a part.

Limits of Mediation

ADR is not a panacea to the incapacity of the 21st-century state to resolve disputes that are, in part, the consequence of its actions. Its strengths as a private and voluntary process are also its limitations. Mediation suffers from unrealistic expectations, especially when it is offered as a solution to structural problems in the court system, legal process, or the inadequacy of legal aid. Mediation presupposes a willingness to negotiate a resolution and an 'entanglement of interests' of sufficient intensity and durability to make the collaboration worthwhile. In mediation, legal rights and social conflict may be muted in a 'coercive harmony' which hides hegemony 'behind the notions of persuasion and mutual accord' (Nader 1993) and is hidden from scrutiny as significant public issues are dealt with in private (Fiss 1984; Luban 1995).

Some critics suggest that this may involve unjust compromises of rights and the subjugation or subordination of those who are already disempowered (Delgado 1985; Bryan 1994; Lerman 1984; Grillo 1991). When parties have unequal legal knowledge and litigation expertise, procedural fairness may result in substantive unfairness. At best, mediation empowers parties to take part in a dialogue that has the potential to create solutions to problems that would not be possible in the courts. At worst, it reproduces social inequality by achieving 'unfair results for parties who don't know what happened to them or whom to blame' (Menkel-Meadow 1995).

Where mediation is practiced with a 'big stick' (Fuller 1963) or ADR is imposed as a way of managing dockets or rationing access to scarce legal resources, it can be a barrier to justice in which vulnerable parties compromise their legal rights without the protection of a judge. Forms of adjudicative ADR typically offer applicants lower rates of compensation than they would find in the courts. In the case of mediation between an unrepresented and a represented party, which is frequently the case in low-value claims in the UK, a mediator's neutrality (a pivotal aspect of their ethical responsibility in UK/US codes of conduct) (Chapter 12) prevents them from robustly challenging the assertions of a lawyer for the person with whom they are in dispute, while their third-party role legitimates the settlement of a case from the perspective of a claimant.

Advocates of mediation (Menkel-Meadow 1991) recognised the danger of 'formalisation' long before mediation was incorporated as an aspect of civil procedure. A process created to offer flexible and informal dispute resolution loses its unique identity when it becomes, rigid, formalised, and inflexible. Mediation *may* sometimes be part of a neo-liberal strategy to limit the arena for public litigation – for instance, in relation to taking consumer disputes out of the courts – but it may equally be an emancipatory process that empowers participants in challenging these policies. All depends on the nature and design of the process, the quality of the mediator, and the conditions of the dialogue they generate in mediation.

As a private dispute mechanism, mediation is not generally appropriate in cases involving the rights of the individual against those of the state. Mulcahy (2013) refers to disputes, including racial discrimination by an incarcerated prisoner, British soldiers being killed in non-combat situations, and PI claims by litigants who alleged they had been bullied into taking part in experiments relating to chemical warfare at Porton Down, in which there would be a clear public interest in open justice but in which there were mediated settlements. Such potentially precedent-bearing litigation inevitably involves enmeshing private interests and the collective good. Recent cases such as *Bates and Others v the Post Office* (2023) illustrate the importance of public adjudication of such private claims, when these are against an emanation of the state.

Mediation in the Shadow of the Law and Society

Mediation (Pavlich 1996) has been described as a form of 'secular confession' and can offer a way of healing relationships if an individual has become estranged from the community. Mediation attests to the abiding significance of Simmel's third element – a representative of society – as an agent of collective solidarity. Mediation is part of a continuum which stretches from the individual to the political.

There are very real conflicts in the practice of ADR and sharp differences over the ends to which it is applied. While mediation offers an alternative to an adversarial court-based adjudication. it has increasingly become imbricated into the court systems in both civil and common law. While, at best, mediation may have a 'dialogic,' 'symbiotic,' or 'complementary' role in litigation, there is a danger that it may become co-opted as a simulacrum by the system it is challenging (Chapter 10).

Law is not the only or necessarily the primary factor that shapes negotiation in mediation. In community mediation (Chapter 5), there may be little prospect of any legal adjudication of a dispute. Mediation takes place in the shadow of many other factors. At a community level, it is shaped by the state and local agencies of control; civil mediation is shaped by commercial pragmatism and the shadow of the market. Business reality, industry norms, and what is financially possible may be more exigent than any legal entitlement. Mediation takes place under the umbrella of the community and, at times, in the religious context of the church, mosque, synagogue, gurdwara, or temple. In the complexity of international relations, it takes place in the penumbra of diplomacy, and with political mediation, in the presence of an underlying threat of coercion or the shadow of war.

The UK/US model of facilitative mediation with its ground rules of party autonomy, professional integrity, confidentiality, and impartiality positions the mediator as an invulnerable or impassible facilitator, who stands outside the conflict as an analogy to judicial impartiality. This fails to fully capture the human complexity of the situation or my experience of observing many community, civil, and family mediations. Simply by their presence, mediators ineluctably become a part of the process of negotiation, just as an interpreter or expert may do. In supposedly confidential mediations, while never explicitly revealing parties' bottom lines, mediators often inadvertently (or advertently) use a process of noisy translation to reveal what the other party is thinking. In some ostensibly facilitative negotiations, mediators browbeat both sides into a compromise that is not of their own making.

Forms of court-annexed mediation, post *Churchill*, will inevitably change the relationship of mediation with the courts. Self-regulation will be inadequate to safeguard litigants who may feel they have been pressured into mediation without understanding exactly what it involves and that coercion into mediation creates an obligation to settle in mediation. By incorporating mediation into the court system, judges assume an obligation for its conduct. With an unrepresented litigant, a judge has a responsibility to challenge inaccurate assertions of a legally represented party's lawyer in a way that would be outside a mediator's role. In these kinds of cases, judges may need to look behind 'Consent Orders' arising from a mediation to ensure they are the result of genuinely informed consent made with the knowledge of legal rights.

There can be no single right style of mediation. Whereas confidentiality is axiomatic in mediating a dispute of a private nature between individuals, it is anathema to a public dispute about environmental or social conditions, in which the decisions of parties privy to the mediation affect those who are not party to the process (Susskind 1981).

While adjudication offers the application of legal norms and the consequent articulation of public values in providing state-sponsored and binding decisions, mediation offers the private resolution of disputes through appeal to the democratic values of equality, solidarity, participation, autonomy, and consent.

Mediation and Cultural Change

Mediation and other forms of ADR have adapted to the cultural niches in which they operate. Their meaning and scope will take on very different inflections in individual-centred or community-centred cultures. (Grande 1999) Mediation and other forms of ADR are perhaps best considered as one genus but many species. Rules and ethics of community, family, and civil mediation need to be developed to meet the specific needs of each of these contexts.

Mediation has a role to play in changing the culture of disputing (Allport 2023) and deliberative democracy itself (Menkel-Meadow 2011). But it cannot perform this independently of the political context in which it operates. At its best, the values of mediation in multi-party disputes are those of democracy itself. A range of academics in the 1980s offered a critique of mediation as being co-opted by the state (De Sousa Santos 1980; Nader 1979). Recent steps towards mandatory mediation have reignited that debate. Online dispute resolution, with increasing use of AI, is both an opportunity and a threat. If applied in a one-size-fits-all format, it risks undermining its unique role in re-establishing and re-orienting relationships. For mediation to fulfil its potential, it must be voluntary, affordable, and conducted by mediators who are sensitive to the issues of the mediation balance of power.

Mediation has developed over the last 50 years to become central to the administration of civil justice. At the apex of the civil justice system, judges have moved from reticence to being among the greatest enthusiasts for ADR. In his McNair lecture (2023), Sir Geoffrey Voss, Master of Rolls, endorses a fusion of court and ADR processes that would effectively incorporate ADR into the court system as part of a single dispute resolution system. This would imply a far more evaluative intervention than the current facilitative style of mediation and one in which the role of mediation in affirming party autonomy and control of the negotiation in mediation would be curtailed. Where mediation becomes an adjunct to the court process, judges cannot wash their hands of responsibility for its conduct as it loses its essentially private nature.

Mediation as practiced by skilled mediators, attentive to the contours of power – for instance, in mediation between parties with diverging cultural expectations – can be an emancipatory process that gives a voice to the vulnerable. Community mediation may at best be a form of popular justice that fulfills its early promise. Except where there is the need for the binding authority of precedent, civil mediation conducted in good faith offers the most effective way of resolving disputes between parties of broadly equal bargaining power. It remains vital that those practicing and studying the art of mediation remain alert to developments that could subvert the process in ways that entrench inequality or make it harder for vulnerable litigants to exercise their constitutional right of access to justice and the courts.

Appendices

Appendix 1

CEDR Model Mediation Agreement*

* Reproduced with permission from CEDR

Better conflicts, Better outcomes, Better world

Model Mediation Agreement

2023 Edition

Centre for Effective Dispute Resolution
100 St Paul's Churchyard
London
EC4M 8BU

T: +44 (0)20 7536 6060
W: www.cedr.com
E: adr@cedr.com

Twitter @cedrsays
linkedin.com/company/cedr

Better conflicts, Better outcomes, Better world

CEDR Model Mediation Agreement

2023 Edition

THIS AGREEMENT dated ....[/ as per the date the last signatory affixed their electronic signature, below]

IS MADE BETWEEN

Party A

Party B

(together referred to as '**the Parties**')

The Mediator

c/o CEDR, 100 St. Paul's Churchyard, London EC4M 8BU

(a term which includes any agreed **Mediator Observer**)

and

CEDR of 100 St. Paul's Churchyard, London EC4M 8BU

(together the principal participants of **"the Mediation"** scheduled for the date/s of...)

Better conflicts, Better outcomes, Better world

IT IS AGREED by those signing this Agreement THAT:

"The Mediation"

1. The Parties agree to attempt in good faith to settle their dispute during the Mediation. The Mediator agrees to conduct and the Parties to participate in the Mediation in accordance with this Agreement to mediate and consistent with the CEDR Model Mediation Procedure and the CEDR Code of Conduct for Third Party Neutrals as published on CEDR's website as at the date of this Agreement.
2. The Mediation will begin and the terms of this agreement will apply from the moment that the Mediator first communicates with either of the Parties and will continue until the date agreed by the Mediator and the Parties.
3. The Mediation may take place in person, remotely using telephone or video conferencing technology, or any combination of the aforementioned (or other media which is compliant with the CEDR Model Mediation Procedure) as agreed by the Parties and the Mediator.

Online/Remote Mediations

4. The Parties agree that for the purposes of the Mediation the Mediator will be the Host and/or Organiser of any video conferencing software used, unless otherwise agreed by all Parties.

Authority

5.

5.1 The person signing this Agreement on behalf of each Party warrants having authority to bind that Party to observe the terms of this Agreement

5.2 Each party warrants that a person with authority will participate in the mediation to authorise any settlement.

Confidentiality and without prejudice status

6. Each Party shall ensure that Mediation participants attending on their behalf are informed and agree to the confidentiality provisions set out in this section.

7. Every person involved in the Mediation:

7.1 will keep confidential all information arising out of or in connection with the Mediation (in accordance with Section 8 of the CEDR Model Mediation Procedure), including but not limited to communications relating to the set-up and scheduling of the Mediation, the discussions leading up to and at the Mediation, and terms of any settlement, unless otherwise agreed by the Parties in writing but not including the fact that the Mediation is to take place or has taken place or where disclosure is required by law, to prevent physical harm to self or to others, or to implement or to enforce terms of settlement or to notify their insurers, insurance brokers and/or accountants;

7.2 agrees that all such information passing between the Parties, the Mediator and/or CEDR, however communicated, is to be without prejudice to any Party's legal position and may not be produced as evidence or disclosed to any judge, arbitrator or other decision-maker in any legal or other formal process, except where otherwise disclosable in law;

Centre for Effective Dispute Resolution
100 St Paul's Churchyard
London
EC4M 8BU

T: +44 (0)20 7536 6060
W: www.cedr.com
E: adr@cedr.com

Twitter @cedrsays
linkedin.com/company/cedr

CEDR Better conflicts, Better outcomes, Better world

7.3 will not make any attempt to, or make any audio or video recording, of any part of the Mediation; and

7.4 will ensure that where the Mediation or a portion thereof is taking place using video conferencing software or other remote means of communication, the only person(s) present in the room where the computer, phone or other communication device is located will be those persons notified in writing as attending to the Mediator and any and all other Party or Parties.

8. Where a Party privately discloses to the Mediator or CEDR any information in confidence before, during or after the Mediation, the Mediator or CEDR will not disclose that information to any other Party or person without the consent of the Party disclosing it, except under the circumstances provided in Section 8 of the CEDR Model Mediation Procedure. The Parties agree, however, that the Mediator may disclose such information to CEDR provided that such disclosure is made by the Mediator and received by CEDR in confidence.

Settlement formalities

9. No terms of settlement reached at the Mediation will be legally binding until set out in writing and agreed to either in writing (including by email) or by wet or electronic signature, by or on behalf of each of the Parties.

Fees and costs of the Mediation

10. The Parties will be responsible for the fees and expenses of CEDR and the Mediator ('the Mediation Fees') in accordance with CEDR's Terms and Conditions of Business current at the date of this Agreement (including any provision for additional hours if the Mediation process extends beyond the allocated hours).

11. Unless otherwise agreed by the Parties and CEDR in writing, each Party agrees to share the Mediation Fees equally and also to bear its own legal and other costs and expenses of preparing for and attending the Mediation ('each Party's Legal Costs'). However, each Party further agrees that any court or tribunal may treat both the Mediation Fees and each Party's Legal Costs as costs in the case in relation to any litigation or arbitration where that court or tribunal has power to assess or make orders as to costs, whether or not the Mediation results in settlement of their dispute.

Liability of CEDR and the Mediator

12. Neither the Mediator nor CEDR shall be liable to the Parties for any act or omission in relation to the Mediation, including the use and operation of the video conferencing platform, unless the act or omission is proved to have been fraudulent or involved wilful misconduct.

13. The Parties understand that neither the Mediator nor CEDR give legal advice and agree that they will not make any claim against the Mediator or CEDR in connection with this Mediation. The Parties will not make an application to call the Mediator or any employee or consultant of CEDR, as a witness, nor require them to produce in evidence any records or notes relating to the Mediation, in any litigation, arbitration or other formal process arising out of or in connection with their dispute and the Mediation. Neither the Mediator nor any CEDR employee or consultant will agree to act as a witness, expert, arbitrator or consultant in any such process. If any Party does make such an application (as listed above), that Party will fully indemnify the Mediator, CEDR or the employee or consultant of CEDR in respect of any costs any of them incur in resisting and/or responding to such an application, including reimbursement at the Mediator's standard hourly rate for the Mediator's time spent in resisting and/or responding to such an application.

Centre for Effective Dispute Resolution
100 St Paul's Churchyard
London
EC4M 8BU

T: +44 (0)20 7536 6060
W: www.cedr.com
E: adr@cedr.com

Twitter @cedrsays
linkedin.com/company/cedr

Better conflicts, Better outcomes, Better world

Law and Jurisdiction

14. This Agreement is governed by the law of England and Wales and the courts of England and Wales shall have exclusive jurisdiction to decide any matters arising out of or in connection with this Agreement and the Mediation.

15. The referral of the dispute to the Mediation does not affect any rights that exist under Article 6 of the European Convention of Human Rights, and if their dispute does not settle through the Mediation, the Parties' right to a fair trial remains unaffected.

Changes to this Agreement

Any changes to this Agreement must be agreed in writing by the Parties, CEDR and the Mediator.

Signed

Party A ....

[Sign and Print Name]

Party B ....

[Sign and Print Name]

Mediator ....

CEDR ....

Centre for Effective Dispute Resolution
100 St Paul's Churchyard
London
EC4M 8BU

T: +44 (0)20 7536 6060
W: www.cedr.com
E: adr@cedr.com

Twitter @cedrsays
linkedin.com/company/cedr

Appendix 2

European Code of Conduct for Mediation Providers

4 December 2018

CEPEJ(2018)24

EUROPEAN COMMISSION FOR THE EFFICIENCY OF JUSTICE
(CEPEJ)

Mediation Development Toolkit
Ensuring implementation of the CEPEJ Guidelines on mediation

European Code of Conduct for Mediation Providers

Ad adopted at the 31st plenary meeting of the CEPEJ, Strasbourg, 3-4 December 2018

This tool has been developed in reference to point 1. Availibility of the CEPEJ Guildelines on mediation.

This code of conduct sets out a number of principles to which mediation centers, institutes or other mediation providers may voluntarily decide to commit themselves. It may be used by mediation providers (including all their employees and affiliated persons) that offer mediation services in different fields of disputes such as civil, commercial, family, administrative and penal matters. This code is coherent and may be used in conjuction with the European Code of Conduct for Mediators developed in 2004 under the auspices of the European Union[1], and with the Council of Europe and the European Commission for the Efficiency of Justice (CEPEJ) reccommendations, guidelines and other instruments on mediation and ADR[2]. Legislators of the Council of Europe Member States may opt to incorporate rules of this code in respective national mediation legal environment as a baseline standard for mediation providers.

With a view to improving the present document, the CEPEJ-GT-MED invites mediation providers which commit to use this document to bring their feedback to the Secretariat of the CEPEJ.

1. DEFINITION

"**Mediation Provider**" means any public or private entity (including court-related mediation schemes) which manages or administers a mediation process conducted by a third party neutral mediator of whatever denomination or profession, (hereafter "mediator") who provides service under its auspicies in assisting parties to amicably resolve their dispute.

2. QUALITY AND COMPETENCE OF THE SERVICE

Mediation providers should take all reasonable steps to ensure an adequate level in the quality and the competence of its services by ensuring that:

a. it maintains sufficient funds, administrative capacity and an adequate number of affiliated mediators to provide relevant services;
b. it complies with all relevant domestic laws and rules;
c. mediators who work under its auspicies are qualified in conducting quality mediation processes by having undertaken proper basic and continuing training in dispute resolution and mediation techniques, having due regard to applicable accreditation and/or certification schemes and/or standards;
d. mediators who work under its auspicies are competent to handle specific types of disputes that may be referred to them;
e. transparent, fair and efficient mediators' selection and assignment procedures are in place;
f. monitoring is applied to ensure adequate and efficient performance of the mediation provider and its affiliated mediators, using client satisfaction surveys as appropriate;
g. statistical data on key indicators is collected;
h. personnel in its secretariat or case management office are properly trained to assist parties and mediators along the entire mediation process;
i. the premises and mediation rooms that it provides are easy accessible, signposted, adequately equipped and comfortable to hold mediation sessions;
j. parties can easily access the service by filing mediation requests online or by any proper means of communications and participate in the process;
k. an adequate quality management system is in place, monitored and effectively applied.

[1] European Code of Conduct for Mediators can be consulted on the internet at http://ec.europa.eu/civiljustice/adr/adr_ec_code_conduct_en.pdf.
[2] Can be consulted on the internet at https://www.coe.int/en/web/cepej/cepej-work/mediation.

3. TRANSPARENCY AND COMMUNICATION

Mediation providers should have an up-to-date and user-friendly website and/or other means available in order to provide mediation users with accurate and easy understandable information about:

a. the nature and history of the provider, names of partners, affiliated, management and main stakeholders;
b. names, accurate up-to-date curriculum vitae and professional competences of the mediators who provide service under its auspicies;
c. the mediation process, mediation rules and relevant legislation applied to the mediation process;
d. fees and criteria of calculation applied to provide the services and how it can be split between the parties;
e. the code of conduct endorsed by mediators.

The mediation provider should not make false, unfair or misleading statements in it communications or marketing about its services and the services of its affiliated mediators.

4. RULES AND ETHICS OF MEDIATION

Mediation providers should ensure that they apply the European Code of Conduct for Mediators as a minimum standard in the provision of mediation services.

Mediation providers shall abide by the rules and procedures concerning their performance and provision of mediation services, as established by domestic laws.

5. INDEPENDENCE, IMPARTIALITY AND NEUTRALITY

Mediation providers must be independent and unbiased towards all disputants and legal practitioners.

All mediation processes shall be managed in an impartial, neutral and independent manner.

Mediation providers may not offer mediation services mixed with any other professional or commercial activities unrelated to dispute resolution. A mediation provider's staff, shareholders, stakeholders and affiliated mediators cannot act as attorneys, counsellors, consultants, trainers, or judges in the same dispute or for one of the parties before the end of the dispute or within a reasonable time after it is finished.

Mediation providers shall comply with all other restrictions and procedures in order to safeguard independence and impartiality.

6. CONFLICT OF INTERESTS

Mediation providers should set in place procedures to detect and eliminate potential conflicts of interest.

Mediation providers should disclose the existence of any facts, interests or relationships which are reasonably likely to affect its impartiality or independence, or which might reasonably create the appearance that the provider is biased against a party or favorable to another, including:

a. any relevant economic interests or sources of revenues (eg. ownerships, sponsorships, annual contributions, fundings, etc.) with any parties or their associations or counsel that could affect its impartiality;
b. any interests in the outcome of the mediation process;
c. any facts or relationships with the parties and their counsel that may affect impartiality or create an appearance of partiality or bias.

7. COMPLAINTS, DISCIPLINARY PROCEDURES AND RESOLUTION OF DISPUTES

Mediation providers should establish and maintain fair and effective complaints and disciplinary mechanisms to deal with disputes concerning mediators or administrators of mediation processes.

Mediation providers should subscribe primarily to amicable dispute settlement in their own matters through negotiation and mediation.

8. CONFIDENTIALITY

Taking due note that as a general standard all information associated with the mediation is confidential, mediation providers should take all reasonable steps to protect the level of confidentiality stipulated by the relevant laws and rules and/or agreed by the parties.

Appendix 3

FMC Code of Practice for Family Mediators*

* Reproduced with permission from FMC

Code of Practice for Family Mediators

Preamble

It is the policy of the FMC to keep this Code under review. Not all aspects of review will fall to take place at the same time, but the FMC is keen to avoid issuing a revised version of the entire Code every time a change is made. Furthermore, the wording for any detailed changes will always be carefully considered before those changes are incorporated, and that will take time. For those reasons, and to allow changes to be brought into effect meanwhile, the FMC will - as occasion may require - issue short-form Practice Directions, setting out, in simple form, the principles of each change. Mediators should comply with those Practice Directions in the same way as they comply with the body of the Code. Each Practice Direction will be superseded once its terms have been incorporated into the Code itself.

1 DEFINITIONS

1.1 In this Code of Practice:

"Code" means this Code of Practice

"FMC" means The Family Mediation Council

"FMCA" means Family Mediation Council Accreditation

"Information and Assessment Meeting" means a pre-mediation meeting or meetings held between a mediator and the potential participants in a mediation for the purpose of explaining the mediation processes and assessing whether mediation is appropriate for the participants and includes statutory Mediation Information and Assessment Meetings under s. 10(1), Children and Families Act 2014, which are known as MIAMs

"Mediation" means the family Mediation to which this Code applies

"Mediator" means any person offering such Mediation

"MO" means an entity which is a Member Organisation of the FMC

"Participant" means any person taking part in Mediation or an Information and Assessment Meeting.

1.2 This Code applies to all Information and Assessment Meetings and Mediation conducted or offered by Mediators who are members of the MOs.

1.3 Mediation is a process in which those involved in family relationship breakdown, change, transitions or disputes, whether or not they are a couple or other family members, appoint an impartial third person, a Mediator, to assist them to communicate better with one another and reach their own agreed and informed decisions typically relating to some, or all, of the issues relating to separation, divorce, children, finance or property by negotiation.

1.4 An Information and Assessment Meeting is a meeting that provides information about Mediation as a way of resolving disputes conducted by a trained mediator who will also assess whether Mediation is appropriate in the circumstances.

1.5 This Code applies whether or not there are or have been legal proceedings between the Participants and whether or not any, or all of them, are legally represented.

2. AIMS AND OBJECTIVES

2.1 Mediation aims to assist Participants to reach the decisions they consider appropriate to their own particular circumstances.

2.2 Mediation also aims to assist Participants to communicate with one another now and in the future and to reduce the scope or intensity of dispute and conflict within the family.

2.3 Where a marriage or relationship has irretrievably broken down, Mediation has regard to the principles that the marriage or relationship should be brought to an end in a way that:

a. minimises distress to the Participants and to any children;
b. promotes as good a relationship between the Participants and any children as is possible;

c. removes or diminishes any risk of abuse to any of the Participants or children from the other Participants; and
d. avoids any unnecessary cost to Participants.

2.4 An Information and Assessment Meeting aims to inform individuals about mediation (and other forms of resolving disputes away from the Court) and to assess whether a mediation process may be suitable in the circumstances. Any individual who intends to make an application to obtain a court order in certain family proceedings is required to attend a statutory Mediation Information and Assessment Meeting unless an exemption applies. Individual respondents are expected to attend a Mediation Information and Assessment Meeting.

3. QUALIFICATIONS AND TRAINING

3.1 Mediators must either be accredited by the FMC (i.e. hold FMCA status), or have completed a foundation training programme approved by the FMC and be currently registered with the FMC as working towards FMCA.

3.2 Mediators must abide by the FMC's current requirements for accredited and registered Mediators, including being a current member of an MO and maintaining the required levels of practice, professional practice consultancy, and ongoing professional development.

3.3 Mediators may undertake child-inclusive Mediation only when they:

a. have registered to do so with the FMC; and
b. have met the requirements as may be laid down by the FMC or, if none exist, are approved to carry out child-inclusive Mediation by an MO.

3.4 Mediators undertaking publicly-funded Mediation must hold FMCA status.

3.5 Mediators must not mediate unless they are covered by adequate professional indemnity insurance.

3.6 Mediators must abide by the complaints and disciplinary procedures laid down by the MO of which they are members. A Mediator who is a member of more than one MO must make clear to Participants which MO's complaints and disciplinary procedures will apply.

3.7 Mediators must have appropriate safeguarding policies and procedures in place.

4. SCOPE OF MEDIATION

4.1 Mediation may cover any or all of the following matters:

a. options for maintaining or ending the marital or other relationship between the adult Participants and the consequences of doing so;

b. arrangements for dependent children: arrangements for parenting between parents and/or careers and extended family as appropriate; any other aspect of parental responsibility such as, but not exhaustively, schooling, holidays or religious education;

c. the future of the family home and any other property or assets, including pensions, belonging to the adult Participants; issues of child maintenance and spousal maintenance; issues relating to debts;

d. how adjustments to these arrangements are to be decided upon in the future.

4.2 The Participants and the Mediator may agree that Mediation will cover any other matters which it would be helpful to resolve in connection with relationship breakdown between the Participants and which the Mediator considers suitable for Mediation.

5. GENERAL PRINCIPLES which apply to Information and Assessment Meetings and to Mediation

5.1 Conflicts of Interest

5.1.1 The Mediator must act impartially in conducting any process of Mediation and with integrity and fairness towards each of the Participants. The Mediator must also ensure that any conflicts of interest are identified, considered and addressed.

5.1.2 The Mediator must not have any personal interest in the outcome of the Mediation.

5.1.3 The Mediator must not mediate in any case in which he or she has acquired or may acquire relevant information in any private or other professional capacity.

5.1.4 Where Mediation services are offered as part of a practice/consortium ("Practice") offering other professional services or where an individual Mediator carries out work for a Practice on a consultancy basis, a Mediator from that Practice or a consultant to that Practice may not act as a Mediator for any Participant who has received other professional services from that Practice unless the Mediator is satisfied that:

a. the information given to other professionals at the Practice has no bearing on the issues to be addressed in the Mediation; and

b. the Participants have been informed of the potential conflict of interest and have given consent in writing to the Mediator conducting the Mediation

The consent of the Participants does not lessen the Mediator's duty as set out in 5.1.1 above.

5.1.5 Mediation must be conducted as an independent professional activity and must be distinguished from any other professional role in which the Mediator may practise.

5.2 Confidentiality

5.2.1 Subject to paragraphs 5.2.2, 5.2.3 and 5.2.4 below, the Mediator must not disclose any information about, or obtained in the course of an Information and Assessment Meeting or during a mediation process to the other participant or to anyone including a court appointed officer or the court, without the express consent of each Participant, an order of the court or where the law imposes an overriding obligation of disclosure on Mediators to do so.

5.2.2 Where it appears necessary so that a specific allegation that a child has suffered significant harm may be properly investigated, or where the Mediator suspects that a child is suffering or is likely to suffer significant harm, the Mediator must ensure that the appropriate agency or authority is notified. Wherever possible, the Mediator should make such a notification after consultation with his or her PPC.

5.2.3 The Mediator may notify the appropriate agency if he or she considers that other public policy considerations prevail, such as an adult suffering or likely to suffer significant harm. Wherever possible, the Mediator should make such a notification after consultation with his or her PPC.

5.2.4 Where a Mediator suspects that he or she may be required to make disclosure to the appropriate government authority under the Proceeds of Crime Act 2002 as updated and/or relevant money laundering regulations, the Mediator must stop the Information and Assessment Meeting or Mediation immediately without informing the Participants of the reason

5.3 Welfare of children

At all times the Mediator must have particular regard to the welfare of any children of the family, and should encourage the Participants to focus on the needs and interests of the children as well as on their own.

5.4 Abuse and power imbalances within the family

5.4.1 The Mediator must be alert to the likelihood of power imbalances existing between Participants, including but not limited to those resulting from emotional or physical abuse, manipulation, coercion or controlling behaviour.

5.4.2 In all cases, the Mediator must seek to ensure that the Participants take part in the Mediation willingly and without fear of violence or harm. The Mediator must seek to discover through a screening procedure whether or not there is fear of abuse or any other harm and whether or not it is alleged that any Participant has been or is likely to be abusive towards another (or towards a child). Where abuse is alleged or suspected, the Mediator must discuss with the Participant believed to be adversely affected whether that Participant wishes to take part (or to continue to take part) in the Mediation, and information about available support services should be provided.

6. GENERAL PRINCIPLES which apply to Mediation

In addition to the clause 5, the following provisions also apply to Mediation.

6.1 Voluntary Participation

Participation in Mediation is voluntary and must be the free choice of each Participant at all times. The Participants and the Mediator are always free to withdraw. Where the Mediator considers that a Participant is unable or unwilling to take part in the process freely and fully, the Mediator must raise the issue and where necessary suspend or terminate the Mediation.

6.2 Neutrality as to Outcome

The Mediator must remain neutral as to the outcome of the Mediation at all times. The Mediator must not seek to impose any preferred outcome on Participants, or to influence them to adopt it, whether by attempting to predict the outcome of court proceedings or otherwise. However, if the Participants consent, the Mediator may inform them (if it be the case) that he or she considers that the resolutions they are considering might fall outside the parameters which a court might approve or order. The Mediator may inform

Participants of possible courses of action, their legal or other implications, and assist them to explore these, but must make it clear that he or she is not giving advice.

6.3 Impartiality

6.3.1 The Mediator must at all times remain impartial as between the Participants and conduct the Mediation process in a fair and even-handed way.

6.3.2 The Mediator must seek to prevent manipulative, threatening or intimidating behaviour by any Participant, and must conduct the process in such a way as to redress, as far as possible, any imbalance of power between the Participants. If such behaviour or any other imbalance seems likely to render the Mediation unfair or ineffective, the Mediator must take appropriate steps to seek to prevent this, including terminating the Mediation if necessary.

6.4 Confidentiality

The Mediator must not discuss the Mediation or correspond with any Participant's legal advisor without the express consent of each Participant. When communicating with the Participants or their legal advisers, the Mediator must maintain professional impartiality.

6.5 Without Prejudice to Legal Proceedings

6.5.1 Subject to paragraph 6.5.2 below, all discussions and negotiations in the Mediation must be conducted without prejudice to legal proceedings. Before the Mediation commences, the Participants must agree in writing that discussions and negotiations in Mediation are not to be referred to in any legal proceedings, and that the Mediator cannot be required to give evidence or produce any notes or records made in the course of the Mediation, unless the Participants agree to waive the without prejudice basis on which the Mediation is conducted or the law imposes an overriding obligation of disclosure upon the Mediator.

6.5.2 The Participants must agree that all factual information material to financial issue must be provided on an open basis, so that it can be referred to in legal proceedings.

6.5.3 In general, information provided by one Participant should be shared openly with other Participants and not withheld, except any address or telephone number or as the Participants may agree otherwise. This requirement does not apply to information which, if shared, could lead to a child or other person suffering harm, or where other public policy considerations prevail.

6.5.4 The without prejudice basis on which the Mediation is conducted and the confidentiality which would otherwise apply will not apply in relation to communications indicating that a child or other person is suffering or likely to suffer significant harm, or where other public policy considerations prevail.

6.6 Welfare of children

6.6.1 The Mediator must encourage the Participants to consider the children's wishes and feelings. All children and young people aged 10 and above should be offered the opportunity to have their voices heard directly during the Mediation, if they wish.

6.6.2 Where the Mediator and the Participants agree that it is appropriate to consult any children directly, the consent of those children must first be obtained. A Mediator intending to consult directly with any children must have been specifically trained to do so. Such Mediators must provide appropriate facilities for direct consultation.

6.6.3 Where a qualified Mediator undertakes direct consultation with any child, he or she must offer that child confidentiality as to any disclosure that that child may make to him or her. This must be explained to the Participants before they agree to the direct consultation. Confidentiality in direct consultation with children must always be exercised subject to paragraphs 5.2.2, 5.2.3, 5.2.4 and 6.5.4.

6.6.4 Where the Mediator suspects that any child is suffering or likely to suffer significant harm, he or she must advise the Participants to seek help from the appropriate agency. The Mediator must also advise the Participants that, in any event, he or she is obliged to report the matter to the appropriate agency in accordance with paragraph 5.2.2.

6.6.5 Where the Mediator considers that the Participants are acting, or are proposing to act, in a manner likely to be seriously detrimental to the welfare of any child of the family or family member, the Mediator may withdraw from the Mediation. The reason for doing this must be outlined promptly, in writing.

6.7 Abuse and power imbalances within the family

6.7.1 The Mediator must uphold throughout the principles of voluntary participation, fairness and safety and must conduct the process in accordance with this section. In addition, steps must be taken to ensure the safety of the Participants on arrival at and departure from the Mediation.

6.7.2 The Mediator must seek to prevent manipulative, threatening or intimidating behaviour by any Participant during the Mediation.

7. CONDUCT OF MEDIATION INFORMATION AND ASSESSMENT MEETINGS

All assessments for suitability for Mediation should be conducted by a Mediator at meetings and, where possible, on a face-to-face basis. Assessment and Mediation may include meetings via an online video connection. Statutory Mediation Information and Assessment Meetings may also be conducted via an online video connection. Assessments, including statutory Mediation Information and Assessment Meetings, should not be carried out via voice only connections except where there are specific problems about access to an online video link. The Mediator must record in writing what those specific problems are. Assessment meetings can be conducted jointly or separately, but must include an individual element with each Participant to allow the Mediator to undertake domestic abuse screening. If assessments or Mediation meetings are conducted via online video connection, the Mediator must act appropriately having regard to all the current practice guidance issued by the FMC.

8. CONDUCT OF THE MEDIATION

8.1 The Mediator must manage the Mediation process. The Mediator should consult the Participants on management decisions such as the ordering of issues and the agenda for each Mediation session but must not relinquish control of the process to the Participants.

8.2 Throughout the Mediation, the Mediator must keep the possibility of reconciliation of the Participants under review.

8.3 The Mediator must advise the Participants clearly at the outset of the nature and purpose of Mediation and how it differs from other services such as marriage or relationship counselling, therapy or legal representation.

8.4 At the same time, the Mediator must inform the Participants of all the general principles set out in Section 5 above, including the nature and limits of the principles of confidentiality, the without prejudice basis of the Mediation and the Mediator's special concern for the welfare of any children of the family.

8.5 The Mediator must inform the Participants of the extent of any disclosure which will be required in cases relating to their property and finances.

8.6 Each Participant must be supplied with written information covering the main points in this Code and given the opportunity to ask questions about it.

8.7 The Mediator must ensure that the Participants agree the terms and conditions regulating the Mediation before dealing with the substantive issues, by means of a written agreement which reflects the main principles of this Code. The agreement must also set out the Mediator's fees.

8.8 Participants must be requested to notify any legal advisors acting for them of the appointment of the Mediator.

8.9 Where, during a privately funded Mediation, the Mediator becomes aware that one or more of the Participants may qualify for public funding, the Mediator must inform the Participants of this and, if the Mediator does not undertake publicly funded work, of the services of a Mediation practice with a Legal Aid Agency contract.

8.10 The Mediator must assist the Participants to define the issues, identify areas of consensus, explore the options and seek to reach agreement upon them.

8.11 The Mediator must seek to ensure that the Participants reach their decision upon sufficient information and knowledge. The Mediator must inform the Participants of the need to give full and frank disclosure of all material relevant to the issues being mediated and assist them where necessary in identifying the relevant information and supporting documentation.

8.12 The Mediator must ensure each Participant is given the opportunity to make enquiries about information disclosed by any other Participant and to seek further information and documentation when required. The Mediator must promote the Participants' equal understanding of such information before any final agreement is reached.

8.13 The Mediator must make it clear that he or she does not make further enquiries to verify the information provided by any Participant; that each Participant may seek independent legal advice as to the adequacy of the information disclosed before reaching a decision; that in any court proceedings an affidavit, written statement or oral evidence may be required; and that authoritative calculations of liability under the Child Support Act 1991 can be made only by the Child Support Agency, Child Maintenance Service or any replacement organisation established under the Child Maintenance and Other Payments Act 2008 or subsequent related legislation.

8.14 The Mediator must inform the Participants of the advantages of seeking independent legal or other appropriate advice whenever this appears desirable during the course of the Mediation. The Mediator must advise the Participants that it is in their own interests to seek independent legal advice before reaching any final agreement, and warn them of the risks and disadvantages if they do not do so.

8.15 Mediation meetings are commonly conducted without lawyers present. However, solicitors or counsel acting for the Participants may be invited to participate in the Mediation process and in any communications if the Participants agree and the Mediator considers that it would be appropriate.

8.16 When appropriate and with the consent of the Participants, arrangements may be made for the attendance of professional third parties other than lawyers, such as interpreters, accountants, actuaries, independent financial advisors, and other advisors.

8.17 When appropriate and with the consent of the Participants, arrangements may be made for the attendance of third parties with an interest in the proceedings, such as new partners, parties with a legal or beneficial interest in property that is the subject of dispute, or other family members.

8.18 The Mediator must seek to ensure that proposals reached by the Participants are fully informed and freely made. The Participants must have as good an understanding as is practicable of the consequences of their decisions for themselves, their children and other relevant family members.

Bibliography

Books and Articles Cited

Abel, R., ed (1982) *The Politics of Informal Justice, Volume 1: The American Experience* (Academic Press).

Adler, N. J. (1996) *International Dimensions of Organisational Behaviour Boston PWS-Kent* (PWS-Kent Publication Co).

Agapiou, A. & Clark, B. (2018) 'The Practical Significance of Confidentiality in Mediation', *Civil Justice Quarterly* 37 (1), 74–97.

Ahmed, M. (2012) 'Implied Compulsory Mediation', *Civil Justice Quarterly* 31 (2), 1–8.

Ahorsu, K. & Ame, R. (2011) 'Mediation with a Traditional Flavor in the Fodome Chieftaincy and Communal Conflicts', *African Conflict & Peacebuilding Review* 6 (1), 7.

Alexander, N. (2014) *The Mediation Manual: Hong Kong Edition* (LexisNexis).

Allen, T. (2018) *Mediation Law and Civil Practice* (2nd ed, Bloomsbury).

Allen, T. & Mackie, K. (2020) 'Moves in Mediation: Confidentiality, the EU Directive and Regulation', *The Barrister* 43.

Allport, L. (2023) 'Mediation and Cultural Change', *Amicus Curiae*, Series 2, 4 (2), 367–390.

Andrews, H. (2018) *Mediation: International Experience and Global Trends* (University of Cambridge Faculty of Law Research Paper No. 42/2018).

Argen, R. (2015) 'Ending Blind Spot Justice: Broadening the Transparency Trend in International Arbitration', *Brooklyn Journal of International Law* 40 (1).

Aris, M. (1994) 'Conflict and Conciliation in Traditional Bhutan', in Michael Hutt, ed. *Bhutan: Perspectives on Conflict and Dissent* (Asgard Publications), pp. 21–41.

Artificial Lawyer (2019) *Online Dispute Resolution Faces Major Challenges Survey Artificial Lawyer*, 19 March 2019. https://www.artificiallawyer.com/2019/03/19/online-dispute-resolution-faces-major-challenges-survey/

Auerbach, J. S. (1983) *Justice Without the Law* (Oxford University Press).

Augsburger, D. W. (1992) *Conflict Mediation Across Cultures: Pathways and Patterns* (Westminster/John Knox Press).

Austin, J. (1832) *The Province of Jurisprudence Determined* (Murray).

Avruch, K. (1998) *Culture and Conflict Resolution* (United States Institute of Peace Press).

Axelrod, R. (1980) 'Effective Choice in the Prisoner's Dilemma', *Journal for Conflict Resolution* 24 (1).

Baker, B. (2013) 'Where Formal and Informal Justice Meet: Ethiopia's Justice Pluralism', *African Journal of International and Comparative Law* 21 (2), 202–218.

Bano, S. (2012) *Muslim Women and Shari'ah Councils – Transcending the Boundaries of Community and Law* (Palgrave Macmillan).

Bano, S. & Webley, L. (2024) 'Family Mediators and Family Mediation Where Norms Collide', *Oxford Journal of Law and Religion*, 1–16.

Barnes, B. E (2007) *Culture, Conflict, and Mediation in the Asian Pacific* (Rowman & Littlefield).

Bar Standards Board (2023) *BSB Handbook* (London).
Bartlet, M. (2009) 'Forgiveness, Reconciliation, and Judicial Process in Northern Uganda: The Lord's Resistance Army and the International Criminal Court', *African Peace and Conflict Journal* 2 (2).
Bartlet, M. (2015) 'Mandatory Mediation and the Rule of Law', *Amicus Curiae*, Series 2, 1 (1), 50–83.
Bartlet, M. (2019) 'Mandatory and the Rule of Law', *Amicus Curiae*, Series 2, 1 (1), 52–83.
Barton, R. F. (1919) *The Kalingas: Their Institutions and Customary Law* (University of Chicago Press).
Basu, S. (2012) 'Judges of Normality: Mediating Marriage in the Family Courts of Kolkata, India', *Journal of Women in Culture and Society* 37 (2).
Bazemore, G. & Walgrave, L., eds (1999) *Restorative Juvenile Justice: Repairing the Harm of Youth Crime* (Criminal Justice Press).
Billiet, J. & Migmatullina, D. (2012) 'Recent Developments in European Mediation and ADR', in *European Mediation Training for Practitioners of Justice – A Guide to European Mediation* (Association of International Arbitration).
Birke, R. & Fox, C. (1999) 'Psychological Principles in Negotiating Civil Settlements', *Harvard Negotiation Law Review* 4 (1).
Birnbaum, R. (2009) *The Voice of the Child in Separation/Divorce Mediation and Other Alternative Dispute Resolution Processes: A Literature Review* (Department of Justice Canada).
Blake, R. & Mouton, J. (1964) *The Managerial Grid: The Key to Leadership Excellence* (Gulf Publishing Company).
Blake, S. (2016) *A Practical Approach to Alternative Dispute Resolution* (4th ed, Oxford University Press).
Blakey, R. (2022) 'Mediators Mediating Themselves': Tensions Within the Family Mediator Profession', *Legal Studies*, 1–20.
Blankley, K. (2020) 'Online Resources and Family Cases: Access to Justice through ADR Fact or Fiction?', *Fordham Law Review* 88 (2019–2020), 2121–2126.
Bohannan, P., ed (1971) *Divorce and After* (Doubleday).
Bolitho, J., Bruce, J. & Mason, G. (2012) *Restorative Justice: Adults and Emerging Practice* (Sydney Institute of Criminology Series).
Boorman, F. (2022) 'Developments in the History of Arbitration: A Past for the Present?', *Amicus Curiae*, Series 2, 4 (1).
Booth Committee (1985) *Report of the Committee on Matrimonial Causes* (HMSO).
Boulding, K. (1977) 'Twelve Friendly Quarrels with Johan Galtung', *Journal of Peace Research* 14 (1), 75–86.
Boulle, L. & Nesic, M. (2001) *Mediation, Principles, Process, Practice* (Butterworths).
Boulle, L. & Nesic, M. (2009) *Mediator Skills and Techniques: Triangle of Influence* (Bloomsbury Professional).
Boyes-Watson, C. (2000) 'What Is Restorative Justice?' *Suffolk UniversityCenter for Restorative Justice*. https://www.suffolk.edu/cas/center-for-restorative-justice/what-is-restorative-justice
Briggs, M. (2009) 'Mediation Privilege', *New Law Journal*, 3rd and 10th April.
Brock-Utne, B. (2001) 'Indigenous Conflict Resolution in Africa', *A Draft Presented to Week-End Seminar on Indigenous Solutions to Conflicts*, The University of Oslo, Institute of Educational Research, Oslo, 23–24.
Broderick, R. (1989) 'Court-annexed Compulsory Arbitration', *Judicature* 72 (4), 219–222.
Brown, H. & Marriot, A. (2011) *ADR: Principles and Practice* (3rd ed, Sweet & Maxwell).
Bryan, P. (1994) 'Reclaiming Professionalism: The Lawyers Role in Divorce Mediation', *Family Law Quarterly*, 177–222.
Burchill, F. (1999) 'Walton and McKersie, A Behavioral Theory of Labor Negotiations (1965)', *Historical Studies in Industrial Relations*, 137–168.
Burger, W. E. (1982) 'Isn't There a Better Way', *American Bar Association Journal* 68, 274–277.
Bush, R., Baruch, A. & Folger, J. P. (2004) *The Promise of Mediation: Responding to Conflict Through Empowerment and Recognition* (Jossey-Bass Publishers).

Capelletti, M. (1978) *Access to Justice, IV Anthropological Perspectives* (Giuffre).
Carroll, E. & Mackie, K. (2021) *The Mediator's Tale: The CEDR Story of Better Conflicts* (Bloomsbury Professional).
Case, S. (2021) 'Responding to Youth Offending: New Labour and the New Youth Justice', in *Youth Justice: A critical Introduction* (Routledge).
CEDR (2003) 'Mediator Handbook', *The: Effective Resolution of Commercial Disputes* (Centre for Effective Dispute Resolution).
CEDR (2019) 'Mediator Handbook' 7th Edition (2019).
CEDR (2021) *Ninth Mediation Audit.*
CEDR (2022) *Model Protocol 12th Edition Centre for Effective Dispute Resolution* (London).
CEDR (2023) *Model Mediation Agreement.*
CEDR Conciliation Procedure (2023) https://www.cedr.com/wp-content/uploads/2023/01/CEDR-Conciliation-Procedure-2023.pdf (accessed 28.9.23)
Centre for Effective Dispute Resolution (CEDR) (2023) *Model Mediation Agreement.*
Civil Courts Structure Review (2015) *Interim Report by Lord Justice Briggs.*
Civil Courts Structure Review (2016) *Final Report by Lord Justice Briggs.*
Civil Justice Council (2017) 'ADR and Civil Justice' (CJC ADR Working Group Interim Report, Civil Justice Council).
Civil Justice Council (2021) *Compulsory ADR.*
Civil Justice Council Advisory Group on ODR Report (2015) Online Dispute Resolution (ODR) – Courts and Tribunals Judiciary.
Civil Justice Statistics Quarterly: January to March (2022) GOV.UK.
Civil Procedure Rules Committee Rules Committee (2024) *CPRC – Consultation, Alternative Dispute Resolution in the Light of Churchill v Merthyr Tudfil: Proposed Changes.*
Clanchy, M. T. (1983) 'Law and Love in the Middle Ages', in John Bossy, ed. *Disputes and Settlements* (Cambridge University Press).
Clark, B. (2022) 'Mandatory Mediation in England and Wales: Much Ado About Nothing?', *Amicus Curiae* 4 (1), 92–108.
'Code of Practice for Conditional Cautions' (2013) Ministry of Justice.
College of Mediators (2018) *Domestic Abuse Screening Policy.*
Colvin, A. J. S. (2014) 'Mandatory Arbitration and Inequality of Justice in Employment', *Berkeley Journal of Employment and Labor Law* 35, 71–90.
Cornes, D. (2008) 'Mediation Privilege and Confidentiality and the EU Directive', *Arbitration* 74, 395.
Coser, L. A. (1956) *The Functions of Social Conflict* (Free Press).
Courts and Tribunals Judiciary (2019) 'Technology and Construction Court Guide', Section 7 [2019] 1 WLR 6527 Paragraph 6.1, Family Practice Direction 9A.
Cunningham, R. B. & Sarayrah, Y. (1994) *Wasta-The Hidden Force in Middle Eastern Society* (Praegar).
Curle, A. (1971) *Making Peace* (Tavistock).
Curle, A. (1990) *Tools for Transformation: A Personal Study* (Stroud Hawthorne Press).
Daly, K. (2002) 'Restorative Justice: The Real Story', *Punishment & Society* 4 (1), 55–79. https://doi.org/10.1177/14624740222228464
Davis, G. et al. (2000) *Monitoring Publicly Funded Family Mediation – Report to the Legal Services Commission* (Legal Services Commission), p. 20.
De Girolamo, D. (2013) 'The Negotiation Process: Exploring Negotiator Moves through a Processual Framework', *Ohio State Journal on Dispute Resolution* 28 (2), 353.
De Girolamo, D. (2016) 'Rhetoric and Civil Justice: A Commentary on the Promotion of Mediation Without Conviction in England and Wales', *Civil Justice Quarterly* 35 (2), 162–185.
Delgado, R., Dunn, C., Brown, P. & Lee, H. (1985) 'Fairness and Formality: Minimizing the Risk of Prejudice in Alternative Dispute Resolution', *Wisconsin Law Review* 1359.
De Paio, G. (2014) 'Rebooting the Mediation Directive: Assessing the Limited Impact of Its Implementation and Proposing Measures to Increase the Number of Mediations in the EU' (Directorate General For Internal Policies Policy Department C: Citizens' Rights and Constitutional Affairs Legal Affairs).

De Sousa Santos, B. (1980) 'Nature of State Power in Late Capitalism', *International Journal of Sociology of Law* 8, 379–397.
Deutsch, M. (1973) *The Resolution of Conflict: Constructive and Destructive Processes* (Yale University Press).
Deutsch, M. (2017) 'Mediation and Difficult Conflicts', in *The Blackwell Handbook of Mediation: Bridging Theory, Research, and Practice* (Wiley), pp. 355–373.
Deutsch, M., Coleman, P. & Marcus, E. D. (2014) *The Handbook of Conflict Resolution: Theory and Practice* (3rd ed, Jossey Bass Publishers).
Dickens, C. (1853) *Bleak House* (Penguin).
Dignan, J. (1995) *Community Mediation Service: General Survey 1995* (Interim Report, Mediation UK), p. 4.
Dignan, J., Sorsby, A. & Hibbert, J. (1996) *Neighbour Disputes, Comparing the Cost-Effectiveness of Mediation and Alternative Approaches* (Centre for Criminological and Legal Research).
Dispute Resolution: Mandatory Arbitration Agreements Under Fire (2016) Program on Negotiation at Harvard Law School.
Douglas, M. (1973) *Natural Symbols: Explorations in Cosmology*(Routledge, University of Michigan Reprinted 2003).
Ekvall, R. (1964) 'Peace and War among the Tibetan Nomads', *American Anthropologist* 66, 1119–1148.
Emery, R. & Wyer, M. (1987) 'Child Custody Mediation and Litigation: An Experimental Evaluation of the Experience of Parents', *Journal of Consulting and Clinical Psychology* 55 (2), 179–186.
Etzioni, A. (1995) *The spirit of Community* (Fontana).
European Code of Conduct for Mediators CEPEJ (2018) *24 European Commission for the Efficiency of Justice* (CEPEJ).
European Code of Conduct for Mediation Providers (2018). http://ec.europa.eu/civiljustice/adr/adr_ec_code_conduct_en.pdf.
Evans-Pritchard, E. (1940) *The Nuer* (Oxford University Press).
Family Justice Review Final Report (2011) (Ministry of Justice).
Family Law Arbitration Financial Scheme (2012).
Family Law Arbitration Scheme Arbitration Rules (2012) Institute of Family Law Arbitrators. https://ifla.org.uk/cms/wp-content/uploads/2012/02/Rules-Final-22.02.12.pdf
Family Mediation Council (FMC) (2018) *Code of Practice for Family Mediators*.
Family Mediators Association (2012) *Teaching Manual*. https://thefma.co.uk/
Felstiner, W. L. F. et al. (1980–1981) 'The Emergence and Transformation of Disputes: Naming, Blaming, Claiming', *Law & Society Review, Special Issue on Dispute Processing and Civil Litigation* 15 (3/4), 631–654.
Fiadjoe, A. (2013) *Alternative Dispute Resolution: A Developing World Perspective* (Routledge).
Finer Report (1974) *Report of the Committee on One Parent Families*, Cmnd 5629 (HMSO).
Fisher, R. & Shapiro, D. (2005) *Beyond Reason: Using Emotions as You Negotiate* (Viking Penguin).
Fisher, R. & Ury, W. (1981) *Getting to Yes: Negotiating Agreement Without Giving* (Houghton Mifflin, Penguin).
Fisher, R. & Ury, W. (1983) *Getting to Yes* (Penguin Books), pp. 17–99.
Fiss, O. (1984) 'Against Settlement', *Yale Law Journal* 93, 1073.
Frankel, V. (1997) *Man's Search for Meaning* (Penguin).
Frankel, V. (2006) *Man's Search for Meaning* (Beacon Press), ISBN 978-0807014264.
Freire, P. (1970) *Pedagogy of the Oppressed* (Continuum).
Freud, S. (1930) *Civilization and Its Discontents* (Penguin Freud Library).
Freud, S. (1985) *The Complete Letters of Sigmund Freud to Wilhelm Fliess, 1887–1904*. Translated and Edited by Jeffrey Moussaieff Masson (The Belknap Press of Harvard University Press).

Fu, H. & Palmer, M. (2017) *Mediation in Contemporary China, Continuity and Change* (Wildy, Simmonds and Hill).
Fuller, L. (1963) 'Collective Arbitration and the Arbitration', *Wisconsin Law Review* 18 (3), 39–42.
Fuller, L. (1971) 'Mediation: Its Forms and Functions', *Southern California Law Review* 44.
Fuller, L. (1978) 'The Forms and Limits of Adjudication', *Harvard Law Review* 92 (2), 353–409.
Galanter, M. (1984) 'World of Deals: Using Negotiation to Teach about Legal Process', *Journal of Legal Education* 34, 268–276.
Galtung, J. (1969) 'Violence, Peace and Peace Research', *Journal of Peace Research* 3, 167–191.
Galtung, J. (1987) 'One Friendly Quarrel with Kenneth Boulding', *Journal of Peace Research* 24 (2), 199–203.
Galtung, J. (1990) 'Cultural Violence', *Journal of Peace Research* 24 (2), 199–203.
Galtung, J. (2004) *Transcend and Transform: An Introduction to Conflict Work* (Peace by Peaceful Means) (Pluto).
Gavrielides, T. (2007) *Restorative Justice Theory & Practice: Addressing the Discrepancy* (HEUNI).
Gavrielides, T. (2008) 'Restorative Justice: The Perplexing Concept. Conceptual Fault Lines and Power Battles within the Restorative Justice Movement', *Criminology and Criminal Justice Journal* 8 (2), 165–183.
General Council of the Bar (1993) 'Civil Justice on Trial: The Case for Change', Report by the Independent Working Party Set Up by the General Council of the Bar and the Law Society (General Council of the Bar).
Genn, H. (2009) *Judging Civil Justice* (Cambridge University Press).
Genn, H. (2012a) 'What Is Civil Justice for – Reform, ADR, and Access to Justice', *Yale Journal of Law & Human Rights* 24, 397–411.
Genn, H. (2012b) 'Why the Privatisation of Civil Justice is a Rule of Law Issue', 36th F.A. Mann Lecture, Lincoln's Inn, London, 19 November.
Gerhardt, S. (2004) *Why Love Matters: How Affection Shapes a Baby's Brain* (Routledge/Taylor & Francis Group).
Gifford, D. H. (1985) 'A Context Based Theory of Selection Strategy in Legal Negotiations', *Ohio State Law Journal* 46, 41–95.
Golbert, R. (2009) 'An Anthropologist's Approach to Mediation', *Cardozo Journal of Conflict Resolution* 11, 81.
Goldberg, S. et al. (1985) 'The Life of a Mediator to Be or Not to be Accountable', *Negotiation Journal* 1 (3), 263–268.
Goldberg, S., Sanders, F., Rogers, N. & Cole, S. (2012) *Dispute Resolution: Negotiation, Mediation, Arbitration, and Other Processes* (Wolters Kluwer Law & Business).
Goleman, D. (1995) *Emotional Intelligence* (Bantam Books).
Grande, E. (1999) 'Alternative Dispute Resolution, Africa and the Structure of Law and Power: The Horn in Context', *Journal of African Law* 43 (1), 63–70.
Green, E. D. (1986) 'A Heretical View of the Mediation Privilege', *Ohio State Journal on Dispute Resolution* 2, 1–36.
Grillo, T. (1991) 'The Mediation Alternative: Process Dangers for Women', *Yale Law Journal* 100 (6), 1545–1610.
Gross, J. (2020) 'Arbitration Archetypes for Enhancing Access to Justice', *Fordham Law Review* 88, 2319. https://ir.lawnet.fordham.edu/flr/vol88/iss6/8.
Gu, W. (2021) *Dispute Resolution in China: Litigation, Arbitration, Mediation, and Their Interaction* (Routledge).
Gulliver, P. H. (1971) *Neighbours and Networks: The Idiom of Kinship in Social Action Among the Ndendeuli of Tanzania* (University of California Press).
Gulliver, P. (1979) *Disputes and Negotiations: A Cross-Cultural Perspective* (Academic Press).
Gulliver, P. H. (1988) 'Anthropological Contributions to the Study of Negotiations', *Negotiation Journal* 4 (3), 247–255.

Habermas, J. (1979) *Communication and the Evolution of Society* (Beacon Press).
Habermas, J. (1990) 'Discourse Ethics: Notes on a Program of Philosophical Justification', in *Moral Consciousness and Communicative Action*. Translated by Christian Lenhart and Shierry Weber Nicholson (MIT Press).
Habermas, J. (1996) *Between Facts and Norms*. Translated by Rehg William (Polity Press). ISBN 978-0-7456-2011-4.
Hall, E. T. (1976) *Beyond Culture* (Anchor).
Hanaway, M., (2021) *Psychologically Informed Mediation* (Routledge).
Hanks, M. (2012) 'Perspectives on Mandatory Mediation', *UNSW Law Journal* 35 (3), 929–952.
Harris, V. (2021) *Transforming Community Conflict* (Mediation Hertfordshire).
Harris, V. (2023) *The Cost of Community Conflict* (Mediation Hertfordshire).
Haynes, J. (1992) 'Mediation and Therapy: An Alternative View', *Mediation Quarterly* 10 (1), 3–19.
Heilbron, H. & Hodge, H. (1993) *Civil Justice on Trial: The Case for Change* (Joint Report of the Bar Council and Law Society, United Kingdom).
Hoffman, D. A. (2000) 'Ten Principles of Mediation Ethics', *Alt High Cost Litig* 18, 147–169. https://doi.org/10.1002/alt.3810180803
Hofrichter, R. (1978) *Neighbourhood Justice and Social Control Problems of American Capitalism: A Perspective* (Greenwood Press).
Hofstede, G. (2001) *Culture's Consequences: Comparing Values, Behaviors, Institutions, and Organizations Across Nations* (2nd ed, Sage).
Hofstede, G. (2011) 'Dimensionalizing Cultures: The Hofstede Model in Context', *Online Readings in Psychology and Culture* 2 (1).
Hussain v Chowdhury (2020) EWHC 790 (Ch).
Hynes, J. (2019) '"Hello Dungavel!" Observations on the Use of Video Link Technology in Immigration, Bail Hearings', UK Admin. Just. Inst May 6.
Irving, H. & Benjamin, M. (1995) *Research in Family Mediation – An Integrative Review in Family Mediation* (Contemporary Issues Sage).
Janis, I. (1982) *Groupthink, Psychological Studies of Policy Decisions and Fiascoes* (Yale University Press).
Kallipetis, K. (2015) 'Mediation Ethics', in D. Richbell, ed. *How to Master Commercial Mediation* (Bloomsbury Professional).
Katch, E. & Rabinovich-Einy, O. (2017) *Digital Justice: Technology and the Internet of Disputes* (Oxford University Press).
Keane, A. & McKeown, P. (2014) *Modern Law of Evidence* (10th ed, Oxford University Press).
Kelly, J. B. & Duryee, M. A. (1995) 'Women's and Men's Views of Mediation in Voluntary and Mandatory Mediation Settings', *Family and Conciliation Courts Review*, 1st January 1992, 30 (1).
Kelsall, Tim (2005) 'Truth, Lies, Ritual', *Human Rights Quarterly* 27, 361–391.
Kilmann, R. H. & Thomas, K. W. (1977) 'Developing a Forced-Choice Measure of Conflict-Handling Behavior: The "MODE" Instrument', *Educational and Psychological Measurement* 37 (2), 309–325.
Koch, K.-F., ed (1979) *Access to Justice Vol. IV: The Anthropological Perspective. Patterns of Conflict Management: Essays in the Ethnography of Law* (Giuffre).
Koo, A. (2015) 'Ten Years after Halsey', *Civil Justice Quarterly* 34 (1), 77–95.
Koo, A. K. C. & Zhao, Y (2011) 'The Development of Legal Protection for Mediation Confidentiality in Hong Kong', *Common Law World Review* 40 (3), 263–277.
Kraybill, R. (2013) *The Conflict Styles Inventory* (River House Press).
Lawyer (2019) *Online Dispute Resolution Faces Major Challenges Survey Artificial Lawyer*, 19 March 2019. http://www.artificiallawyer.com/2019/03/19/online-dispute-resolution-faces-major-challenges-survey/
Lax, D. A. & Sebenius, J. K. (1986) *The Manager as Negotiator: Bargaining for Cooperation and Competitive Gain* (Free Press).

Lax, D. A. & Sebenius, J. K. (2006) *3-d Negotiation: Powerful Tools to Change the Game in Your Most Important Deals* (Harvard Business Review Press).
Lederach, J. P. (1997) *Building Peace: Sustainable Peace in Divided Societies* (US Institute of Peace).
Lederach, J. P. (2005) *The Moral Imagination: The Art and Soul of Building Peace* (Oxford University Press).
Lerman, L. G. (1984) 'Mediation of Wife Abuse Cases: The Adverse Impact of Informal Dispute Processes on Women', *Harvard Women's Law Journal* 7, 57–113.
Liao, Yong'an & Cong, W. (2023) *Mediation and Law in China Vol 1* (Routledge).
Liao Yong'an Mediation Course (China Renmin University Press, 2019), p. 30.
Lieberman, J. & Henry, J. (1986) 'Lessons from the Alternative Dispute Resolution Movement', *University of Chicago Law Review* 53 (2), Article 7.
Liebmann, M., ed (1998) *Community and Neighbour Mediation* (Cavendish Publishing).
Liebmann, M. (2007) *Restorative Justice: How It Works* (Jessica Kingsley).
Long, D. (1973) 'The Board of Governors in Saudi Arabia', *Middle East Journal* 27 (1), 71–75.
Love, L. P (1997) 'The Top Ten Reasons Why Mediators Should not Evaluate', *Florida State University Law Review* 24, 937–948.
Lowenthal, G. (1982) 'A General Theory of Negotiation Process, Strategy and Behaviour', *University of Kansas Law Review* 24, 937–948.
Luban, D. (1995) 'Settlements and the Erosion of the Public Realm', *Georgetown Law Journal* 83, 2619–2662.
Mackie, K. et al. (2007) *The ADR Practical Guide: Commercial Dispute Resolution* (3rd ed, Bloomsbury Professional).
Mania, K. (2015) 'Online Dispute Resolution: The Future of Justice', *International Comparative Jurisprudence* 1, 76–86.
Marshall, T. F. (1984) 'Reparation, Conciliation and Mediation: Home Office Research and Planning Unit', *Paper 27* (HMSO).
Marshall, T. F. (1999) *Restorative Justice: An Overview* (Home Office Research Development and Statistics Directorate Report).
Matsumoto, D. R. (1996) *Culture and Psychology* (Brooks/Cole).
Maxwell, G. & Morris, A. (2001) 'Implementing Restorative Justice: What Works?', in A. Morris & G. Maxwell, eds. *Restorative Justice for Juveniles Conferencing, Mediation and Circle* (Portland).
McCrory, J. P. (1981) 'Environmental Mediation – Another Piece for the Puzzle', *Vermont Law Review* 6 (1), 49–84.
McEwen, Craig A. & Maiman, R. J. (1984) 'Mediation in Small Claims Court: Achieving Compliance Through Consent', *Law & Society Review* 18 (1), 11–49. JSTOR, https://doi.org/10.2307/3053479 (accessed 30.7.24).
McIntosh, J., Smyth, B., Kelaher, M., Wells, Y. & Long, C. (2008) 'Child Focused and Child Inclusive Divorce Mediation: Comparative Outcomes from a Prospective Study of Post-Separation Adjustment', *Family Court Review* 46 (1), 105–124.
McNair Lecture (2023) *Sir Geoffrey Vos* (MR).
Mediationsgesetz (2012) Mediation Act of 21 July 2012 (BGBl. 2012 I, p. 1577), as amended by Article 135 of the Ordinance of 31 August 2015 (BGBl. 2015 I, p. 1474).
Meggitt, G. (2014) 'PGF II SA v OMFS Co and Compulsory Mediation', *Civil Justice Quarterly* 33 (2014), 335.
Meggitt, G. (2020) 'Mediation Privilege', in F. Moscati, M. Palmer & R. Roberts, eds. *Comparative Dispute Resolution: A Research Handbook* (Edward Elgar Publishing).
Menkel-Meadow, C. (1991) 'Pursuing Settlement in an Adversary Culture: A Tale of Innovation Co-Opted or the Law of ADR', *Florida State University Law Review* 19 (1).
Menkel-Meadow, C. (1993) 'Lawyer Negotiations: Theories and Realities – What We Learn from Mediation', *Modern Law Review* 56, 361–367.
Menkel-Meadow, C. (1995) 'The Many Ways of Meditation: The Transformation of Traditions, Ideologies, Paradigms, and Practices', *Negotiation Journal* 11, 217.

Menkel-Meadow, C. (1997) 'Ethics in Alternative Dispute Resolution, No Answers from the Adversary Conception of Lawyer's Responsibilities', *South Texas Law Review* 38, 407.

Menkel-Meadow, C. (2007) 'The Lawyer as a Consensus: Ethics for a New Practice', *Tennessee Law Review* 70, 63–119.

Menkel-Meadow, C. (2011) 'Scaling up Deliberative Democracy as Dispute Resolution as Dispute Resolution in Health Care Reform: A Work in Progress.' https://scholarship.law.duke.edu/cgi/viewcontent (accessed 19.12.23).

Menkel-Meadow, C., ed (2012) *Complex Dispute Resolution. Foundations of Dispute Resolution*, Vol. I, Foundations of Dispute Resolution; Vol. II, Multi-Party Dispute Resolution, Vol. III, International Dispute Resolution (Ashgate).

Menkel-Meadow, C. (2016) 'Is ODR ADR? Reflections of an ADR Founder from the 15th ODR Conference' The Hague, 22-23 May 2016', *International Journal of Online Dispute Resolution* 3 (1), 4–7.

Menkel-Meadow, C. (2017) 'Conflict Resolution by the Numbers', *Negotiation Journal* 33, 317–322.

Menkel-Meadow, C. et al. (2005) *Dispute Resolution: Beyond the Adversarial Model* (Aspen).

Mentschikoff, S. (1961) 'Commercial Arbitration', *Columbia Law Review* 61, 846.

Merry, S. (1993) 'Sorting Out Popular Justice', in S. Merry & N. Milner, eds. *The Possibility of Popular Justice: A Case Study of American Community Mediation* (University of Michigan Press).

Mills, O. (2008) 'Effects of Domestic Violence on Children', *The Family in Law* 38 165.

Ministry of Justice. (2011 November) *Family Justice Review Final Report* (Ministry of Justice).

Mnookin, R. H. (2003) 'Strategic Barriers to Dispute Resolution', *Harvard Negotiation Review* 8 (1).

Mnookin, R. H. & Kornhauser, L. (1979) 'Bargaining in the Shadow of the Law: The Case of Divorce', *The Yale Law Journal* 88 (5).

Moe (2022) 'Unpublished LLM Essay'.

Monk, G. & Winslade, J. (2000) *Narrative Mediation, a New Approach to Conflict Resolution* (John Wiley & Sons).

Moore, C. (2014) *The Mediation Process: Practical Strategies for Resolving Conflict* (John Wiley & Sons).

Moscati, F., Palmer, M. & Roberts, R., eds (2020) *Comparative Dispute Resolution: A Research Handbook* (Edward Elgar Publishing).

Mr Justice Eder (2014) *Challenges to Arbitral Awards at the Seat*, Address to Mauritius International Arbitration Conference 15 December 2014. http://www.judiciary.uk/wp-content/uploads/2015/10/Eder-Speech-Dec-2014.pdf

Mulcahy, L. (2000) 'The Devil and the Deep Blue Sea? A Critique of the Ability of Community Mediation to Suppress and Facilitate Participation in Civil Life', *Journal of Law and Society* 27 (1), 133–150.

Mulcahy, L. (2013) 'The Collective Interest in Private Dispute Resolution', *Oxford Journal of Legal Studies* 33 (1), 59–80.

Murithi, T. (2006) 'African Approaches to Building Peace and Social Solidarity', *African Journal on Conflict Resolution* 6 (2), 24–27.

Nader, L. (1979) 'Disputing without the Force of Law', *The Yale Law Journal* 88 (5), 998–1021.

Nader, L. (1993) 'Controlling Processes in the Practice of Law: Hierarchy and Pacification in the Movement to Re-Form Dispute Ideology', *Ohio State Journal of Dispute Resolution* 9 (1), 1–25.

National Advisory Council on Violence against Women (2004) 'Chapter 3: Enhancing the Response of the Justice System: Civil Remedies', in *Toolkit to End Violence Against Women* (US Dept of Justice, Office on Violence Against Women).

National Audit Office Report (2007) *Legal Aid and Mediation for People Involved in Family Breakdown* (HMSO).

Neill Lecture (2022) *Sir Geoffrey Vos* (MR).

Neuberger, L. (2010) 'Has Mediation Had Its Day?', *Gordon Slynn Memorial Lecture*, 10th November 2010. https://www.bailii.org/uk/other/speeches/2010/Z43SZ.html

Neuberger, L. (2015) *Keynote Address: A View from on High*, Civil Mediation Conference 12 May 2015. https://www.supremecourt.uk/docs/speech-150512-civil-mediation-conference-2015.pdf

Newell, T. & Edgar, K. (2006) *Restorative Justice in Prisons: A Guide to Making It Happen* (Waterside Press).

Nolan-Haley, J. (2015) 'Mediation and Access to Justice in Africa: Perspectives from Ghana', *Harvard Negotiation Law Review* 21, 59.

Nolan-Haley, J. (2018) 'Does ADR's "Access to Justice" Come at the Expense of Meaningful Consent?', *Ohio State Journal on Dispute Resolution* 33, 373, 386, 388–389, 396.

Nolan-Haley, J. (2020) 'International Dispute Resolution and Access to Justice: Comparative Law Perspectives', *Journal of Dispute Resolution* 2. https://scholarship.law.missouri.edu/jdr/vol2020/iss2/11.

Northern Ireland Courts and Tribunals Service (2019) *Judicial Statistics 2018*. https://www.gov.uk/government/statistics/judicial-statistics-2018 (accessed 8.1.24).

Orna, R.-E. & Ethan, K. (2017) 'A New Relationship Between Public and Private Dispute Resolution: Lessons from Online Dispute Resolution', *Ohio State Journal on Dispute Resolution* 32, 695.

Palmer, M. (2014) *The Politics of Law and Stability in China*. Edited by Susan Trevaskes (Edward Elgar Publishing).

Palmer, M. & Roberts, S. (2020) *Dispute Processes, ADR and the Primary Forms of Decision-making* (3rd ed, Cambridge University Press).

Parkinson, L. (1986) 'Conciliation in Britain', *Mediation Quarterly*, 69–82.

Parkinson, L. (2004) 'A Happy Concatenation?', in J. Westcot, ed. *Family Mediation – Past, Present and Future Family Law* (Jordan Publishing).

Parkinson, L. (2011) *Family Mediation: Appropriate Dispute Resolution a New Family Justice System* (2nd ed, Jordans Publishing).

Parkinson, L. (2020) *Family Mediation* (4th ed, Jordan Publishing).

Pavlich, G. (1996) 'The Power of Community Mediation: Government and Form of Self Identity', *Law and Society Review* 30.

Pease, A. (1984) *Body Language: How to Read Others Thoughts by Their Gestures* (Sheldon Press).

Pirie, F. (2013) *Moral Order: Aspiration and Emulation: The Anthropology of Law* (Clarendon Law Series Oxford), p. 20.

Price C. (2018) 'Alternative Dispute Resolution in Africa: Is ADR the Bridge between Traditional and Modern Dispute Resolution?', *Pepperdine Dispute Resolution Law Journal* 18, 393.

Prince, S. (2019) '"Fine Words Butter No Parsnips": Can the Principle of Open Justice Survive the Introduction of an Online Court?', *Civil Justice Quarterly* 38 (1), 111–125.

Program on Negotiation (2016) *Harvard Law School*. Dispute Resolution: Mandatory Arbitration Agreements Under Fire – PON – Program on Negotiation at Harvard Law School.

Quek, D. (2010) 'Mandatory Mediation: An Oxymoron – Examining the Feasibility of Implementing a Court-Mandated Mediation Program', *Cardozo Journal of Conflict Resolution* 11 (2), 479.

Quek, D. (2019) 'The Convergence of ADR and ODR within the Courts', *Civil Justice Quarterly* 38, 142.

Rabinovich-Einy, O. & Katsh, E. (2017) 'A New Relationship Between Public and Private Dispute Resolution: Lessons from Online Dispute Resolution', *Ohio State Journal of Dispute Resolution* 32 (4), 695–724.

Raiffa, H. (1982) *The Art and Science of Negotiation* (Harvard University; Press/Belknap).

Ramsbotham, O., Woodhouse, T. & Miall, H., eds (2016) *Contemporary Conflict Resolution* (4th ed, Polity Press).

Reich, J. B. (2001) 'A Call for Intellectual Honesty: A Response to the Uniform Mediation Act's Privilege against Disclosure', *Journal of Dispute Resolution* 2001 (2).

Resnik, J. (2014) 'The Privatization of Process: Requiem for and Celebration of the Federal Rules of Civil Procedure at 75', *University of Pennsylvania Law Review* 162 (1793), 1809–1814.

Restorative Justice Action Plan (2019) (Scottish Government).
Richbell, D. (2015) *How to Master Commercial Mediation* (Bloomsbury Professional).
Riskin, L. L. (1996) 'Understanding Mediators' Orientations, Strategies, and Techniques: A Grid for the Perplexed', *Harvard Negotiation Law Review* 1, 7–51.
Ritchie, J. (1986) 'Planning: A Perspective on the Māori World', *Planning Quarterly* 82.
Roberts, M. (1992) 'Systems or Selves, Some Ethical Issues in Family Mediation', *Mediation Quarterly* 10 (3), 4–10.
Roberts, M. (2014) *Mediation in Family Disputes: Principle of Practice* (4th ed, Routledge).
Roebuck, D. (2001) *Ancient Greek Arbitration* (Oxford University Press).
Roebuck, D. (2007) 'The Myth of Modern Mediation', *Arbitration* 73, 1–9.
Rosenberg, M. (2015) *Nonviolent Communication: A Language of Life* (3rd ed, PuddleDancer Press).
Royal Commission on Marriage and Divorce, Morton Fergus, HMSO (1956) Marriage and Divorce: Great Britain. Royal Commission on Marriage and Divorce: Free Download, Borrow, and Streaming: Internet Archive.
Sander, F. (1985) 'Alternative Methods of Dispute Resolution: An Overview', *University of Florida Law Review* 37.
Sander, F. E. A. (2007) 'Another View of Mandatory Mediation' *Dispute Resolution Magazine* 13, 16.
Sander, F. E. A. & Goldberg, S. (1994) 'Fitting the Forum to the Fuss: A User Friendly Guide to Selecting an ADR Procedure', *Negotiation Journal* 10 (1), 49–68.
Schaffer, D. (2018) 'An Examination of Mandatory Court-Based Mediation', *Arbitration* 84 (3), 229–238.
Schelling, T. C. (1960) *The Strategy of Conflict* (Harvard University Press).
Schmitz, A. J. (2020) 'Measuring "Access to Justice" in the Rush to Digitize', *Fordham Law Review* 88 (2019–2020), 2382.
Scottish Law Commission (1991) 'Confidentiality in Family Mediation' *Paper 92*. dp92.pdf (scotlawcom.gov.uk) (accessed online 13.9.23).
Shah-Kazemi, S. N. (2000) 'Cross-Cultural Mediation: A Critical View of the Dynamics of Culture in Family Disputes', *International Journal of Law, Policy and the Family* 14, 302–325.
Shapira, O. (2012) 'Conceptions and Perceptions of Fairness in Mediation', *South Texas Law Review*, 281–341.
Shapira, O. (2016) *A Theory of Mediators' Ethics, Foundations, Rationale and Application* (Cambridge University Press).
Shapira, O., ed (2021) *Mediation Ethics: A Practioners Guide* (American Bar Association).
Shapiro, D. (2010) 'From Signal to Semantic: Uncovering the Emotional Dimension of Negotiation', *Nevada Law Journal* 10, 461–471.
Shapland, J. et al. (2004) *Implementing Restorative Justice Schemes* (Crime Reduction Programme) (Home Office).
Shapland, J. et al. (2006) *Restorative Justice in Practice – Findings from the Second Phase of the Evaluation of Three Schemes* (Home Office) www.homeoffice.gov.uk/rds/pdfs06/r274.pdf
Shapland, J. et al. (2007) 'Restorative Justice: The Views of Victims', *The Third Report from the Evaluation of Three Schemes Ministry of Justice Research Series 3/07* (Ministry of Justice).
Shapland, J. et al. (2008) 'Restorative Justice: Does Restorative Justice Affect Reconviction', *The Fourth Report from the Evaluation of Three Schemes* (Home Office).
Shapland, J. et al. (2011) *Restorative Justice in Practice. Evaluating What Works for Victims and Offenders* (Routledge).
Sheeran, M. (1991) *Beyond Majority Rule: Voteless Decisions in the Religious Society of Friends* (Philadelphia Yearly Meeting).
Sherman, E. (1993) '"Court Mandated Alternative Dispute Resolution" What Form of Participation Should Be Required?', *Southern Methodist University Law Review* 46, 2079.
Sherman, L. & Strang, H. (2007) 'Restorative Justice the Evidence' (Smith Institute). https://www.iirp.edu/images/pdf/RJ_full_report.pdf (accessed 8.1.24).

Shipman, S. (2006) 'Court Approaches to ADR in the Civil Justice System', *Civil Justice Quarterly* 25 (April), 181–218.
Shipman, S. (2011) 'Compulsory Mediation: The Elephant in the Room', *Civil Justice Quarterly* 30, 163.
Shipman, S. et al. (2019) *Brown and Marriot's ADR Principles and Practice* (4th ed, Sweet & Maxwell).
Simmel, G. (1950) *The Sociology of George Simmel*. Edited by K. Wolff (Free Press).
Solicitors Regulation Authority (2018) *SRS Principles*. https://www.sra.org.uk/solicitors/standards-regulations/principles/ (accessed 8.1.24).
Solicitors Regulation Authority Code of Conduct (2019). https://www.sra.org.uk/solicitors/standards-regulations/code-conduct-solicitors/
Sternlight, J. (1996) 'Panacea or Corporate Tool? Debunking the Supreme Court's Preference for Binding Arbitration', *Washington University Law Review* 74 (3).
Storr, A. (1989) *Freud* (Oxford University Press).
Strasser, F. & Randolph, P. (2004) *Mediation: A Psychological Insight into Conflict Resolution* (Bloomsbury Continuum).
Susskind, L. (1981) 'Environmental Mediation and the Accountability Problem', *Vermont Law Review* 6 (1), 1.
Susskind, L. & Cruikshank, J. (2006) 'What Is Consensus?', in *Breaking Roberts Rules: The New Way to Run Your Meeting, Build Consensus, and Get Results* (Oxford University Press), pp. 18–35.
Susskind, L. et al. (2005) 'What We Have Learned About Teaching Multiparty Negotiation', *Negotiation Journal* 21 (3), 395.
Tauri, J. M. (2018) 'The Master's Tools Will Never Dismantle the Master's House: An Indigenous Critique of Criminology', *Journal of Global Indigeneity* 3 (1), 1–18. https://www.jstor.org/stable/48717653
Taylor, A. (1969) *War by Timetable* (Macdonald & Co).
Tinsley, C. & Pillutla, M. (1998) 'Negotiating in the United States and Hong Kong', *Journal of International Business Studies* 29 (4), 711–728.
Tinsley, C. et al. (1999) 'Adopting a Dual Lens Approach for Examining the Dilemma of Differences in International Business Negotiations', *International Negotiation* 4, 5–22.
Tversky, A. & Kahneman, D. (1974) 'Judgment under Uncertainty: Heuristics and Biases', *Science* 185 (4157), 1124–1131.
Wall, A. J. (1985) *Negotiation: Theory and Practice* (Scott Foresman).
Walton, R. E., & McKersie, R. B. (1965) *A Behavioral Theory of Labor Negotiations* (McGraw-Hill).
Ware, S. J. (2021) 'Lasting Lessons from Mentschikoff's Commercial Arbitration', in A. Hinshaw, A. K. Schneider & S. R. Cole, eds. *Discussions in Dispute Resolution* (Oxford University Press).
Wehr, P. & Lederach, J. (1991) 'Mediating Conflict in Central America', *Journal of Peace Resolution* 28 (1), 85–87.
Weitekamp, E. G. M. (1999) 'The History of Restorative Justice', in Walgrave, L. & Bazemore, G., eds. *Restorative Juvenile Justice: Repairing the Harm of Youth Crime* (Criminal Justice Press).
Welsh, N. (2011) 'Mandatory Mediation and Its Variations (2011)', in Susan Franck & Anna Joubin-Bret, eds. *Investor-State Disputes: Prevention and Alternative to Arbitration*, Vol. 2, Proceedings of the Washington and Lee University and UNCTAD Joint Symposium on International Investment and Alliterative Dispute Resolution. https://ssrn.com/abstract=3300161
White, J. J. (1984) 'The Pros and Cons of Getting to Yes', *Journal of Legal Education* 34 (1), 115–129.
Whyatt, S. J. (1961) *The Citizen and the Administration. The Redress of Grievances. A Report by Justice* (Stevens & Sons, Ltd). Now Published online by Cambridge University Press, 17 January 2008.

Winkelmann, J. (2011) 'ADR and the Civil Justice System' (Speech at AMINZ Conference on Taking Charge of the Future, 6th August 2011). https://www.courtsofnz.govt.nz/assets/speechpapers/adrw.pdf
Winslade, J. & Monk, G. (2000) *Narrative Mediation: A New Approach to Conflict Resolution* (Jossey Bass).
Woolf, L. (1995) *Access to Justice: Interim Report to the Lord Chancellor on the Civil Justice System in England and Wales* (Lord Chancellors Dept).
Woolf, L. (1996) *Access to Justice: Final Report to the Lord Chancellor on the Civil Justice System in England and Wales* (HMSO).
Xavier, A. (2006) 'Mediation: Its Origin and Growth in India', *Hamline Journal of Public Law & Policy* 27, 275.
Yong'an, L. & Cong, W. (2023) *Mediation and Law in China*, Vol. 1 (Routledge).
Yong'an, L. & Ming, D. (2023) *Mediation and Law in China*, Vol. 2 (Routledge).
Zehr, H. (2005) *Changing Lenses – A New Focus on Crime and Justice* (Scottdale).
Zehr, H. (2015) *The Little Book of Restorative Justice* (Good Books).
Zhiping, L. (1991) *Searching for Harmony in the Natural Order* (Shanghai People's Publishing House).
Zuckerman, A. (2013) *Civil Procedure: Principles of Practice* (3rd ed, Sweet & Maxwell), para.17.7.

Index

Note: Page numbers in *italics* indicate a figure and page numbers in **bold** indicate a table on the corresponding page. Page numbers followed by "n" with numbers refer to notes.

Kolibri 360 GmbH
Ferdinand-Jühlke-Straße 7
99095 Erfurt, Deutschland
produktsicherheit@kolibri360.de